Give God the Glory

ANCIENT PRAYER AND WORSHIP IN CULTURAL PERSPECTIVE

Jerome H. Neyrey, S.J.

WILLIAM B. EERDMANS PUBLISHING COMPANY
GRAND RAPIDS, MICHIGAN / CAMBRIDGE, U.K.

Published 2007 by

Wm. B. Eerdmans Publishing Co.

2140 Oak Industrial Drive N.E., Grand Rapids, Michigan 49505 /

P.O. Box 163, Cambridge CB3 9PU U.K.

www.eerdmans.com

Printed in the United States of America

12 11 10 09 08 07   7 6 5 4 3 2 1

Library of Congress Cataloging-in-Publication Data

Neyrey, Jerome H., 1940-
    Give God the glory: ancient prayer and worship in cultural perspective /
    Jerome H. Neyrey.
        p.   cm.
    Includes bibliographical references and index.
    ISBN 978-0-8028-4015-8 (pbk.: alk. paper)
    1. Public worship.   2. Public worship — Biblical teaching.
    3. Prayer — Christianity.   I. Title.

    BV5.N49   2007
    264 — dc22

                                            2007018936

Chapter Four appeared as "'First,' 'Only,' 'One of a Few,' and 'No One Else': The Rhetoric of
    Uniqueness and the Doxologies in 1 Timothy," *Biblica* 86 (2005): 59-87. It appears here with
    the kind permission of the journal.

Chapter Six originally appeared as "Worship in the Fourth Gospel: A Cultural Interpretation
    of John 14–17," *Biblical Theology Bulletin* 36 (2006): 107-17 and 155-63. It appears here with
    the kind permission of the journal.

To those with whom I pray:

Jesuits of the New Orleans Province
   Teams of Our Lady (Winchester MA; Mishawaka IN)
      St. Monica's Parish

CONTENTS

ABBREVIATIONS   ix

INTRODUCTION   1

1. "Supplications, Prayers, Intercessions, and Thanksgivings"
   (1 Timothy 2:1)   5

2. Prayer, in Other Words: Reading with Cultural Lenses   31

3. Five New Testament Prayers, in Other Words   63

4. Praise of God's Uniqueness,
   Who Is "First," "Only," and "No One Else"   112

5. Worship, in Other Words: Appropriate Cultural Models   144

6. Worship in the Fourth Gospel:
   A Cultural Interpretation of John 14–17   167

7. The *Didache* and Justin's *First Apology:*
   Descriptions of Christian Worship   206

CONCLUSION   245

BIBLIOGRAPHY   249

INDEX OF SUBJECTS   263

INDEX OF SCRIPTURE AND OTHER ANCIENT TEXTS   266

ABBREVIATIONS

AB	Anchor Bible
ABD	*Anchor Bible Dictionary*
ANRW	*Aufstieg und Niedergang der Römischen Welt*
BAGD	Bauer, Arndt, Gingrich, and Danker, *Greek-English Lexicon of the New Testament and Other Early Christian Literature*
Bib	*Biblica*
BJRL	*Bulletin of the John Rylands University Library of Manchester*
BTB	*Biblical Theology Bulletin*
CBQ	*Catholic Biblical Quarterly*
CRINT	Compendia rerum iudaicarum ad Novum Testamentum
CurTM	*Currents in Theology and Ministry*
ETL	*Ephemerides theologicae lovanienses*
EvQ	*Evangelical Quarterly*
ExpT	*Expository Times*
Greg	*Gregorianum*
HSCP	*Harvard Studies in Classical Philology*
HTR	*Harvard Theological Review*
HUCA	*Hebrew Union College Annual*
IBS	*Irish Biblical Studies*
ICC	International Critical Commentary
IDB	*The Interpreter's Dictionary of the Bible*
IESS	*International Encyclopedia of the Social Sciences*
JAAR	*Journal of the American Academy of Religion*
JBL	*Journal of Biblical Literature*
JETS	*Journal of the Evangelical Theological Society*

JHS	*Journal of Hellenic Studies*
JJS	*Journal of Jewish Studies*
JR	*Journal of Religion*
JSJ	*Journal for the Study of Judaism*
JSNT	*Journal for the Study of the New Testament*
JSOTSup	Journal for the Study of the Old Testament: Supplement Series
JTS	*Journal of Theological Studies*
NDIEC	*New Documents Illustrating Early Christianity*
NTA	*New Testament Abstracts*
NTS	*New Testament Studies*
OTP	*Old Testament Pseudepigrapha*
Phil	*Philologus*
PSB	*Princeton Seminary Bulletin*
RB	*Revue Biblique*
ResQ	*Restoration Quarterly*
RSR	*Recherches de science religieuse*
RSRev	*Religious Studies Review*
RTR	*Reformed Theological Review*
SBLSP	Society of Biblical Literature Seminar Papers
StPat	*Studia Patristica*
TAPA	*Transactions and Proceedings of the American Philological Association*
TBT	*The Bible Today*
TDNT	*Theological Dictionary of the New Testament*
TLZ	*Theologische Literaturzeitung*
TS	*Theological Studies*
TU	Texte und Untersuchungen
TynBul	*Tyndale Bulletin*
TZ	*Theologische Zeitschrift*
ZNW	*Zeitschrift für die Neutestamentliche Wissenschaft*
ZRGG	*Zeitschrift für Religions- und Geistesgeschichte*

INTRODUCTION

T he library of scholarly materials on prayer and worship is particularly rich. Whether monographs on worship or dictionary articles on the topic, we do not lack for wise interpreters.[1] Seminars at the conventions of the Society of Biblical Literature produced excellent guides and introductions to various ancient prayers, including those of the New Testament.[2] And there are many collections of studies of New Testament authors and prayers.[3] Then why another book? What does this volume bring to the conversation?

I have frequently used the tag "in other words" to describe my approach to biblical study, and have included that phrase in the title of several of my own writings. Same documents and often the same data, but interpreted "in other words."[4] The otherness in "other words" refers to the

1. Oscar Cullmann, *Early Christian Worship* (London: SCM, 1953); C. C. Richardson, "Worship in New Testament Times, Christian," in *IDB* 4:883-94; Gerhard Delling, *Worship in the New Testament* (London: Darton, Longman and Todd, 1962); Ralph P. Martin, *Worship in the Early Church* (London: Marshall, Morgan and Scott, 1964); Ferdinand Hahn, *The Worship of the Early Church* (Philadelphia: Fortress, 1973); David E. Aune, "Worship, Early Christian," in *ABD* 6:973-89.

2. James H. Charlesworth, ed., *The Lord's Prayer and Other Prayer Texts from the Greco-Roman Era* (Valley Forge, Pa.: Trinity, 1994); and Mark Kiley et al., eds., *Prayer from Alexander to Constantine: A Critical Anthology* (New York: Routledge, 1997).

3. D. A. Carson, ed., *Teach Us to Pray: Prayer in the Bible and the World* (Grand Rapids: Baker, 1990); Richard N. Longenecker, ed., *Into God's Presence: Prayer in the New Testament* (Grand Rapids: Eerdmans, 2001).

4. Jerome H. Neyrey, *Paul, in Other Words: A Cultural Reading of His Letters* (Louisville: Westminster John Knox, 1990); Neyrey, "Prayer, in Other Words: A Social-Science Model for

use of materials from the social sciences to interpret a culture that is radically "other" in regard to ours — so much so that Americans can hardly understand what the Middle East is like. So the aim of this book is to bring readers to understand and appreciate the "otherness" of the Christian Scriptures and their worship. The best way I know to recognize and then interpret the "otherness" of the New Testament is to employ models and concepts from the social sciences, in particular, cultural anthropology. Sensitive readers and listeners do not presume to understand what an "other" is saying, although as full a comprehension as possible is the desired aim of communication.

But how can we know the cultural world of early Christianity? What materials do we have? Since the issue is one of culture, we do best to turn to cultural studies of the Middle East. It is not claimed that there is a simple equation of ancient culture to modern Islamic or Mediterranean culture, but those are at least the most likely places to begin looking for cultural patterns that can be appropriated and developed to understand the ancients in those regions. Do we need to do this? No, unless readers wish to interpret the ancient documents on their own terms and in the context of their cultures. To be sure, the Western world has ample proof that we do not understand the Levant and the Middle East. But by using appropriate cultural lenses we can begin to see and understand the world of the New Testament. Cultural studies all employ models. But what models? What concepts?

A cultural world is comprised of institutions, modal personality, pivotal values, and the like. As natives of the West, we have some knowledge of our institutions (economics, education, politics, finance), our personality type (individualistic), our values (money, above all), and our family pattern (nuclear). But every piece of this system differs from that of the Middle East. The human person there was group oriented; he took his identity, trade, and even his enemies and friends from his father. Kinship, not politics or economics or education, was his basic institution; he was born into it, was nurtured there, supported family marriages and business deals, depended on it entirely for sustenance, affection, protection, and health care, especially in his senior years. He was in no way a Western individualist, for his basic education by his family schooled him to know and live up to what was expected of him, that is, honor concerns or purity rules. Living in a

---

Interpreting Prayers," in *Social Scientific Models for Interpreting the Bible: Essays by the Context Group in Honor of Bruce J. Malina*, ed. John J. Pilch (Leiden: Brill, 2001), 349-80.

patron-client relationship, he knew he was constantly indebted to others; as part of a radically divided gender world, he knew in what place to be found, what tools belonged to him, what animals were his, what male ideals he was expected to uphold. If God is called "Father," then we enter a world where we must know what male roles were, especially as pertains to a father, to whom honor and respect were due; what duties one incurred and to whom one was indebted. How else can one understand doxologies that state: "To the only God our Savior, through Jesus Christ our Lord, be glory, majesty, power, and authority, before all time and now and forever. Amen" (Jude 25)?[5] Embedded here is a model of social relations known as patron-client relations expressed in praising God as "our Savior." This patronal deity is owed the only thing we can give, namely, praise, which here is expressed as "glory, majesty, power, and authority."

Reading "in other words" is simply not an option for us. It is axiomatic that languages have no meaning independent of the cultures in which they are spoken. "Honor your father and your mother" seems quite straightforward; after all, all of us know "father" and "mother." Aren't these universal concepts? Frankly, no! Nor have we a clue what "honor" means as something owed a father or mother. Languages can have meaning only in their own cultures. If we want to read "honor father and mother" in its own culture, we must first appreciate that that world was totally gender divided: males and females had different spaces, tools, tasks, animals, etc. "Father," moreover, presided over a patriarchal household, and was owed obedience, especially by his sons. "Honor" refers both to submission to the regnant father and to support of him in his last years. Honor was the premier value of antiquity; wealth is ours. But God is often addressed as "Father," and many prayers give God "praise, honor, and glory." This complex of meaning, then, needs to be understood to appreciate that "Abba isn't Daddy."

But will the use of cultural models take the spirit out of prayers to be studied, of worship to be examined? On the contrary, merely to repeat current wisdom about prayer and worship is to put another coat of varnish on the art object. But if a reader takes pleasure in learning another culture and studying how life is lived there, that reader will patiently discover the cultural world of the New Testament in a way that builds but does not tear down, that burnishes but does not diminish.

---

5. All biblical quotations in this book are taken from the New Revised Standard Version, unless otherwise noted.

What readers will not find in this book are the traditional historical-critical treatments of documents and prayers. This is by no means because such studies lack merit, but simply because this book is about interpretation, not history. Readers have at their fingertips a library of scholarship to supplement the readings presented here.

Therefore, this is not just another book on prayer and worship, because it brings new materials to the task of interpretation. It brings cultural materials to the task, not for the sake of novelty, but because they seem to be the most appropriate tools to allow us to recognize the "otherness" of the world of early Christianity and also to begin seeing things the way early Christians did.

CHAPTER ONE

"Supplications, Prayers, Intercessions, and Thanksgivings" (1 Timothy 2:1)

W hat is prayer? How do we interpret individual prayers? Should we, in fact, be so analytical? Inasmuch as human ability to learn, analyze, and describe is itself a gift from God, yes, we should strive to learn as much as possible about human communication with God, which we describe as worship and prayer. This is by no means the first attempt to understand biblical prayer. Biblical interpreters are all grateful heirs of Hermann Gunkel's description of the Psalms.[1] His work and that of his followers provide us with analyses of various types of psalms, identifications of their formal elements and indications of their different purposes. In addition, productive attention has been given both in antiquity and in modern criticism to understanding the premier Christian prayer, the Our Father.[2] Scholars have also examined topics related to prayer, such as the Israelite roots of Christian prayer,[3] the prayers of

1. Hermann Gunkel, *The Psalms: A Form-Critical Introduction* (Philadelphia: Fortress, 1967); B. W. Anderson, *Out of the Depths: The Psalms Speak for Us Today* (Philadelphia: Westminster, 1983); Claus Westermann, *Praise and Lament in the Psalms* (Atlanta: John Knox, 1981); and Hans-Joachim Kraus, *Psalms 1–59: A Commentary* (Minneapolis: Augsburg, 1988); see also Patrick Miller, *They Cried to the Lord: The Form and Theology of Biblical Prayer* (Minneapolis: Fortress, 1994).

2. Gordon J. Bahr, "The Use of the Lord's Prayer in the Primitive Church," *JBL* 84 (1965): 153-59; Eric George Jay, "Prayer in the New Testament and Apostolic Fathers," in his *Origen's Treatise on Prayer* (London: SPCK, 1954), 3-43.

3. Roger T. Beckwith, "The Daily and Weekly Worship of the Primitive Church in Relation to Its Jewish Antecedents. Pt 1," *EvQ* 56 (1984): 65-80; James H. Charlesworth, "A Prolegomenon to the Study of the Jewish Background of the Hymns and Prayers in the New Testament," *JJS* 33 (1982): 264-85; Charlesworth, "Prayer in the New Testament in Light of

Jesus,[4] prayer in the Pauline letters,[5] the function of prayer in Luke's Gospel,[6] and the shape of New Testament doxologies.[7] Of course, there are many fine works examining prayer in the Bible,[8] the Greco-Roman world,[9] and the early church.[10] Recently a working group in the Society of Biblical Literature studied prayer in the Greco-Roman period (1989-92), the results of which appeared in *The Lord's Prayer and Other Prayer Texts from the Greco-Roman Era.*[11] While this volume contains seven articles on different ancient authors and their prayers, its major contribution lies in the rich bibliography for studying a given prayer and the history of interpretation of these select prayers. Yet it is fair to say that in terms of methods of interpreting prayer, even this latest effort brings little new to the table. Current scholarship on biblical prayer operates from the perspective of form criticism and history-of-religions examination of background, but not necessarily from the perspective of inter-

---

Contemporary Jewish Prayers," in SBLSP (1993): 773-86; Charlesworth, "Jewish Hymns, Odes, and Prayers (ca. 167 B.C.E–135 C.E.)," in *Early Judaism and Its Modern Interpreters,* ed. R. A. Kraft and G. W. E. Nicklesburg (Atlanta: Scholars, 1986), 411-36. See also Michael Wyschogrod, "The 'Shema Israel' in Judaism and the New Testament (Deut 6:4-9; 11:13-21; Num 15:37-41)," in *The Roots of Our Common Faith,* ed. H. G. Link (Geneva: World Council of Churches, 1984), 23-32; and T. Zahavy, "Three Stages in the Development of Early Rabbinic Prayer," in *From Ancient Israel to Modern Judaism: Essays in Honor of Marvin Fox,* vol. 1, ed. Jacob Neusner, Ernest Frerichs, and Nahum Sarna (Atlanta: Scholars, 1989), 233-65.

4. For example, Joachim Jeremias, *The Prayers of Jesus* (Philadelphia: Fortress, 1978); and Jeremias, *The Lord's Prayer* (Philadelphia: Fortress, 1980).

5. Gordon P. Wiles, *Paul's Intercessory Prayers: The Significance of the Intercessory Prayer Passages in Paul's Letters* (Cambridge: Cambridge University Press, 1974).

6. Allison A. Trites, "The Prayer Motif in Luke-Acts," in *Perspectives on Luke-Acts,* ed. Charles H. Talbert (Danville, Va.: Association of Baptist Professors of Religion, 1978), 168-86; and Steven F. Plymale, *The Prayer Texts of Luke-Acts* (New York: Peter Lang, 1991).

7. Reinhard Deichgräber, *Gotteshymnus und Christushymnus in der frühen Christenheit* (Göttingen: Vandenhoeck & Ruprecht, 1967), 25-40, 97-102; Matthew Black, "The Doxology to the *Pater Noster* with a Note on Matthew 6:13b," in *A Tribute to Geza Vermes,* ed. Philip Davies and Richard White (Sheffield: JSOT Press, 1991), 327-38.

8. Samuel E. Balentine, *Prayer in the Hebrew Bible* (Minneapolis: Fortress, 1993); and Miller, *They Cried to the Lord.*

9. Simon Pulleyn, *Prayer in Greek Religion* (Oxford: Clarendon, 1997).

10. See Carl A. Volz, "Prayer in the Early Church," in *A Primer on Prayer,* ed. Paul R. Sponheim (Philadelphia: Fortress, 1988), 36-50.

11. This volume was edited by James H. Charlesworth with Mark Harding and Mark Kiley (Valley Forge, Pa.: Trinity, 1994). See also Mark Kiley et al., eds., *Prayer from Alexander to Constantine: A Critical Anthology* (New York: Routledge, 1997).

pretation, since its aim continues to be some form of history, not interpretation.

Yet there are available to scholars fresh and productive ways of interpreting prayers, namely, the resources of cultural anthropology. Bruce Malina in particular has digested and made available to biblical scholars many of the basic, reliable models from the social sciences for understanding the communication that is prayer and the social exchange that occurs during it. Hence, if imitation is the best form of praise, then using the material Bruce Malina has introduced to scholars is the finest, sincerest praise I can give to a colleague and mentor. Social science models for interpretation have also been employed by other scholars, whose suggestions will be considered as well.[12] Our aim, then, is to systematically introduce readers to these cultural ways of interpreting prayers by providing an appropriate set of social and cultural lenses. Prayer, then, in other words.

What Is Prayer?

In modern Christian history, spiritual writers discussing prayer have tended to begin their works by attempting to define what prayer is, how it might differ from similar speech directed to a sovereign, and how we can describe various kinds of prayers. This threefold task is both necessary and profitable. If, for example, we wanted to know what "apple" means, we would want to know how "apple" differs from "orange" and then how many kinds of apples are available. If we think apples are "red," such as Red Delicious, Northern Spy, and McIntosh, then we miss out on "green" apples such as Granny Smith and "yellow" apples such as Golden Delicious and "mottled red/yellow" apples such as Gala and Braeburn. We regularly make such definitions and classifications in our lives, which can be very profitable in examining prayer and prayers.

---

12. Jerome H. Neyrey, *2 Peter, Jude*, AB 37C (New York: Doubleday, 1993), 94-101; Douglas E. Oakman, "The Lord's Prayer in Social Perspective," in *Authenticating the Words of Jesus*, ed. Bruce Chilton and Craig Evans (Leiden: Brill, 1999), 137-86; and John J. Pilch, "Prayer in Luke," *TBT* 18 (1980): 221-25.

Traditional Definitions of Prayer

Many factors go into defining what prayer is. One traditional way has been to gather a list of the terms used for prayer in the Scriptures. Such lists tend to be long in the number of terms found but short on analysis of the prayers identified as such. Moreover, this type of inquiry is more likely to find lexical items that may or may not refer to an identifiable form or type. Let us take, for example, the list of synonyms surfaced by the author of the article on prayer found in the *New Catholic Encyclopedia (NCE):*

> The words used to express it in Scripture are: to call up (Gen., iv,26); to intercede (Job, xxii,10); to mediate (Is., liii,10); to consult (I Kings, xxviii,6); to beseech (Ex., xxxii,11); and, very commonly, to cry out to. The Fathers speak of it as the elevation of the mind to God with a view to asking proper things from Him (St. John Damascene, "De fide," III, xxiv, in *P.G.,* XCIV, 1090); communing and conversing with God (St. Gregory of Nyssa, "De oratione dom.," in *P.G.,* XLIV, 1125); talking with God (St. John Chrysostom, "Hom. xxx in Gen.," n. 5, in *P.G.,* LIII, 280). It is therefore the expression of our desires to God whether for ourselves or others.

A very rich harvest of terms, but merely descriptive — no definition is offered. The list ultimately begs for a model to organize and interpret these data. This list is long, perhaps too long; compared to it is the exceptionally lean definition of prayer as "an address to or celebration of a deity."[13] If the *NCE*'s descriptive definition seems too expansive, Kiley's is too lean to be helpful. Nevertheless, both seem to agree that prayer is a distinctive communication with God, which invites a fuller analytical description of the phenomenon of prayer from the sociology of communication.

Malina's Operative Definition of Prayer

Twenty years ago in an article much too large for the journal in which it was printed,[14] Bruce Malina analyzed prayer as an "act of communication." His definition immediately sets him apart from other authors, such

---

13. Kiley et al., *Prayer,* 1.
14. Bruce J. Malina, "What Is Prayer?" *TBT* 18, no. 4 (1980): 214-20.

as the one who wrote the article on prayer in the *NCE;* he defined prayer as "an act of the virtue of religion which consists in asking proper gifts or graces from God." Malina's description as an "act of communication," however, aims to widen the horizon for understanding prayer and to engage in a cross-cultural examination of it. Typical of Malina, he provides a definition of prayer that describes all types of prayers and is rooted in the human phenomenon of communication. "Prayer is a socially meaningful act of communication, bearing directly upon persons perceived as somehow supporting, maintaining, and controlling the order of existence of the one praying, and performed with the purpose of getting results from or in the interaction of communication."[15] This definition identifies the nature of the communication activity, its object and its purpose. In the act of communicating, we can identify five regular, characteristic elements.

1. The *sender* of the prayer, a person or group. Their sending of a communication presumes a prior relationship between themselves and God.[16]
2. The *message* they communicate might be petition, adoration, contrition, or thanksgiving.
3. The *medium* of their message, moreover, might be verbal or substantive or both. Although we tend to consider prayer as only verbal activity, there are many nonverbal forms of communication: (a) petition or praise may be carved on amulets that are then worn; (b) prayers may be written and stuffed into cracks in the temple wall in Jerusalem or tied to prayer trees, such as I have found both in the American Southwest and in Muslim countries; (c) prayers may be carved on prayer wheels or painted on kites; (d) sacrifices, incense, and libations (all nonverbal) may be offered to God.
4. The *receiver* of the prayer is the person perceived as "supporting, maintaining, and controlling the order of existence of the one praying," which presupposes a superior/subordinate relationship.
5. The *purpose* of prayer is to have some effect on the person with whom the pray-er communicates; that is, it seeks results, which may for the time being be classified as petitions for goods and services or as maintenance of relationships.

15. Malina, "What Is Prayer?" 215.
16. Lawrence S. Cunningham, *Catholic Prayer* (New York: Crossroad, 1992), 9.

This resembles what one finds in the sociology of knowledge about communication: Who says what to whom, when, how, and why? There is nothing controversial about this definition, except perhaps how Malina goes on to discuss many different purposes of prayer. The values of his definition include: (1) comprehensive identification of five distinct elements in prayer; (2) sensitivity to other verbal as well as written material media of communication; (3) definition of the recipient of prayer, which excludes potentates, popes, and presidents; and (4) broad description of the function of prayer as seeking "results" and "interaction," which invite a generous expansion of types of prayers beyond petition and praise. Moreover, reflection on our normal patterns of communication immediately verifies his definition. Who? Says what? To Whom? When and how? And why?

A Typology of Prayers

Why do people pray? What effect(s) do they seek to have upon God? Or, to put it another way, what types of prayers do people pray? Many of us were raised to think of either two or four types of prayers. How, then, to make a full accounting of the types of prayers?

How Many Types of Prayers? One, Two, or Four?

Let us start with what we know. In times past, scholars of ancient prayer made their own surveys of Greco-Roman prayers. An author may recognize several types of prayers but try to reduce them all to one type. Wolfson, for example, finds that while Philo talks about a variety of prayers, he lifts one type to such a position of prominence that he seems to compress many other types into this one type, which is "praise":

> Under the head of the preservation offering is embraced what is called the praise-offering (αἰνέσεως) . . . (the blessed person) has as his bounded duty to requite God . . . with hymns (ὕμνοις) and benedictions (εὐδαιμονισμοῖς) and prayers (εὐχαῖς) and sacrifices (θυσίαις) and the other expressions of gratitude (εὐχαριστίαις) as religion demands. *All these collected and summed up have obtained the single name*

of praise (αἰνέσεως). (*On the Special Laws* 1.224, emphasis added; see *On Planting* 135)[17]

And while Philo knows of petitionary prayer ("Prayer is an asking for good things," *On Agriculture* 99), "praise" is his chief, best, and most inclusive prayer. Were Philo our only ancient voice, prayer would basically be the praise of God by the world's philosophical elites.

Wolfson, however, in his comprehensive reading of Philo, balanced the remark about one type of prayer with a summary of other types of prayers, each with a characteristic purpose. "In Greek, the principal terms for prayer are four. (1) εὔχεσθαι, referring primarily to the prayer of petition, (2) προσεύχεσθαι, normally meaning a prayer of thanksgiving, (3) . . . ἐπεύχεσθαι, having also the meaning of praying a curse, and (4) λιτέσθαι, chiefly used in the sense of praying for forgiveness."[18] Depending on how wide we cast our net, we find many authors, ancient and modern, who would collapse these four into two categories, petition and praise. Going back in time, we find Socrates remarking that Greeks typically distinguish two types of prayers: "It is the case that sacrificing is making a gift to the gods and praying is making a request of them" (Plato, *Euthyphro* 14c). A "gift" to the gods, of course, could be both verbal praise and a sacrificed animal. But Plato seems to reduce "prayer" to petition, that is, "asking for good things for us" (*Politics* 290d). Several modern studies of Greek prayers likewise argue the thesis that real prayer was prayer in need, that is, petitionary or supplicatory request; they argue that "ancient prayer accords little space to true gratitude."[19] While there is no disagreement about petitionary prayer, the phenomenon of "thanksgiving" is receiving considerable attention.[20] It is argued that "thanks" can be misleading, for in the culture of honor and shame, such pray-ers are really seeking to honor and praise god, a nuance often lost on moderns. The tendency of this material,

17. Readers are asked for their patience when Greek terms occasionally appear; the problem for us lies in the English translations of these words, which might need some tweaking. Hence, it is good to have the original Greek.

18. Harry A. Wolfson, *Philo: Foundations of Religion Philosophy in Judaism, Christianity, and Islam* (Cambridge: Harvard University Press, 1947), 2:237.

19. H. S. Versnel, ed., *Faith, Hope, and Worship: Aspects of Religious Mentality in the Ancient World* (Leiden: Brill, 1981), 2.

20. Pulleyn, *Prayer in Greek Religion*, 39-55; Versnel, "Religious Mentality in Ancient Prayer," in *Faith, Hope, and Worship*, 34-62.

then, seems both to identify two or four types of prayers and to contract them into two types, petition and praise.

What of the Psalms? What types of prayers do they include? The book of Psalms, a collection of 150 psalms, provides us with another important fountain of information about types of prayers. Scholars who study the psalms generally tend to classify the prayers in the psalms into hymns of (1) praise, (2) thanksgiving, (3) lament, (4) petition, and (5) confession and penance.[21] But as with Greek prayers, scholars feel the urge to reduce this list to two categories: "The result is then, that in the Psalter there are two dominant categories, the hymn (including the Psalm of thanks) and the lament."[22] Later on in his study, Westermann expressed this generalization more clearly: "This analysis is determined by the two basic modes of speaking to God: praise and petition,"[23] or "prayers (words directed to God in supplication or rejoicing)."[24]

Yet scholars have also conducted their own investigations of the forms of prayer and the rich vocabulary of prayer in the Christian Scriptures. Does this advance our question of the types of prayers? Because a harvest of this material may advance our inquiry, we gathered a sample of New Testament terms for prayer, which yields the following list:

1. "Sing a song" (ᾄδω, ᾠδή): "They sang a new song" (Rev 5:9).
2. "Psalm" (ψαλμός): "Sing psalms and hymns and spiritual songs with thanksgiving in your hearts to God" (Col 3:16; Eph 5:19; Rom 15:9).
3. "Hymn" (ὕμνος) or song of praise: "in psalms and hymns and spiritual songs" (Eph 5:19; Matt 26:30).
4. "Paean" (δοξολογία) (Rom 11:36; 16:25-27; Eph 3:20-21; Phil 4:20; Jude 24-25).
5. "Bless" (εὐλογέω) and "blessing" (εὐλογία): "With it [tongue] we bless the Lord and Father, and with it we curse men" (James 3:9; Luke 1:64; 2:28; Rev 5:12-13).
6. "Praise" (αἰνέω, αἴνεσις): "a great army of heavenly angels praising God" (Luke 2:13; 18:43; Heb 13:15; Eph 1:6).
7. "Gratitude" or "appreciation" (εὐχαριστία): "By prayer and supplica-

21. Claus Westermann, *The Praise of God in the Psalms* (Richmond, Va.: John Knox, 1965), 15-35; Miller, *They Cried to the Lord*.
22. Westermann, *Praise of God*, 18.
23. Westermann, *Praise of God*, 35.
24. Westermann, *Praise of God*, 11.

tion with thanksgiving let your request be made known to God" (Phil 4:6; Rev 4:9; 7:12).

7. "Confession as praise" (ἐξομολογέω): "Confess that Jesus is Lord to the glory of God" (Phil 2:11; Matt 11:25; Rom 15:9).

8. "Confession of sins" (ἐξομολογέω): "Confess your sins to one another" (James 5:16; Mark 1:5).

9. "Petitionary prayer" (εὐχή): "The prayer of faith will save the sick man" (James 5:15), and (προσευχή): "Pray at all times in the Spirit, with all prayer and supplication" (Eph 6:18; Rom 15:30).

Seven of these terms have as their purpose "praise," and two are "petition-ary" prayer. Yet, problems arise with such a list, for it implies that just be-cause we have a label (e.g., "song," "psalm," "hymn," or "paean"), it must represent a distinctive kind of prayer essentially different from other prayers. Moreover, while some of these labels belong to a recognizable lit-erary form, most do not. Finally, what terms are synonymous or overlap in meaning? Which is a genus, which are species?

Not to prolong this, but we should examine Origen's interpretation of 1 Timothy 2:1 where he provides a fourfold classification of prayer, which he claims he finds in 1 Timothy.

> This is what he says, "First of all, then, I urge that supplications (δεήσεις), prayers (προσευχάς), intercessions (ἐντεύξεις), and thanksgivings (εὐχαριστίας) be made for all men and so forth" (1 Tim. 2:1). I think that *supplication* is a prayer offered with entreaty to get something a person lacks, while *prayer* is something nobler offered by a person with praise and for greater objects. And I think that *intercession* is a petition for certain things addressed to God by someone who has some greater boldness, while *thanksgiving* is a statement of gratitude made with prayers for receiving good things from God. (Origen, *On Prayer* 14.2, emphasis added)

"Supplications" and "intercessions" seem to refer to the same kind of prayer, namely, petitionary. Zechariah's "supplication" for a son had been heard (Luke 1:13), and Moses supplicated God when the golden calf was manifested (Exod 32:11). "Intercession," Origen says, describes the action of the Spirit interceding for us (Rom 8:26-27) and the requests made by Joshua for the sun to stand still (Josh 10:12) or by Samson to die destroying the Philistines (Judg 16:30). The only difference seems to be that a broker or mediator "intercedes" for the pray-er. As was the case with Philo, Origen's premier type of "prayer" is "praise," which is similar to "thanksgiving," which is a "statement of gratitude." Origen allows "supplication, intercession, and thanksgiving" (14.6) to be given to the saints as well as to God. Origen comes to his task with a conventional notion of four types of prayer, which he sees all too conveniently in 1 Timothy 2:1. So many types of prayers, so many names for prayers. But there is a higher way of reading.

Malina's Full Typology

Let us turn back to the analysis of Bruce Malina for suggestions on a classification of prayers that is both sufficiently inclusive of what various cultures actually do and discriminating enough to discern many basic purposes for addressing God. Malina classified prayers in terms of their purposes, identifying seven results or aims the pray-er desires through the communication that is prayer:

1. *Petitionary* ("I want . . ."): prayers to obtain goods and services for individual and social needs.
2. *Regulatory* ("Do as I tell you . . ."): prayers to control the activity of God, to command God to order people and things about on behalf of the one praying.
3. *Interactional* ("Where are you when I need you?"): prayers to maintain emotional ties with God, especially in the psalms of lament.
4. *Self-focused* ("I gave them your word . . . I kept them safe"): prayers that identify the self — individual and social — to God; prayers of confession, as well as boasting and superiority.
5. *Heuristic* ("Tell me why . . . ?" "Should I marry?"): prayers that explore the world of God and God's workings within us individually and collectively; meditative prayers, perceptions of the spirit in prayer.
6. *Imaginative/Contemplative* ("I was caught up to the second heaven"): prayers to create an environment of one's own with God; prayers in tongues and those recited in languages unknown to the pray-er.
7. *Acknowledgment* ("I have something to tell you"). In this category we place all speech that (1) acknowledges God's sovereignty or glory,

(2) praises and honors God, and (3) expresses gratitude and appreciation for divine benefaction.[25]

Malina next classified prayers in terms of those that seek to have an effect on God. He identifies seven results or aims the pray-er desires through
the communication that is prayer. It is worth our while to examine each of
these types in greater detail.

Petitionary ("I need . . ."). This type of prayer requests goods and
services. For example, "Now, Lord, look at their threats, and grant to
your servants to speak your word with all boldness" (Acts 4:29). Note,
moreover, Jesus' instruction to make petitionary prayer: "Ask, and it will
be given you; search, and you will find; knock, and the door will be
opened for you" (Matt 7:7). Words frequently used to express this type of
prayer include: (1) to ask with urgency, based on presumed need
(δέησις), e.g., Luke 1:13; (2) to speak to or make requests of God
(προσεύχομαι), e.g., Acts 26:29; 2 Corinthians 13:7, 9; James 5:16; (3) to
ask (ἐρωτάω), e.g., John 16:26; 17:9; (4) to ask for with urgency, even to
the point of demanding (αἰτέω), e.g., James 1:5 and 4:3; (5) to supplicate
or beseech God (ἱκετεύω), e.g., Isocrates 7.69; and (6) to pray or to request (εὔχομαι), e.g., Acts 27:29.

Regulatory ("Do as I tell you . . ."). This type of prayer seeks to control the activity of God, commanding God to order people and things
about on behalf of the one praying.[26] Scholars distinguish the verb "to
pray (for)" (εὔχομαι) from "to pray against" (ἀράομαι), the latter being
conveniently translated as "to curse."[27] The former expresses one's
wishes for oneself, and the latter one's wishes regarding other people.
Moreover, two kinds of "curses" are distinguished. The civic curse petitions punishment on crimes considered bad by all and that should not
go unpunished; it was intended to uphold the just order of the cosmos.
Second, the personal or domestic "curse" seeks to harm or restrain some-

25. Malina, "What Is Prayer?" 217-18.

26. Included here are curses, spells, incantations, and the like. See Christopher A.
Faraone and Dirk Obgink, eds., *Magika Hiera: Ancient Greek Magic and Religion* (New York:
Oxford University Press, 1991); Hans Dieter Betz, ed., *The Greek Magical Papyri in Transla-
tion*, 2nd ed. (Chicago: University of Chicago Press, 1986); and Martin Meyer and Richard
Smith, eds., *Ancient Christian Magic: Coptic Texts of Ritual Power* (San Francisco: Harper,
1994).

27. Pulleyn, *Prayer in Greek Religion*, 70-77.

one whom an individual perceives as threatening his good fortune; it may be considered a "pre-emptive strike."[28] Those who study these matters identify four contexts or life situations in which domestic curses are found: (1) judicial, against one's courtroom enemies; (2) against thieves and calumniators; (3) amatory curses; and (4) sporting curses against players and charioteers.[29] For example, someone wrote this curse against his rival in the hippodrome: "Bind, tie down, fetter, strike with a javelin, overturn, finish off, destroy, kill, crush Eucherius the charioteer and all the horses."[30]

Interactional ("Where are you when I need you?"). This prayer seeks to maintain emotional ties with God. The "lament," which is found in the Psalter, is an apt illustration of it, namely, a complaint to God. The pray-er asks a question of God, which is not a request for information but a protest at God's seeming inactivity:

Why do you hide your face?
    Why do you forget our affliction? (Ps 44:24)

How long, O LORD? Will you forget me forever? (Ps 13:1)

O God, why do you cast us off forever? (Ps 74:1)

These and other questions of complaint directly challenge the way God has acted, in particular the perceived failure of God to provide what God has promised. For example, Israel tells God how ironic it is that having delivered them from slavery in Egypt, God will let them die in the desert or at the hands of other enemies. The pray-er interprets current distress to be an inexcusable inconsistency on God's part, which seems most inappropriate to the faithfulness and compassion that are God's hallmark. Hence, the pray-er complains to God: "Why are you doing this or allowing it to happen?"[31] Hence, interactional prayer seeks a result, namely, the restoration of a previously good relationship with God.

Self-focused ("I gave them your word . . . I kept them safe"). The person

28. Pulleyn, *Prayer in Greek Religion,* 80-89.

29. Pulleyn, *Prayer in Greek Religion,* 87.

30. Pulleyn, *Prayer in Greek Religion,* 83. H. S. Versnel itemizes many of the types we are covering here, including "offensive, indecent and improper prayers," in *Faith, Hope, and Worship,* 21-26.

31. Miller, *They Cried,* 71-71.

praying identifies the self — individual and social — to God.[32] The posture toward God may be humility or boasting, confession of a job finished or of superiority to others. Occasionally we find this in the psalms in which God is addressed, not in petition or praise, but in innocent confidence:

> For God alone my soul waits in silence;
>> from him comes my salvation.
> He alone is my rock and my salvation,
>> my fortress; I shall never be shaken. . . .
> For God alone my soul waits in silence,
>> for my hope is from him.
> He alone is my rock and my salvation,
>> my fortress; I shall not be shaken. (Ps 62:1-2, 5-6)

Clearer is the psalm whose entire address to God is a self-focused expression of one's right relationship with God:

> O Lord, my heart is not lifted up,
>> my eyes are not raised too high;
> I do not occupy myself with things
>> too great and too marvelous for me.
> But I have calmed and quieted my soul,
>> like a weaned child with its mother;
>> so is my soul within me.
> O Israel, hope in the Lord
>> from this time on and forevermore.
>>>> (Ps 131:1-3; see also Pss 40:10-11 and 108:1)

As we shall see later in this study, the best sample of this type of prayer is found in Jesus' Great Prayer in John 17. The following sample from that source illustrates what it looks like and what it aims to do.

> I have glorified you on earth (v 4). I have manifested your name (vv 6, 26).

> I have given them the words you have given me (vv 8, 14).

---

32. Versnel ("Religious Mentality," 6-8, especially n. 70) discusses what we call "self-focused" under the label *"Gebetsegoismus,"* thus drawing on an old German conversation.

I have kept them in your name (v 12a). I have guarded them (v 12b).

I have sent them into the world (v 18). I have consecrated myself (v 19).

I have given them the glory you have given me (v 22).

In all these statements Jesus addresses God and manifests the current state of his agency: he has done God's will, both by laboring for God's glory and by shepherding the flock God gave him.[33]

Jesus' parable in Luke 18:9-14 contrasts two men praying: a Pharisee prays a self-focused prayer and a tax collector petitions for mercy. We are not interested in justifying which kind of speech is acceptable to God, because all that matters here is that people in fact talk to God this way.[34] Long ago Joachim Jeremias pointed to a talmudic prayer (*b. Ber* 28b), which we cite to establish the fact of self-focused prayer: "I thank you, O Lord my God, that you have given me my lot with those who sit in the seat of learning, and not with those who sit at the street corners; for I am early to work, and they are early to work; I am early to work on the words of the Torah, and they are early to work on things of no moment. I weary myself and they weary themselves; I weary myself and profit by it, while they weary themselves to no profit. I run, and they run; I run toward the life of the Age to Come, and they run towards the pit of destruction."[35] While the pray-er begins with "thanks" for God's favor, he then declares to God in a

---

33. Although he seems to consider "prayer" only as "petitionary" speech, Ernst Käsemann (*The Testament of Jesus: A Study of John in the Light of Chapter 17* [London: SCM, 1968], 5) commented on the variety of Jesus' speech in John 17. Yet he writes: "This is not a supplication, but a proclamation directed to the Father in such manner that his disciples can hear it also. The speaker is not a needy petitioner but the divine revealer and therefore the prayer moves over into being an address, admonition, consolation and prophecy." Other examples of self-focused prayers would include Pss 23; 84; 91; 131, and in the New Testament, Luke 2:29-32.

34. F. Gerald Downing, "The Ambiguity of 'The Pharisee and the Toll-Collector' (Luke 18:9-14) in the Greco-Roman World of Late Antiquity," *CBQ* 54 (1992): 80-99.

35. Joachim Jeremias, *The Parables of Jesus*, rev. ed. (New York: Scribner, 1963), 142. He points to another example of this type of prayer: "I (who study the law) am a creature of God, and my fellow man is a creature (of God). My work is in the city, his in the field; I rise early to my work, he rises early to his. Just as he cannot excel in my work, so I cannot excel in his. Perhaps you will say, I do much and he does little (for the Torah). But we have learned . . . he who offers much and he who offers little are equal, provided that each directs his heart to heaven" (*b. Ber* 17a).

self-focused way that he has cooperated with this favor and so has walked the way of righteousness, in contrast to those who walk the way of evil.

Self-focused prayer, then, is found in the Talmud, but we find instances of it in ancient Egyptian prayers, indicating both temporal and geographical continuity. In this prayer a deceased Egyptian stands before god and communicates his innocence.

> Behold, "*Sati-merfiti*, Lord of Justice,"
> I have brought you justice;
> I have expelled deceit for you.
> I have not committed evil against men.
> I have not mistreated cattle.
> I have not done violence to a poor man.
> I have not defamed a slave to his superior.
> I have not made anyone sick.
> I have not killed.
> I have not had sexual relations with a boy.
> I have not defiled myself.
> I have neither increased or decreased the grain measure.
> I am pure! I am pure! I am pure! I am pure!
> My purity is the purity of the great *benu* bird in Herakleopolis.[36]

Heuristic ("Tell me why . . . ?"). Job, who best exemplifies this kind of speech to God, searches relentlessly to know God and God's ways. Many times Job asks heuristic questions about God and God's ways (3:11-15; 6:8-13; 9:1-10; 12:2-25), but at the end of the book he speaks directly to God, which we identify as a prayer, a heuristic prayer:

> Then Job answered the LORD:
> "I know that you can do all things,
> and that no purpose of yours can be thwarted.
> 'Who is this that hides counsel without knowledge?'
> Therefore I have uttered what I did not understand,
> things too wonderful for me, which I did not know. . . .
> I had heard of you by the hearing of the ear,
> but now my eye sees you;

36. James B. Pritchard, *Ancient Near Eastern Texts* (Princeton: Princeton University Press, 1950), 34. The citation in our text is less than half of the whole confession and is more straightforward.

therefore I despise myself,
and repent in dust and ashes." (Job 42:1-6)[37]

Perhaps the best illustration of heuristic prayer is found in Plutarch's treatise on oracles, in which he enumerates the kinds of interrogations made by low-status and elite people of the oracle. He informs us of the kinds of questions put to god: "The interrogations are on slight and commonplace matters, like the hypothetical questions in school: if one ought to marry, or to start on a voyage, or to make a loan; and the most important consultations on the part of States concern the yield from crops, the increase of herds, and public health" (Plutarch, *Oracles at Delphi* 408C).

Imaginative/Contemplative ("I was caught up to the second heaven"). Occasionally those praying find themselves having out-of-body experiences.[38] They might be taken up to the heavens (2 Cor 12:1-3) or receive visions on earth.[39] They may pray to God in "tongues," a language known only to them, unless an interpreter is present (1 Cor 14:6-26).

Acknowledgment ("I bless you . . . I name you Sovereign Lord"). In this category we find speech addressed to God that (1) acknowledges God's sovereignty or glory, (2) praises and declares God's worthiness, or (3) expresses gratitude for divine benefaction. God in the Christian Scriptures cannot be ascribed honor, because there is no person above God to bestow honor on him. Neither does God acquire honor, but rather has it acknowledged.

Excursus: Does God Enjoy Ascribed and/or Achieved Honor?

Whether Israelites think God does or does not achieve glory and honor depends on whether the people's theology was henotheistic or monotheistic. Henotheism implies that there are many gods in the cosmos, but Israel

37. Versnel ("Religious Mentality," 6-8) indicates that the gods were called upon at times in some detective capacity: "Did D steal the gown?" "Has so and so kidnapped my slave?" He goes on to describe questions asked of various oracles.

38. John J. Pilch, "Altered States of Consciousness in the Synoptics," in *The Social Setting of Jesus and the Gospels,* ed. Wolfgang Stegemann, Bruce J. Malina, and Gerd Theissen (Minneapolis: Fortress, 2002), 103-16; Pilch, "Holy Men and Their Sky Journeys," *BTB* 35 (2005): 106-11.

39. John J. Pilch, "Altered States of Consciousness: A 'Kitbashed' Model," *BTB* 26 (1996): 133-38; Pilch, "Appearances of the Risen Jesus in Cultural Context: Experiences of Alternate Reality," *BTB* 28 (1998): 52-60.

chooses one, Yahweh, with whom to ally itself in covenant. In this context we find references to God at war, manifesting power, routing nations and their gods, and so gaining or achieving honor, just as any earthly monarch might defeat another monarch and his army. Hence, we find many references to God's mighty and outstretched arm (Deut 4:34; 5:15; 2 Kings 17:36; Pss 44:3; 89:10, 13). Isaiah describes God viewing injustice, putting on armor, and then "his own arm brought him victory" (59:16-17). Another body part, the right hand, always expresses honor, including honor gained by military prowess (Exod 3:20; 15:6, 9, 12; Ps 89:13). God's right hand might liberate (and thus defeat those enslaving God's people) or defeat the enemy outright, but "victory" attends God's right hand:

> There are glad songs of victory in the tents of the righteous:
> "The right hand of the LORD does valiantly;
>   the right hand of the LORD is exalted;
>   the right hand of the LORD does valiantly." (Ps 118:15-16)

But in a monotheistic perspective, because there is only one God and no other, God has no one to battle, and so is no longer thought of as achieving honor. Furthermore, under the pressure of anti-anthropomorphic criticism, God is never changed and so does not increase in honor.

"Acknowledgment" may be found on the pray-ers' lips, or expressed by their posture (bend the knee; prostration) or in their hearts. All prayers of acknowledgment "inform" God of something, not in the sense that they provide God with new knowledge. God makes claims by virtue of creative powers, benefaction, and virtue, which are acknowledged by his devotees as right and just. Thus acknowledgment expresses itself by way of celebrating the powers, names, and deeds of God. Fundamentally prayers of acknowledgment honor God in different but related ways: (1) by acknowledging and confessing God's sovereignty and majesty; (2) by naming God by a unique and special name, such as Savior, Lord, Father, and the like; and (3) by praising, glorifying, blessing, magnifying God for his deeds and powers. The acknowledgment factor of this type of prayer is highlighted in the following examples from the Psalter:

> *Know* that the LORD is God.
>   It is he that made us, and we are his. (Ps 100:3)

I will *confess* you among the Gentiles,
  and *sing* praises to your name. (Rom 15:9//Ps 18:49)

Let all the earth *fear* the LORD;
  . . . *stand in awe* of him. (Ps 33:8)

Although Israelites and Christians acclaim the name of the Lord ("O
LORD, our Sovereign, / how majestic is your *name* in all the earth!" Ps 8:1),
the same phenomenon was found throughout the Greco-Roman world, as
is instanced by Seneca: "You may address the author of this world by *different names* . . . call him Jupiter Best and Greatest, and the Thunderer and
the Stayer. . . . Any name you choose will be properly applied to him if it
connotes some force that operates in the domain of heaven — *his titles
may be as countless as are his benefits*" (Seneca, *Benefits* 4.7.1, emphasis
added). Finally, the Psalter again provides a variety of different ways in
which Israel glorified, praised, and exalted God. Alleluia!

The heavens *declare* the *glory* of God. (Ps 19:1 KJV)

Great is the LORD and greatly to be *praised*
  in the city of our God. (Ps 48:1)

Clap your hands, all you peoples;
shout to God with *loud songs of joy.* (Ps 47:1)

Sing to the LORD, *bless* his name; . . .
Declare his glory among the nations,
  his marvelous works among all the peoples. (Ps 96:2-3)

Bless the LORD, O my soul,
  and all that is within me,
    bless his holy name. (Ps 103:1)

Praise the LORD!
Praise the LORD from the heavens. (Ps 148:1)

Acknowledgment prayer, then, honors God in the ways in which any
earthly person was honored, shown respect, and revered. The semantic
word field of individual verbs expressing honor indicates the rich and
manifold garden of praise whereby Greeks, Romans, and Israelites addressed prayers of praise to God.

Appreciation and Gratitude. We offer this eighth type of prayer as a further refinement of the prayer of *acknowledgment.* We seek to indicate that praise, glory, and worship include "giving thanks," but that giving thanks is a special kind of acknowledgment. Just as interactional prayer is lament but also petition that the relationship be renewed, and heuristic prayer at bottom is also petitionary prayer to know, comparably *appreciation/gratitude* is a species of *acknowledgment.* Throughout this study we prefer the terms "appreciation" and "gratitude" to the more popular English word "thanksgiving," for reasons that will shortly appear.

Whereas New Testament gratitude is expressed by the verb εὐχαριστέω *(eucharisteō),* Hebrew has no equivalent. Gratitude is expressed "in the thanksoffering *tdh* and the psalm of thanksgiving."[40] In other words, "thanks" is united with sacrifice: together they reciprocate for favors received. To express gratitude, ancient Israel used the Hebrew words *brk* and *brkh,* words that come into English as *berakah* or *berakot.*[41] In the Greek translation of the Scriptures, *brk* is translated as "blessing" (εὐλογητός).[42] Hermann Beyer provides a needed insight: "The Israelite cannot find any better expression for his faith and gratitude and hope than by giving God the glory . . . this prayer is a declaration of God's works to His glory."[43] Put simply, one does not give thanks to God, but rather glorifies and praises God. Appreciation and gratitude, then, are expressed in terms of praise and glory. Even though most English translators of the Hebrew term *brk* render it as "thanks," we should understand that word in terms of praise of God and appreciation.

I will *give thanks* to the LORD with my whole heart. (Ps 9:1)

O *give thanks* to the LORD, call on his name. (Ps 105:1)

40. Hans Conzelmann, "εὐχαριστέω," in *TDNT* 9:409.

41. The initial tractate in the Mishnah is *Berakot.* It discusses when and how benediction to God should be made, but it provides no definition of "blessing" or right and wrong understandings of it.

42. Another caution: we are accustomed to read that a superior blesses an inferior, just as Isaac blessed Jacob or God blessed Israel; the prayer of Aaron expresses this most clearly: "The Lord bless you and keep you . . ." (Num 6:24-26). When humans "bless the Lord," they certainly do not act in the role of a superior blessing an inferior. In fact, God is never *blest* (passive recipient of blessing) but always *blessed,* that is honorable, praiseworthy, and glorious.

43. Hermann Beyer, "εὐλογέω," in *TDNT* 2:758-59.

O *give thanks* to the Lord, for he is good. . . .
O *give thanks* to the God of gods. (Ps 136:1-2)

Give thanks to the God of praise. (Sir 51:12)

The prayer in Tobit 12:6 is an excellent case in point. An angel instructs Tobias and Tobit how to pray, formulating for them an acceptable prayer. "Praise God and give thanks to him; exalt him and give thanks to him in the presence of all the living for what he has done for you. It is good to praise God and to exalt his name, worthily declaring the works of God. Do not be slow to give him thanks" (Tob 12:6). The father and son are told to "praise," "give thanks," "praise and exalt," "worthily declare," "give thanks." Sounds normal, but the English translation of "give thanks" swallows and homogenizes many rich Greek words simply as "thanks." The Septuagintal version of this passage tells a different story. For example, the first instance of "praise" masks the term for "bless" (εὐλογεῖτε τὸν θεόν); "give thanks" obscures the command to "acknowledge" or "praise" (ἐξομολογεῖσθε); next, "exalt and give thanks" are originally "give God majesty" (i.e., "acknowledge God's preeminence, μεγαλωσύνην δίδοτε) and "acknowledge [him]" (ἐξομολογεῖσθε); the statement "it is good to praise God and to exalt his name" is not true to the Greek words, which mean "bless" God (εὐλογεῖν τὸν θεόν) and "sing a song in cultic setting" (i.e., "'hymn' God's name," ὑψοῦν τὸ ὄνομα αὐτοῦ). "Worthily declaring the works of God" accurately renders the verb that means "to call attention to" (ὑποδεικνύοντες). Finally, "do not be slow to give him thanks" again does not express the original "bless" (ἐξομολογεῖσθαι). Our lexica urge us to revise the impulse to call everything "thanksgiving" to more shades of praise and acknowledgment.

Similarly, in the New Testament, the reaction of the healing of the woman bent over for twelve years is described as "she praised God" (Luke 13:13). Similarly in the incident of the ten lepers, Luke uses "glory" and "praise" to express gratitude: "One of them, when he saw that he was healed, turned back, praising (δοξάζων, literally, 'glorifying') God with a loud voice; and he fell on his face at Jesus' feet, showing gratitude (εὐχαριστῶν). . . . 'Was no one found to return and give praise (δοῦναι δόξαν, literally, "give glory") to God except this foreigner?'" (17:15-18).

EXCURSUS: WHAT DID THE GREEKS MEAN BY "GIVING THANKS"?

The problem begins with English (and French and German) where "thanksgiving" is popularly understood this way: "thanks" is a thing or object humans "give" to God. This suggests that some sort of offering is made, such as a "sacrifice of praise," and that this gesture has overtones of reciprocity. God has given, so we give in return. This is quite different from the way the ancient Greeks understood "thanksgiving," which differences we should note.

First, in classical literature a "response" to a proffered gift or favor could take two forms: (1) negative, as when the designated recipient says, "I am content" (καλῶς ἔχει μοι), where the focus is more on the recipient than on the giver; (2) positive, as when the recipient praises the giver.[44] Embedded in these responses is a sense of obligation to acquit oneself of the inevitable debt that comes with receiving gifts or favors. Quincey concludes: "The Greeks' habit in accepting an offer, service, etc. was to *confer praise and not thanks.* . . . The Greeks saw an *obligation created by a favour received* and sought to discharge it. . . . The service rendered in the ordinary world of business might need to be recorded [for future settlement]. [But] the *debt* created by a service between friends could be *settled* on the spot with ἔπαινος [praise]."[45]

Other classicists emphasize the sense of reciprocity understood in gift giving and gift responding. "Thanksgiving" almost always articulated the meaning of a sacrifice offered for a favor received; gift requires gift, even if asymmetrical. Pulleyn remarks: "One ideally needed to be able to offer a god some sort of *recompense in return for his help.*"[46] Yet he notes that prayers of gratitude are rare in classical Greece. Pulleyn interprets an ancient remark about "favor" and response in terms of reciprocity: "The χάρις [favor/gift] felt by Oenobius was reciprocated by an offering which, itself in turn, would make the god well disposed to help in the future. . . . One presumably made one's request and promised to deliver the quid pro quo as soon as was practicable."[47] Thus we observe the creation of a loop of giving, responding with expectation of more giving and so more responding.

In time another term for "thanksgiving" emerged, which is prominent in New Testament and early Christian literature, εὐχαριστέω

44. J. H. Quincey, "Greek Expressions of Thanks," *JHS* 86 (1966): 133.
45. Quincey, "Greek Expressions of Thanks," 157.
46. Pulleyn, *Prayer in Greek Religion,* 39, emphasis added.
47. Pulleyn, *Prayer in Greek Religion,* 40-41.

(*eucharisteō*, from which we draw the liturgical word "Eucharist"). Frederick Danker, in his culturally informed revision of the classical BAGD, defines the Greek verb εὐχαριστέω in a very nuanced manner: "(1) to show that one is under obligation, feel obligated to thank (common in diplomatic documents in which the recipient of a favor reciprocates with assurances of goodwill); (2) to express appreciation for benefits or blessings."[48] Louw and Nida, who interpret New Testament words in terms of their semantic word fields, concur. They define εὐχαριστέω as "to express gratitude for benefits or blessings. . . . Thanks is often expressed in highly idiomatic ways. For example, in some languages one says thanks by saying 'may God pay you.' In other instances, thankfulness may be expressed as 'you have made my heart warm.'"[49] We should not, however, consider these lexicographers idiosyncratic or egregious on this point, for the same is regularly mentioned by classicists writing on Greek prayer and reciprocity.[50]

Therefore, we must be extrasensitive to the meanings of "thanksgiving" in Greek, for they differ considerably from modern understandings of this word. Better to think of this as "showing appreciation for" or "praising" or "telling of God's wondrous deeds." While notions of obligation remain, particularly in liturgical prayers,[51] gratitude should not be perceived as a form of reciprocity.[52] It is a species of acknowledgment, it is praise pure and

48. Frederick W. Danker, *Greek-English Lexicon of the New Testament and Other Early Christian Literature*, 3rd ed. (Chicago: University of Chicago Press, 2000), 415-16.

49. Johannes Louw and Eugene A. Nida, *Greek-English Lexicon of the New Testament Based on Semantic Domains* (New York: United Bible Societies, 1988), 1:428-29.

50. The pioneer study was done by T. Schermann, "Eucharistein und Eucharistia in ihrem Bedeutungswandel bis 200 n. Chr," *Phil*, n.s., 23 (1910): 375-410. See also Jan-Maarten Bremer, "The Reciprocity of Giving and Thanksgiving in Greek Worship," in *Reciprocity in Ancient Greece*, ed. Christopher Gill, Norman Postlethwaite, and Richard Seaford (Oxford: Oxford University Press, 1998), 127-38.

51. For example, most "prefaces" that introduce the eucharistic prayer in the Roman Catholic liturgy begin with the formula: "Let us give thanks and praise to God. . . . It is right and just to give God thanks and praise."

52. Once again, we find an apt example of this discussion in a liturgical prayer.

Preface Weekday IV
We do well always and everywhere to give you thanks.
You have no need of our praise,
Yet our desire to thank you is itself your gift.
Our prayer of thanksgiving adds nothing to your greatness,

simple. We are in a way engaging in a "traffic" of gifts given and acknowledged with the expectation that God will now give again.

In summary, this taxonomy differs in many ways from the standard classification of psalms, and the differences are worthy of note. On the one hand, psalms are said to be either lament (complaint + petition) or praise-thanksgiving. But "prayer" is a more complex phenomenon than psalms, and needs a more discriminating classification. The two basic classifications of psalms are further broken down by form critics into six or seven types of psalms: (1) praise, (2) petition, (3) royal psalms, (4) songs of Zion, (5) didactic poetry, (6) festival psalms and liturgies.[53] This classification is based on several criteria: (1) instructions to the pray-er ("Praise the Lord!"), (2) repetitive formal characteristics, (3) differing *Sitze-im-Leben* (royal wedding, coronation of the king, festivals), (4) wisdom instructions, and the like. While such criteria are useful in classifying *psalms,* they prove less reliable in sorting out the communication that is *prayer.* Malina's taxonomy, however, builds on previous form-critical insights and provides a more discriminating classificatory system that focuses on the desired results of the communication and the social relationship between pray-ers and deity.

Psalm Types Are Not Enough. Whereas psalm critics speak of psalms of lament, Malina's taxonomy more critically distinguishes the "lament" as *interactive* and *petitionary* prayer. Psalms of "praise," "thanksgiving," and "trust" are prayers of *acknowledgment,* a category that includes acknowledgment, confession, blessing, honor, glory, and the like. Communication classification aids greatly in appreciating prayers such as Psalm 84 ("How lovely is your dwelling place, Lord, God of hosts!") as both *heuristic* meditation that explores the world of God and *imaginative* construction of a personal environment with God.

In regard to prayers that are not psalms, the taxonomy based on communication theory allows those who read biblical prayers to analyze and classify them in more accurate and informative ways. For example,

---

But makes us grow in your grace
Through Jesus Christ our Lord.

According to this, gratitude and appreciation are themselves gifts from God.

53. Kraus, *Psalms 1–59,* 38-62. See Westermann, *The Praise of God in the Psalms* and *The Psalms, Structure, Content, and Message* (Minneapolis: Augsburg, 1980); Patrick D. Miller, *Interpreting the Psalms* (Philadelphia: Fortress, 1986), passim.

petitionary prayer describes the petitions in the Our Father for bread, debt remission, and deliverance (Matt 6:11-13), as well as the charge of Jesus to his disciples in Mark 14:38 that they "pray" to escape the coming crisis. But the first part of the Our Father contains *interactional* prayer of praise and benediction. *Interactional* prayer captures Mary's sentiments of blessedness ("Henceforth all generations will call me blessed; / for he who is mighty has done great things for me," Luke 1:48-49 RSV), as well as her *informative* thanksgiving to God ("My soul magnifies the Lord," Luke 1:46). *Self-focused* prayer describes the communication of the Pharisee in Luke 18:11-12, in contrast to the *petitionary* prayer of the publican in Luke 18:13.[54] *Heuristic* prayer identifies Job's many requests to God to know the reason for his suffering. Speaking in tongues provides an example of *imaginative* prayer (1 Cor 14:6-26); and *informative* communication describes thanksgivings offered to God,[55] doxologies proclaimed,[56] and praise extended to him.[57] Communication taxonomy also aids in interpreting prayers such as Simeon's address to God in Luke 2:29-32 *(informative and interactional)*, Jesus' "acknowledgment" of God in Matthew 11:25-26 *(informative)*, and Zechariah's canticle extolling God's faithfulness in Luke 1:68-79 *(informative)*.

Summary and Conclusion

It matters that we define prayer accurately. While the definition of prayer changes from describer to describer, the use of a cross-cultural model of communication removes the matter from the world of untestable intuition and situates it in a context that makes salient both its parts and its aims.

---

54. In a careful study of Luke 18:9-14, F. Gerald Downing analyzed the prayers of the Pharisee and the tax collector against the background of prayers in the Israelite and Greco-Roman world ("The Ambiguity of 'The Pharisee and the Toll-Collector' (Luke 18:9-14) in the Greco-Roman World of Late Antiquity"). One of Downing's conclusions was that both prayers were "self-absorbed," but he had no broader classification system to sort out the prayers.

55. For example, both psalms of thanksgivings (Ps 116) and epistolary prayers of thanksgiving (Rom 1:8-15; 1 Cor 1:4-9; Phil 1:3-11; Col 1:3-8; 1 Thess 1:2-10) and blessings of God (2 Cor 1:3-7; Eph 1:3-10; 1 Pet 1:3-9).

56. For example, Rom 16:25-27; Phil 4:20; Jude 24-25.

57. Ps 118 is the clearest example of this, but see also Pss 30 and 136.

And the model can be verified, which intuition cannot. The model, moreover, makes more elements of prayer salient because it is less a description and more an X-ray of the phenomenon.

It matters how many types of prayers there are, simply because humans communicate with God for quite diverse reasons. Petitioning and praise, while adequate reductions of types of prayers, do not do justice to what we read and see in the prayers of Israel and the New Testament. It would be like being satisfied with describing the color "red" as either tomato or scarlet.

It matters that one can distinguish variations of petition and praise. Petition may be an outright request for goods and services (food, protection, health, and the like). It may also be an interactional complaint with the implied petition that God regard the faithful pray-er with immediate regard, or a heuristic request for knowledge of one's relationship with God. Self-focused prayer, besides being not that uncommon, expresses one's true status before God, but with the understanding that good behavior praises God while sinful behavior petitions forgiveness. Prayers of acknowledgment resemble the color "yellow" on an artist's palette, ranging from muted expressions of gratitude and appreciation to bright explosions of praise, glory, and honor. Alleluia! makes a very bold statement.

It matters that we take time to gain clarity on what the ancients meant by gratitude. "Giving thanks," for openers, is a misleading expression because of its implication of reciprocity and its incomplete understanding of God; as a sovereign, God needs nothing nor changes. Does this matter? Will it affect how we pray to God? Are these unnecessary distinctions? Obviously we think not. What artist is content to paint with only the primary colors? In fact, trying to sort out the business of prayer of appreciation and gratitude is itself an exercise in theology: Who is God? How do we or should we relate to God? What is it that we do or want to do by expressing prayers of gratitude and appreciation to God?

This study of the definition and typology of prayer needs to be done, but by itself it does not suggest the cultural dynamics occurring in prayer. Inasmuch as our aim is to understand the ancients on their own terms, not only do we need better understandings of the original language but we also need an understanding of it in cultural terms. For words have meaning only in terms of the culture in which we find them. "Abba" is not "paterfamilias" is not "Daddy." Same role, but played quite differently on different stages. We turn now to study six new social science lenses through which we seek to interpret the ancient prayers as closely as possible on their own terms. These lenses (comparative values, honor and shame, exchange theory, forms of reciprocity, patron-client relations, and rituals) are indeed articulated for us by accredited anthropologists, but they adequately interpret the same patterns in the cultural lives of the ancients. Now we are ready to read prayers, in other words.

CHAPTER TWO

Prayer, in Other Words:
Reading with Cultural Lenses

As important as it is to classify prayers as we did in the previous chapter, our task of interpretation is only beginning. What is going on in a
given prayer? What cultural moves does the pray-er make to assure a successful communication in prayer? What, in short, is the cultural world of
the pray-er like? It will surely matter if we learn to read as the ancients
spoke and wrote, for then we will truly be understanding them on their
own terms.

But to do this we must go back to school to learn some of the major
cultural values and patterns that illustrate how the ancients did in fact
view the world and that go a long way to informing us of their cultural system. For in learning these new scenarios we are not just acquainting ourselves with individual ideas or models, but we are putting the various
pieces of the puzzle into an orderly system, a cultural system. And so we
will examine six different but overlapping cultural models that are reliable
windows into the ancient world: (1) value systems in comparison;
(2) honor and shame, the pivotal values of the ancient Mediterranean;
(3) types of exchanges; (4) forms of reciprocity; (5) patron-client relationships; and (6) ritual, in which prayer might change us or confirm us.

The Value System of Addresser and Addressee

In his work on the anthropology of illness and wellness in antiquity,
John Pilch introduced to biblical scholarship a cross-cultural model that
aids in the discovery of different configurations of values that character-

ize social groups.[1] Pilch brings to biblical scholars a model that anthropologists originally developed to differentiate and understand the four different cultures found in New Mexico (Native American, Spanish, Mexican American, and Anglo). Health-care deliverers then successfully utilized it for understanding the cultural variations among a host of immigrant groups in America in regard to illness and health care.[2] Recently John Pilch and Bruce Malina wrote a volume entitled *Biblical Social Values and Their Meanings,* to whose introduction we turn for a mature elaboration of a model of differing cultural values applicable to biblical literature. They define "value" as "some general quality and direction of life that human beings are expected to embody in their behavior. A value is a general, normative orientation of action in a social system."[3] Just as Americans consider money or wealth a "value," so early Christians held kinship and honor as paramount values.[4] What, then, is value comparison all about?

The diagram on page 33 provides a productive way of discovering the value preferences of a group. In a given context and faced with a specific task, individuals prefer to act in certain predictable ways that would be rec-

1. John J. Pilch, "Healing in Mark: A Social-Science Analysis," *BTB* 15 (1985): 142-50; Pilch, "The Health Care System in Matthew," *BTB* 16 (1986): 102-6; Pilch, "Understanding Biblical Healing: Selecting the Appropriate Model," *BTB* 18 (1988): 60-66; Pilch, "Sickness and Healing in Luke-Acts," in *The Social World of Luke-Acts: Models for Interpretation,* ed. Jerome H. Neyrey (Peabody, Mass.: Hendrickson, 1991), 181-210; Pilch, "Understanding Healing in the Social World of Early Christianity," *BTB* 22 (1992): 26-33; and Pilch, "Insights and Models for Understanding the Healing Activity of the Historical Jesus," in SBLSP (1993): 154-77.

2. F. R. Kluckhorn and F. L. Strodbeck, *Variations in Value Orientations* (New York: Harper and Row, 1961); Arthur Kleinman, *Patients and Healers in the Context of Culture* (Berkeley: University of California Press, 1980); and Monica McGoldrick, John K. Pearce, and Joseph Giordano, eds., *Ethnicity and Family Therapy* (New York: Guilford, 1982).

3. John J. Pilch and Bruce J. Malina, *Biblical Social Values and Their Meanings* (Peabody, Mass.: Hendrickson, 1993), xiii.

4. Time and again in an effort to sensitize Euro-American readers to the differences between us moderns and those ancients, Bruce Malina in particular has provided a detailed series of contrasts between modern first-world countries and the ancient world. See, for example, Bruce J. Malina and Jerome H. Neyrey, *Calling Jesus Names: The Social Value of Labels in Matthew* (Sonoma, Calif.: Polebridge, 1988), 145-51; Bruce Malina, *Windows on the World of Jesus: Time Travels to Ancient Judea* (Louisville: Westminster John Knox, 1993); and Bruce J. Malina and Jerome Neyrey, *Portraits of Paul: An Archaeology of Ancient Personality* (Louisville: Westminster John Knox, 1996), 226-31.

Problem	Range of Solutions		
Principal Mode of Human Activity	Being	Being-in-Becoming	Doing
Interpersonal Relationships	Collateral	Hierarchical	Individual
Time Orientation	Present	Past	Future
Relationship of Humans to Nature	Be subject to it	Live in harmony with it	Master it
View of Human Nature	Mixture of good and evil	Evil	Good

ognized and approved by their peers; all three options are theoretically available, but generally one or two are more prevalent.[5] In applying this to prayers from antiquity, one must distinguish the values of those praying from those attributed to the Deity, the object of prayer.

1. Activity

Whereas the ancients themselves may be described as valuing "being," God is almost always described as "doing," whether creating, maintaining the universe, or rising up to fight Israel's enemies (Acts 4:24-30).[6] All prayers of petition, then, ask God to "do something," that is, "be active" on behalf of those praying.

5. This adaptation of the value map appeared first in Pilch's *Introducing the Cultural Context of the New Testament* (New York and Mahwah, N.J.: Paulist, 1991), 244; the version in our text is that of Pilch and Malina, *Biblical Social Values*, xxiii.

6. Especially in the holy war tradition, Israel is told to "be still" while God battles on its behalf (Exod 14:4; Pss 37:7 and 46:10).

2. Relationships

Relationships among mortals are both collateral and hierarchical; for, in addition to the vertical relationships people find themselves in (father/son; landlord/peasant; sovereign/subject), they also enjoy parallel kinship relationships with friends and relatives. God, however, is generally addressed in terms of some hierarchical relationship, "King," "Lord," "God of Israel," "Sovereign," and the like. The sense of social distance separating a pray-er and God is never made clearer than in prayers of petition, where those praying confess that God alone controls the universe, their enemies, or the rain in their valley. Therefore God will be addressed and treated like the various patrons or sovereigns in the life of those praying.

Moreover, we suggest a further observation of vertical relationships by remembering the inscriptions over the portal of the temple at Delphi: "Know thyself" (γνῶθι σεαυτόν), "Nothing overmuch" (μηδὲν ἄγαν), and "A pledge, and ruin is nigh."[7] A man is wise who "knows himself," that is, knows his position in the social hierarchy, who is above him and who is below him. His strategy is to avoid going beyond the limits of what society thinks is appropriate to a person of his social location (Plutarch, *Letter to Apollonius* 116D-E).[8] All the more in considering the deity; humankind is God's creature and servant. God help them if they try to climb the ladder of status. Knowing where one belongs, then, is an axiom of common social and prayerful experience.

3. Time

In regards to time, ancient Judeans both appealed to the past (Israel's legal and wisdom traditions embodied in Scripture) and focused on the present. In contrast, the God of Israel enjoys an eternity that temporally reaches back and forward without limit. It is God alone "who is, who was,

7. Diodor of Sicily 9.10.1-4; Plutarch, *Letter to Apollonius* 116D-E; Plutarch, *Dinner of the Seven Wise Men* 164B-C; Plutarch, *Talkativeness* 511A-B; see Helen North, *Sophrosyne: Self-Knowledge and Self-Restraint in Greek Literature* (Ithaca, N.Y.: Cornell University Press, 1966).

8. See Jerome H. Neyrey and Anselm Hagedorn, "'It Was Out of Envy That They Handed Jesus Over' (Mark 15:10): The Anatomy of Envy and the Gospel of Mark," *JSNT* 69 (1998): 37.

and who will be."[9] Unlike mortals who come into being and inevitably die, God — the immortal one — has no beginning and no end. Yet pray-ers ask God to act in the present; or they call upon God to remember his actions "as of old" and to repeat them once more in the present. The future, however, belongs to God alone, and it is sacrilegious to try to discover it; it belongs to God alone and those to whom it pleases God to disclose it.[10]

4. Nature

Native Americans are reputed to live in harmony with nature, whereas mainstream Americans consider themselves superior to it. Hence they dam rivers, tunnel under seas, and force deserts to bloom. But the ancients thought of themselves as subject to nature: storms wreck their vessels,[11] droughts cause terrible famines,[12] and the like. Yet God the all-powerful rules the sky, the sea, and the earth; God can send rain as well as rescue people from shipwreck. God, who is both pantocrator and sovereign of the universe, can providentially aid pray-ers on land or at sea.[13]

9. See Isa 41:4; Rev 1:4, 8; 4:8; see also Jerome H. Neyrey, "'Without Beginning of Days or End of Life' (Hebrews 7:3): Topos for a True Deity," *CBQ* 53 (1991): 439-55.

10. Bruce Malina ("Christ and Time: Swiss or Mediterranean?" *CBQ* 51 [1989]: 1-31) provided the biblical guild with an excellent anthropological study on the meaning of time as it applies to the Bible. Of the future he writes: "The past and the future as the possible cannot belong and never will belong to human beings. To glimpse the world of the distant past, or of the future, the world of the possible, is to assume divine prerogatives. In Israel such insolence was idolatry, while for Greeks it was hubris. The possible past and the possible future are simply closed to human beings" (15).

11. Jon. 1:4-16; Mark 4:35-41; Acts 27:13-44; storms themselves were thought to be caused by some heavenly being, either the God of Israel or a hostile spirit. Nevertheless, those caught in storms were powerless against them. See Vernon Robbins, "'By Land and by Sea': The We-Passages and Ancient Sea Voyages," in *Perspectives on Luke-Acts*, ed. Charles H. Talbert (Macon, Ga.: Mercer University Press, 1978), 215-42.

12. In addition to the seven-year famine at the end of Genesis, see 1 Kings 17:1-16; Acts 11:27-30.

13. See Wilhelm Michaelis, "παντοκράτωρ," in *TDNT* 3:914-15.

5. Human Nature

Whereas Euro-Americans are socialized to view their children as innocent and good, Sirach advises wise fathers how to deal with a son: "Beat his ribs."[14] Yet certain strains of Christianity likewise believe that children are born in sin, and so must be treated accordingly. Ancient Israel in general seemed to consider human nature as a mixture of good and evil. In petitionary prayer, pray-ers regularly describe their oppressors as evil; yet pray-ers themselves on occasion seek forgiveness and reconciliation and so confess their own sinfulness, error, or failure. Human nature for the ancients was, at best, a mixture of good and evil.

From this value map we draw the following conclusions. (1) In both prayers of thanksgiving and petitioning God, those praying always think of God "doing" something, either in the past or in the present. Many prayers refer to past actions of God as warrants and proof of what God should presently do. Rehearsing them, moreover, seems to give God reason to "do" them again. (2) The vertical relationship between God and Israel or the disciples of Jesus expresses the transcendent distance between the Immortal One and his mortal subjects. In contrast, humans characteristically look laterally to their friends and relatives for aid, as well as hierarchically to their covenant Lord and Patron. This hierarchical relationship, moreover, is likely what is expressed in the acclamation "Holy, holy, holy." If holiness means separation, God, who is immortal, is separated from those who are mortal; God, who is sinless, is distant from sinners; God, who is King of kings and Lord of lords, is immeasurably above and beyond the world of humans; he alone is the Most High. (3) In terms of time, pray-ers in the Bible regularly looked to the past to clarify the present: i.e., reflection on God's faithfulness in the covenants with Abraham and David, the endurance of their ancestral law and the ancient system of worship as evidence of what God has done and should continue doing.[15] Yet, if the roots of hope exist back in God's past actions, pray-ers expect God's assistance today ("Give us this day our daily bread," Matt 6:11; Luke 11:3) or stand under God's judgment today ("O that today you would listen to his

14. Particularly helpful here is the study by John Pilch, "'Beat His Ribs While He Is Young' (Sir 30:12): A Window on the Mediterranean World," *BTB* 23 (1993): 101-13.

15. In Phil 1:6 Paul states his hope in God relative to past and present: "And I am confident of this, that the one who began a good work among you will bring it to completion by the day of Jesus Christ."

voice . . . ," Ps 95:7-11/Heb 3:7–4:13). They might also rejoice today that ancient prophecies or promises are now fulfilled (Luke 2:29; 4:21).[16] (4) All prayers of praise and petition celebrate God's omnipotence over nature, that is, divine power to make the rains fall (or not fall), to multiply food, and to still storms. (5) With the story of Adam's sin, Israelites and early Christians thought of human nature as evil or a mixture of good and evil. In Romans Paul declared that "all have sinned and fall short of the glory of God" (Rom 3:23).[17] But God of course is holy beyond measure; God forgives humans their sins and sends Jesus as their savior. God will also transform corruptible humankind and make it incorruptible, and have humans' mortality changed to immortality so that they may worthily enter the presence of God (1 Cor 15:53-54).

Honor and Prayer

To my knowledge, Bruce Malina pioneered New Testament research on the importance of honor and shame for biblical interpretation.[18] His synthesis of various field studies from countries bordering on the Mediterranean led him to develop a model of this "pivotal value." Honor refers to the *claim* of worth, value, and respect that must be publicly *acknowledged*.[19] The *claim*

16. On the motif of prophecy-fulfillment, see R. H. Gundry, *The Use of the Old Testament in St. Matthew's Gospel* (Leiden: Brill, 1967); G. M. Soares-Prabhu, *The Formula Quotations in the Infancy of Matthew* (Rome: Pontifical Biblical Institute, 1976); on Luke's Gospel, see David L. Tiede, *Prophecy and History in Luke-Acts* (Philadelphia: Fortress, 1980); and Charles H. Talbert, "Prophecy and Fulfillment in Lucan Theology," in *Luke-Acts: New Perspectives from the Society of Biblical Literature Seminar*, ed. Charles H. Talbert (New York: Crossroad, 1984), 91-103.

17. On Rom 5:12-21, see the sage remarks of Joseph A. Fitzmyer, *Romans* (New York: Doubleday, 1993), 405-28.

18. Bruce J. Malina, *The New Testament World: Insights from Cultural Anthropology*, rev. ed. (Louisville: Westminster John Knox, 1993), 28-62. See also Bruce J. Malina and Jerome H. Neyrey, "Honor and Shame in Luke-Acts: Pivotal Values of the Mediterranean World," in *The Social World of Luke-Acts*, 97-124. See also Johannes Pedersen, *Israel: Its Life and Culture*, vol. 1 (Atlanta: Scholars, 1991), 213-44.

19. Julian Pitt-Rivers, "Honour and Social Status," in *Honour and Shame: The Values of Mediterranean Society*, ed. J. G. Peristiany (London: Weidenfeld and Nicolson, 1965), 19-78; Pitt-Rivers, "Honor," in *IESS* (1968), 6:503-11; Pitt-Rivers, *The Fate of Shechem or the Politics of Sex: Essays in the Anthropology of the Mediterranean*, Cambridge Studies in Social Anthropology 19 (Cambridge: Cambridge University Press, 1977), 1.

may be made either by the person demanding respect or by others on his behalf, usually family or fictive-kin (cocitizens, comembers of the army); and the *acknowledgment* must always be public approval of this claim. The ancients used many different verbs to express this *acknowledgment,* such as "glorify," "praise," "acclaim," "exalt," "magnify," "celebrate," "make famous," "declare the name of the Lord," "know the Lord," and the like.[20]

Sources of Honor

A person acquires honor in two basic ways: *ascription* by another or *achievement* by the claimant. Most people in antiquity have honor ascribed to them first and foremost by the parents, family, and clan into which they are born.[21] If the family belongs to the elite stratum and ruling class, the offspring — primarily the male ones — are born with high honor manifested in the family's power, wealth, reputation, and worth. Conversely offspring born of peasants share in their relative honor, symbolized by modest landholdings or modest flocks. We observe constantly that most people are introduced as the "son of so-and-so" or the "wife of so-and-so." Thus children inherit the social worth or honor of their parents. Adoption into a family provides a comparable process, as would commissioning as ambassador or assignment as procurator. On the other hand, individuals may acquire fame, glory, and renown through military, athletic, or aesthetic prowess. A city's benefactor may earn praise for the gift of an aqueduct or theater. Or individuals may engage in the ubiquitous game of challenge and riposte.

20. Malina, *The New Testament World,* 59. The study of "honor" by Johannes Schneider ("Τιμή," in *TDNT* 8:169-80) presents the various meanings of τιμή; but "honor" is expressed by other terms; hence semantic word field studies are needed, such as A. Klose, "Altrömische Wertbegriffe *(honos* und *dignitas),*" *Neue Jahrbücher für Antike und deutsche Bildung* 1 (1938): 268-78; and Emile Benveniste, *Indo-European Language and Society* (Coral Gables, Fla.: University of Miami Press, 1969), 334-45.

21. See Malina, *The New Testament World,* 33-34; see also Malina and Neyrey, *Portraits of Paul,* 16-17, 92-93, 202-5.

Honor and Virtue

Honor in antiquity dealt with "excellence" of some sort, either the prowesses mentioned above or some socially sanctioned virtue or uniqueness. The most common virtues meriting respect and honor are courage (military and athletic prowess) and justice. Because of its importance for assessing behavior in prayer, we take a closer look at what the ancients understood by "justice." Since discourse on virtue was taught by ancient rhetoricians, we take the remarks of a Roman writer close in time to the New Testament to illustrate the traditional understanding of justice. This author represents the utterly conventional, ancient discourse stretching back to Aristotle and forward into Byzantine times.

> We will be using the *topics of justice* if we say that we ought to *pity* innocent persons and suppliants; if we show that it is proper to *repay* the well-deserving with *gratitude;* if we explain that we ought to *punish the guilty;* if we urge that *faith* ought zealously to be *kept;* if we say that the *laws and customs* of the state ought especially to be *preserved;* if we contend that *alliances and friendships* should scrupulously be *honored;* if we make it clear that the *duty* imposed by nature *towards parents, gods, and fatherland* must be religiously *observed;* if we maintain that *ties of hospitality, clientage, kinship,* and *relationship by marriage* must inviolably be *cherished.* (*Rhetorica ad Herennium* 3.3.4, emphasis added; see also Pseudo-Aristotle, *Virtues and Vices* 5.2-3; Cicero, *De inventione rhetorica* 2.160-61; Menander Rhetor 1.361.17-25)

This rhetorician flags as marks of justice: (1) gratitude, (2) fair judgment, (3) fidelity, (4) duty to gods, parents, and fatherland, and (5) maintenance of important social ties. Thus pray-ers are just when they offer thanks for benefaction, keep covenant fidelity with God, fulfill their duty to God by obeying his commandments, and maintain their ties of clientage with their heavenly Patron. Similarly, God will be shown in prayer to be just and worthy of praise when God judges the wicked and rewards the faithful, when God's faithfulness is acknowledged, when God's patronage is seen as reliable and everlasting. Thus the psalmist praises God:

> The LORD is faithful in all his words,
> and gracious in all his deeds. (Ps 145:13)

Honor and Benefaction

Benefaction is one of the most productive concepts for assessing God's honor in the social structure of prayers. The custom whereby powerful and wealthy people in the ancient world provided important public services is well-known.[22] Wealthy aristocrats and monarchs were expected to provide public festivals, fund warships, and build aqueducts and theaters and the like for their cities or kingdoms.[23] Josephus provides the following record of how Athens honored the Judean king Hyrcanus for his benefaction. In it we note the balance between Hyrcanus's benefaction and Athenian public acknowledgment of his noble deed. The acknowledgment took the form of a golden crown, a statue, and the heralding of the Judean king's worth at the most important public events in the city's calendar — both its dramatic and its athletic festivals. Finally, the leaders of Athens make their continued praise and honor contingent upon future benefaction from the king. But in general this proclamation registers their "reward of merit," the acknowledgment of Hyrcanus as a worthy benefactor.

> Inasmuch as Hyrcanus, son of Alexander, the high priest and ethnarch of the Jews, has continued to show his goodwill to our people as a whole and to every individual citizen, and to manifest the greatest zeal on their behalf . . . it has therefore now been decreed to honor this man with a golden crown as the reward of merit fixed by law, and to set up his statue in bronze in the precincts of the temple of Demos and the Graces, and

22. The premier collection of benefaction inscriptions for biblical study is that of Frederick C. Danker, *Benefactor: Epigraphic Study of a Graeco-Roman and New Testament Semantic Field* (St. Louis: Clayton Publishing House, 1982); see also A. R. Hands, *Charities and Social Aid in Greece and Rome* (Ithaca, N.Y.: Cornell University Press, 1968), 175-209. See also S. R. Llewellyn, "The Development of Systems of Liturgies," *NDIEC* 7 (1994): 93-111; Stephen C. Mott, "The Power of Giving and Receiving: Reciprocity in Hellenistic Benevolence," in *Current Issues in Biblical and Patristic Interpretation*, ed. Gerald Hawthorne (Grand Rapids: Eerdmans, 1975), 60-72.

23. Isaeus provides an excellent example of this: "Our forefathers . . . performed every kind of choregic office, contributed large sums for your expenses in war, and never ceased acting as trierarchs. As evidence of all these services, they set up in the temples out of the remainder of their property, as a memorial of their civic worth, dedications, such as tripods which they had received as prizes for choregic victories in the temple of Dionysus, or in the shrine of Pythian Apollo. Furthermore, by dedicating on the Acropolis the first-fruits of their wealth, they have adorned the shrine with bronze and marble statues, numerous, indeed, to have been provided out of a private fortune" (*On the Estate of Dicaeogenes* 5.41-42).

to announce the award of the crown in the theater at the Dionysian festival when the new tragedies are performed, and at the Panathenaean and Eleusinian festivals and at the gymnastic games; and that the magistrates shall take care that so long as he continues to maintain his good will toward us, everything which we can devise shall be done to show honor and gratitude to this man for his zeal and generosity. (Josephus, *Jewish Antiquities* 4.149-55)

This proclamation describes the gifts of a Judean monarch to a Greek city, a relationship in which no "duty" was involved. The same would not be true of elites and populations of the same city-state or region. For them the virtue of justice would indicate a duty to benefit one's own and a corresponding duty by those benefited to acknowledge the gift.[24] In this convention the worthy person might well be addressed as "Benefactor" (εὐεργέτης), "Father," "Friend," or "Savior," names that evoke a kinship relationship even as they mask its harsher aspects.

Honor from Conflict

Another way of acquiring honor and respect deserves closer attention, namely, the game of challenge and riposte. It is regularly observed in Greco-Roman as well as early Christian literature that social games are played in public in which one party challenges another, the purpose of which is to diminish the one challenged and so garner the esteem in which the challenged person basks.[25] These challenges are easily recognized in the rhetorical *chreiai* in which a philosopher or sage is asked a question intended to stump him.[26] A witty riposte dismisses the challenger and confirms the reputation of the wise man.

24. For a clearer sense of the *do ut des* character of benefactions, see Josephus, *Jewish Antiquities* 14.212.

25. One is reminded of the practice of a victorious king putting atop his already-crowned head the crown of the monarch just vanquished. Thus the honor taken from the defeated directly increased that of the victor. The same would be true of the spoils of war.

26. See Ronald F. Hock and Edward N. O'Neil, *The Chreia in Ancient Rhetoric.* Volume I. *The Progymnasmata* (Atlanta: Scholars, 1986); and Jerome H. Neyrey, "Questions, *Chreiai*, and Challenges to Honor: The Interface of Rhetoric and Culture in Mark's Gospel," *CBQ* 60 (1998): 657-81.

This ubiquitous social game of push-and-shove also serves as background for appreciating many prayers. A petitioner might complain to God that he, the petitioner, has been faithful and loyal to God but is now hard pressed. He does not now experience God's beneficent generosity,[27] and his complaint puts God on the spot, so to speak. The pray-er has transformed the challenge from his enemy into a challenge to God. One thinks immediately of Jesus' dying words, which are formally a prayer, i.e., Psalm 22:1, "My God, my God, why have you forsaken me?"[28] God, then, is challenged to honor his loyal benefaction to Jesus. Similarly, if the Davidic monarch, the temple, or Jerusalem were threatened, the pray-er might remind God of God's ancient promises and thus petition the deity to defend his own interests. God, then, is put on the spot; and the pray-er petitions God to deliver the fitting riposte to the foreign monarch and the threatening army, thus fulfilling the divine promise to Israel. God, therefore, is perceived as engaged in a challenge/riposte situation. Divine failure to respond to such challenges might be considered a loss of divine honor as well as a lack of virtue (faithfulness) on God's part.

What do we know if we know all this? First, we recognize that many prayers acknowledge God's worth as the pray-er exclaims "praise to," "glory be to . . . ," "honor be to . . . ," and "alleluia!" Mortals give God nothing God lacks; rather they acknowledge the deity's claims. Second, God's honor is never ascribed, for no one in the universe can be found higher than God to bestow it (see Heb 7:7).[29] Third, one finds in prayers a sense that there is a "more" and "less" to God's honor. For example, the Bible states that God acts so as to win himself glory,[30] which suggests that pray-

27. For an enlightened exposition of these psalms of complaint or lament, see Patrick Miller, *They Cried to the Lord: The Form and Theology of Biblical Prayer* (Minneapolis: Fortress, 1994), 68-86.

28. For a fuller exposition of Ps 22 as Jesus' dying prayer, see my *Honor and Shame in the Gospel of Matthew* (Louisville: Westminster John Knox, 1998), 156-60. The aggressive nature of questions such as "Where is . . . ?" and "Why have you . . . ?" has been splendidly analyzed by Miller, *They Cried*, 68-79 and 99-100.

29. Yet Harold Attridge (*The Epistle to the Hebrews* [Philadelphia: Fortress, 1989], 196) cites biblical examples of lesser people blessing greater ones. Yet his discussion seems innocent of social-science concepts such as ascribed and achieved honor.

30. The premier example is the boast God makes before destroying the Egyptian army at the exodus: "I will gain glory for myself over Pharaoh and all his army" (Exod 14:4; see also vv 17-18; Ezek 28:22).

ers thought God could increase in majesty in some way.[31] Similarly, pray-ers state that should the nation be destroyed or should the pious come to ruin, who then would praise God?[32] Fourth, the virtue of "justice" in its many aspects frequently appears in prayer, and praise is regularly awarded for virtue. God is acclaimed as "faithful" or "faithful and true,"[33] and God's steadfast loyalty to the nation often serves as the reason for or basis of rela-tionship in petitioning God. God's just judgment, especially of foreigners and sinners, redounds to God's honor, for it belongs to justice to judge justly. Fifth, God is frequently understood in prayers as the benefactor par excellence. Hence a rehearsal of God's deeds often precedes acknowledg-ment of God's honor in statements of praise and glory. Sixth, the psalmist occasionally challenges God by calling into question God's loyalty and faithfulness; such challenging questions begin with "How long, O Lord . . . ?"[34] or "Why have you . . . ?"[35] or "Where is our God?"[36] Thus, in terms of this human logic, God is expected to act vigorously to defend God's honor or be shamed as unfaithful or powerless.

Prayer and the Media of Exchange

We saw earlier how Malina brought to our understanding of prayer a model of communication: sender — message — receiver. Later he brought

---

31. In a henotheistic world, Yahweh competes with the gods of the nations for glory and honor; therefore God is in conflict with the gods of the nations as these peoples fight against Israel. In a monotheistic world, Yahweh as the only deity in the universe does not need to battle other deities. Hence, it would seem that notions such as God "getting glory" would be-long to henotheistic times and would have little meaning in a monotheistic world.

32. God is regularly reminded that "The dead do not praise the LORD, / nor do any that go down into silence" (Ps 115:17; see also Isa 38:18-19). The same sentiment appears also at Qumran: "Surely a maggot cannot praise thee nor a grave-worm recount thy lovingkindness, but the living can praise thee" (11QPs-a XIX.1-2). Thus pray-ers, at least, see God as gaining more or less honor in proportion to the number of the living who acknowl-edge the Lord.

33. See Deut 7:9; Pss 31:5; 69:13; 97:10; 111:7; 145:13; Isa 49:7; 1 Cor 1:9; 10:13; 2 Cor 1:18; 1 Thess 5:24; 2 Thess 3:3; 2 Tim 2:13; Heb 10:23; and 1 John 1:9.

34. Pss 13:1-2; 35:17; 74:10; 79:5; 80:4; 89:46; 90:13; 94:3.

35. Pss 10:1; 22:1; 42:9; 44:23-24; 74:1, 11; 88:14.

36. Pss 79:10; 115:2; as mentioned above, an excellent treatment of this questioning ma-terial can be found in Miller, *They Cried*, 71-74.

into conversation a model of communication drawn from Talcott Parsons, this time paying attention to the "channel" by which a source presents a receiver "with goods, services, actions or a range of words."[37]

Talcott Parsons identifies four basic media of communication, which result from his efforts to find meaningful ways to gather and classify diverse social phenomena.[38] They are *power, commitment, inducement,* and *influence,* abstract categories that distinguish the means by which senders seek to have an impact on receivers. (1) *Power* refers to collective effectiveness systems such as government (king, president, ruler, judge); power means the ability to make others act in certain ways. (2) *Commitment* refers to the belonging system — family, extended family, and groups of friends. (3) *Inducement* touches on the economic system, that is, the exchange of things of value (agricultural produce, clothing, money, and the like). (4) *Influence* refers to the meaning system, the reasons for something or the learning amassed in a culture. In his characteristic way, Malina explains how even Euro-American audiences can quickly grasp these four categories: "Consider the following sentence and insert the roles of the persons who asked or told you to do or not to do something that in fact you did or did not do: 'I did it because he or she was: my mother, father, sister, brother, friend, relative (= commitment); a doctor, lawyer, clergy person, teacher (= influence); the police, mayor, president of the U.S. (= power); my boss at work, employer, foreman, customer, client (= inducement).'"[39] Broadly speaking, the Deity addressed in ancient prayers possesses all four of the media of communication, but those praying do not. It is unthinkable that mere mortals would offer God *power,* especially as many prayers acclaim God as "omnipotent," "creator," and "mighty warrior." Pray-ers on the contrary petition God to defeat their enemy, stop a drought, or deliver them from war — all petitions for God's unique *power.* Similarly, mortals have no *influence,* that is, knowledge, wisdom, or secret,

---

37. Bruce J. Malina, *Christian Origins and Cultural Anthropology: Practical Models for Biblical Interpretation* (Atlanta: John Knox, 1986), 75-76; he is digesting Talcott Parsons, *Politics and Social Structure* (New York: Free Press, 1969), 352-429. In his study of benefaction, Danker enumerated the kinds of things for which benefactors were praised, that is, what they did or provided (*Benefactor,* 393-409). His list provides abundant illustration of the general media of exchange abstracted in the works of Parsons and Malina.

38. Parsons, *Politics and Social Structure,* 352-437; see also his earlier article, "On the Concept of Influence," *Public Opinion Quarterly* 27 (1963): 37-62.

39. Malina, *Christian Origins,* 77.

that they can bring to the "omniscient"[40] Deity. They may, however, inform God of sorrow for sin (Ps 51) or, like Job, petition to know the cause of their misfortune. God alone knows all things, especially the secrets of the human heart. Concerning *inducement,* although people have on occasion promised God wealth or vowed offerings to temples if their prayers are heard, this attempt at plying God with *inducement* received mixed reactions in antiquity.[41] On the one hand, Israel's temple system offered *inducement* to God in its vast array of sacrifices (holocausts and thanksgiving sacrifices, grain and wine offerings).[42] We also read of many prophetic denunciations of the temple system as a form of bribery.[43] No, God is the source of *inducement,* which is expressed in the petitions to God to send bread in due season, rain in time of drought, and wealth to deliver them from debt. It is God from whom all goods flow.

Turning to *commitment,* we seem to find here the premier expectation of God by those praying as well as their own unique manner of communicating with God. *Commitment* may express any or all of the following sentiments: obedience, faithfulness, thanksgiving, blessing, praise, acknowledgment, honor, glory, respect, and the like. When we read of relationships expressed as "God and the people he has chosen," "as a father carries his infant," and similar expressions, we recognize that commitment is being appealed to. Similarly, when those praying appeal to God's covenantal faithfulness and beg God to act once more as loyal patron, they express their own *commitment* and seek to activate God's *commitment.* Moreover, many prayers consist of blessing and thanksgiving to God for benefaction received, thanksgiving being another example of commitment; other prayers may pledge faithfulness and loyalty. Therefore, those praying biblical prayers primarily use *commitment* as their medium of communication

40. Earlier we described one of the types of prayers as "informative," in which senders make known sentiments such as sorrow for sins as well as thanksgiving. The pray-er may consider this secret information, yet some psalms indicate that God knows the hearts of all (Ps 139:1: "O Lord, you have searched me and know me").

41. In the case of Saul, "to obey *(commitment)* is better than sacrifice *(inducement)*" (1 Sam 15:10-23); see Ps 40:6-8 LXX.

42. On sacrifice as a form of *inducement,* Bruce J. Malina ("Mediterranean Sacrifice: Dimensions of Domestic and Political Religion," *BTB* 26 [1996]: 37) defined sacrifice as "a ritual in which a deity or deities is/are offered some form of inducement, rendered humanly irretrievable, with a view to some life-effect for the offerer(s)."

43. See Isa 1:11-16; Jer 6:20; 7:3-29; Hos 6:6; 8:11-13; Amos 5:21-24; Mic 6:6-8; Mal 1:6-14.

with God, along with sacrificial *inducement,* but never *power* and *influence.* God, on the other hand, is perceived as having all four of the media at his disposal and in great supply.

Prayer and Reciprocity

Discussion of the media of communication leads to an inquiry about the kind of exchange in which the participants engage. Once again we are indebted to Bruce Malina for digesting the relevant theory of exchange that identifies three kinds: *generalized, balanced,* and *negative* reciprocity.[44] (1) *Generalized* reciprocity refers to the altruistic, asymmetrical attention paid to the wants and needs of another. It characterizes kinship and includes hospitality, gifts, and assistance to kin (i.e., "charity begins at home"). (2) *Balanced* reciprocity looks to the mutual interests of both parties in a symmetrical way (i.e., quid pro quo; *do ut des*). This type of reciprocity characterizes the communication between neighbors, not kin; and its typical forms are trade agreements, fees paid for services, and exchange or barter. (3) *Negative* reciprocity seeks self-interest at the expense of "the other," who probably is a stranger or an enemy. It attempts to get as much as possible for oneself, while giving as little as possible in return. Examples of negative reciprocity include use of fraudulent weights in commerce, as well as devaluation of coinage and theft. Obviously one does not treat either kin or neighbors in this way, but rather strangers or enemies. If *generalized* reciprocity is the "solidarity extreme," then *negative* reciprocity is the "unsocial extreme." The diagram on page 47 may help to distinguish the three types more clearly.[45]

What forms of reciprocity do those praying employ or imply in communicating with God, and what forms do those praying think characterize God's dealing with them? Most frequently in prayers of petition and praise/thanksgiving, God's creatures, whose being, life, and happiness are in God's hands, acknowledge the deity as Creator, Father, Savior, and Benefactor to whom they turn "to give them their food in due season." As

---

44. Malina, *Christian Origins,* 98-106; he draws on the work of Marshall Sahlin, *Stone Age Economics* (Chicago: Aldine-Atherton, 1972). Of considerable importance is the work of Christopher Gill, Norman Postlethwaite, and Richard Seaford, eds., *Reciprocity in Ancient Greece* (Oxford: Clarendon, 1998).

45. Malina, *Christian Origins,* 101-4.

Types of Reciprocity	Comparative Aspects
Generalized reciprocity	1. *characteristic:* give without expectation of return 2. *forms:* child rearing, hospitality 3. *recipients:* parents, children, kin 4. *biblical examples:* Matt 7:11/Luke 11:11-13; Luke 10:33-35
Balanced reciprocity	1. *characteristic:* tit for tat, quid pro quo 2. *forms:* barter, assistance agreements 3. *recipients:* neighbors 4. *biblical examples:* 1 Cor 9:3-12; Matt 10:10/Luke 10:7
Negative reciprocity	1. *characteristic:* exploitation; reap where one does not sow 2. *forms:* robbery, buy-cheap-sell-dear 3. *recipients:* strangers, enemies 4. *biblical examples:* Luke 10:30; 19:22

clients in a patron-client relationship with the deity, they depend on God's election of them (*generalized* reciprocity) and faithful[46] maintenance of the covenant bond. They appreciate the gratuity of God's benefaction of all four symbolic media (power, commitment, inducement, and influence) and respond with their own commitment (loyalty, obedience, praise, thanks, and honor). But do they think they are engaging in some form of *balanced* reciprocity? The data provide a mixed answer: some suggest no balance but express appreciation, while others state and imply some sort of asymmetrical reciprocity.

Several scholars have provided us with a broader understanding of "reciprocity" in prayer.[47] What we find is a range of opinions and practices among the ancients. On one end of the spectrum we find it best to understand that "gratitude," although surprisingly rare, was expressed by praise:

46. This important motif, the "faithfulness" of God, is more fully developed in Jerome H. Neyrey, *Render to God: New Testament Understandings of the Divine* (Minneapolis: Fortress, 2004), 128-34 and 152.

47. H. S. Versnel, "Religious Mentality in Ancient Prayer," in *Faith, Hope, and Worship: Aspects of Religious Mentality in the Ancient World,* ed. H. S. Versnel (Leiden: Brill, 1981), 1-64; Simon Pulleyn, *Prayer in Greek Religion* (Oxford: Clarendon, 1997), 39-55; and Gill, Postlethwaite, and Seaford, *Reciprocity in Ancient Greece,* 105-38.

"The term with which the Greek of the classical period expressed his grati-tude is not so much a word of the family χάρις [gift, benefaction], as, both in religion and secular texts, above all (ἔπ)αινος, ἐπαινεῖν [praise, to praise]."[48] Continuing in this vein, Versnel tries to specify what was meant by "thanks": "acknowledgment which implies the superiority of the bene-factor."[49] Professions of "praise and honor" or "praise and admiration" be-come adequate responses to benefaction, human and divine. On the other end of the spectrum we find material explicitly commenting on a kind of commerce between gods and humans, such as human response to favor and benefaction. Benefactors literally driven by "love of honor" give so as to glory in it when expressed by their clients. Some even say that the client has a duty or obligation to praise the patron. Again, Versnel remarks: "in Antiquity nothing was given free,"[50] with the conclusion that we find much data following from this logic: if earthly benefactors give so as to get, then the same obtains with the heavenly benefactors. In summary, then, both voices are heard: (1) humans do not "give" anything to the gods, but only acknowledge their greatness, and (2) commerce between the gods and humans has much of reciprocity in it, albeit asymmetrical.

When pray-ers communicate with God or the gods, even the ancients agree that *negative* reciprocity is blasphemous. For mortals are shameful who attempt to despoil God by lying, deceiving, cheating, or stealing from him.[51] Yet ancient criticism of superstition acknowledges that indeed some pray-ers do just this, even though such prayers are recognized as shallow and self-serving.[52]

Although some ancients described the petitionary relationship be-tween Deity and pray-er as a *balanced* exchange (*do ut des,* or "give so as to get"), Lucian's famous satire of ancient sacrifice mocks the religious be-havior of those who seek to barter with God, offering something cheap or

---

48. Versnel, "Religious Mentality," 50.

49. Versnel, "Religious Mentality," 51.

50. Versnel, "Religious Mentality," 56.

51. One might profitably think of "regulatory" prayer as in some way being an example of negative reciprocity; the pray-er performs perfunctory rites, bringing as little as is needed to secure a powerful result. God is shamed both by the assertion of the pray-er's power or control and by the desire to reduce contact with the deity to the most minimal level. God loses all around.

52. See James 1:5-8; on the traditions reflected here, see Luke T. Johnson, *The Letter of James,* AB 37A (New York: Doubleday, 1995), 179-81.

mean to secure something of worth, which looks for all intents and purposes like *negative* reciprocity.

> So nothing, it seems, that they [the gods] do is done without compensation. They sell men their blessings, and one can buy from them health, it may be, for a calf, wealth for four oxen, a royal throne for a hundred, a safe return from Troy to Pylos for nine bulls, and a fair voyage from Aulis to Troy for a king's daughter! Hecuba, you know, purchased temporary immunity for Troy from Athena for twelve oxen and a frock. One may imagine, too, that they have many things on sale for the price of a cock or a wreath or nothing more than incense. (Lucian, *On Sacrifices* 2)

At first glance Lucian seems to mock the exchange of sacrificial petitions from mortals for benefactions provided by the gods. This is by no means a *balanced* exchange, but tends rather toward *negative* reciprocity. Mortals give as little as possible for indescribable results: health, wealth, and royal rule can be had for a mere calf or four oxen or a hundred oxen. Although it is bad enough to imagine that one could engage in a balanced exchange of the general symbolic media with God, it is shameful to think that one could trick a deity into bestowing superior goods for a meager offering.

Yet, some pray-ers on occasion imply that their communication with God has an element of *balanced* reciprocity. In some cases we read of complaints against the deity, which express the pray-ers' commitment and even sacrificial inducement to God *in response to which God appears not to be reciprocating.*[53] At least for the moment, such complaints testify both to the pray-er's commitment to God (faithfulness, constant prayer; sacrifice) and to the experience of shame, mockery, and humiliation. An imbalance is perceived, and so God is faulted for failing to respond with divine benefaction to the pray-er's commitment to God. Moreover, although in some situations pray-ers seem to engage in a sort of *balanced* reciprocity when they make promises and vows to God[54] to be fulfilled upon receipt of God's grant of deliverance or health, the psalmist declares that nothing that could be offered would be a sufficient repayment:

53. See Claus Westermann, *Praise and Lament in the Psalms* (Atlanta: John Knox, 1981), 176ff.; Samuel Balentine, *The Hidden God: The Hiding of the Face of God in the Old Testament* (New York: Oxford University Press, 1983), 116-35; Craig Broyles, *The Conflict of Faith and Experience in the Psalms,* JSOTSup 52 (Sheffield: Sheffield Academic Press, 1989), 80-82; and Miller, *They Cried,* 70-76.

54. See Num 21:2; 30:2-3; Deut 23:18, 21; Pss 22:25; 50:14; 56:12; 61:5, 8; 66:13; 116:14, 18.

> What shall I return to the LORD
> for all his bounty to me? (Ps 116:12)

The best that can be done is "to pay my vows to the Lord," a remark that I suggest is but acknowledging God's honorable benefaction, not balancing it with anything. In the main, pray-ers receive God's *generalized* reciprocity, and their public praise only acknowledges God's claims of honor. *Balanced* reciprocity, at best, is but an occasional and illusory suggestion. *Negative* reciprocity, such as Lucian described, is shameful.

According to the definition of justice noted earlier, we often read of virtuous people who fulfill their duties to God, country, and family. Does God have duties and obligations to the world he created and the people he has made his own? Does justice contain an element of *balanced* reciprocity? Just worshipers owe God the fulfillment of their vows, even as justice dictates that benefactions received are to be acknowledged. Commitment, as we saw, is what pray-ers owe the Deity, whether this be hymns of thanksgiving and praise or sacrifices, which acknowledge God's benefaction. Yet this relationship is hardly *balanced*, nor were ancient pray-ers bold enough to say they had satisfied for all time the debt of benefaction from the Creator-Parent, which is implied in *balanced* reciprocity. Mortals can never repay the Lord or balance the scales, but live forever with the duty to praise and thank God. Josephus describes just this sort of piety: "Twice every day, at the dawn thereof, and when the hour comes for turning to repose, let all acknowledge before God the bounties which he has bestowed on them through their deliverance from the land of Egypt: *thanksgiving is a natural duty*, and is rendered alike in gratitude for past mercies and to incline the giver to others yet to come" (*Jewish Antiquities* 14.212, emphasis added). "Duty," the natives' term describing what mortals express in prayer of thanksgiving, encodes a sense of obligation to acknowledge God's benefaction. While it may be viewed by some as reciprocity (see Athens's honoring of Hyrcanus above), it looks more to the protocols of honor claims that are acknowledged than to balanced reciprocity that seeks to equalize the scales of the exchange and thus terminate a particular act of barter. To render God his due, then, is not to engage in balanced reciprocity, but to send a response of commitment in view of altruistic benefactions received.

It may help clarify this consideration of the three types of reciprocity if we turn to a discussion in Philo where he asks the question: "Why did God create?" He begins by citing a pregnant text, "Noah found grace with the Lord God" (Gen 6:8), then asks about this "grace," whether it is something Noah earned or deserved, and thus expressive of a balanced reciprocity between God and Noah. After rejecting any notion of "balance" here, he offered another explanation. "The second explanation ('he was thought worthy of grace') is founded on a not unreasonable idea, that the Cause judges those worthy of His gifts who do not deface with base practices the coin within them which bears the stamp of God, even the sacred mind. And yet perhaps that explanation is not the true one" (*Unchangeableness of God* 105). Since *no balanced reciprocity* whatsoever is appropriate between God and mortals, Philo offers a third explanation, which turns to a different form of reciprocity, not balanced, but generalized:

> [T]he man of worth . . . in all his inquiries found this to be the highest truth, that all things are the grace or gift of God — earth, water, air, fire, sun, stars, heaven, all plants and animals. . . . But God has given His good things in abundance to the All and its parts, not because He judged anything worthy of grace, but looking to His eternal goodness, and thinking that to be beneficent was incumbent upon His blessed and happy nature. So that if anyone should ask me what was the motive for the creation of the world, I will answer that it was the goodness of the Existent, that goodness which is the oldest of His bounties and itself the source of others. (*Unchangeableness of God* 107-8)

Thus God's dealings with us are always done in altruistic generosity or generalized reciprocity. Such is the nature of God: "to be beneficent was incumbent upon His blessed and happy nature."

What do we know if we know this? First, we become aware of the four media of exchange (power, commitment, inducement, and influence), which aid us in appreciating what a sender might communicate to a receiver. In general, mortal pray-ers mostly communicate with God in terms of commitment (but also with inducement-as-sacrifice). God communicates with all four forms of symbolic media. Second, if exchange appropriately describes the communication between pray-er and Deity, it seems best to describe God as exercising *generalized* reciprocity or altruism in bestowing divine benefaction in all four media. The pray-er's petition for or praise of divine benefaction does not seem to be a form of reciprocity of any kind. Pray-ers, we saw, approach God either as needy or as grateful; but they are not exercising any power over God, nor bribing him, nor bringing God anything God lacks. They engage in no reciprocity with God; pray-ers are the recipients of divine benefaction, that is, of divine favoritism or election. As recipients they are thereby indebted to God and have an obligation in justice to offer praise and thanksgiving. But this is hardly what was meant by *balanced* reciprocity, for there is no commensurability between gift and thanksgiving. The commitment of pray-ers is balanced by God's commitment, so to speak, but the Deity's eternal faithfulness and loyalty greatly surpass that of the pray-ers; hence there is no balance here.[55]

Patron-Client Relationships

Classicists have long appreciated the importance of the patron-client relationship in antiquity.[56] Frederick Danker brought to the attention of New Testament interpreters the grand tradition of honoring benefactors, a form of patron-client relations characteristic of the eastern Mediterranean.[57] Bruce Malina, however, pioneered the formal use of the anthropology of patron-client relations for interpreting early Christian literature.[58] His adapted model[59] of patron-client relations describes those that arise among people of unequal status and resources: landlord/vassal, aristocrat/peasant, king/subject, father/son, and God/Israel. Thus patron-client rela-

55. The Sacramentary of the Roman Catholic Church contains a preface prayer for use on weekdays: "You have no need of our praise, yet our desire to thank you is itself your gift. Our prayer of thanksgiving adds nothing to your greatness, but makes us grow in your grace" (Weekdays IV P40).

56. For example, Richard P. Saller, *Personal Patronage under the Early Empire* (Cambridge: Cambridge University Press, 1982); Paul Veyne, *Bread and Circuses: Historical Sociology and Political Pluralism* (London: Penguin Press, 1990); and Andrew Wallace-Hadrill, ed., *Patronage in Ancient Society* (London: Routledge, 1989).

57. Danker, *Benefactor.*

58. The initial study is Bruce J. Malina, "Patron and Client: The Analogy behind Synoptic Theology," *Forum* 4, no. 1 (1988): 2-32; this article was made more widely available in Malina's *The Social World of Jesus and the Gospels* (London: Routledge, 1996), 143-75.

59. The important anthropological literature includes Steffen Schmidt, James Scott, Carl Landé, and Laura Guasti, *Friends, Followers, and Factions: A Reader in Political Clientalism* (Berkeley: University of California Press, 1977); Jeremy Boissevain, *Friends of Friends: Networks, Manipulators, and Coalitions* (New York: St. Martin's Press, 1974); and Shlomo Eisenstadt and Louis Roniger, *Patrons, Clients, and Friends: Interpersonal Relations and the Structure of Trust in Society* (Cambridge: Cambridge University Press, 1984).

tionships describe the vertical dimension of exchange between higher-status and lower-status persons. A full inventory of the standard features of patron-client relationships is found in the following note,[60] but we highlight those pertinent to this discussion.

First, patron-client relations all contain an element of exchange/benefit; otherwise, it would be difficult to know why patron and client engaged in a relationship at all. Malina noted: "Patron-client relations are based on strong inequality and difference between patrons and clients. Patrons monopolize certain positions of crucial importance to clients, especially access to means of production, major markets, and centers of society."[61] What, then, do patrons bestow on clients and what do clients render in return? Patrons are usually wealthy and powerful people, who have first-order goods, that is: (1) *power* to stop agonistic behavior threatening the life and livelihood of a client; (2) *commitment* to support clients by giving them a sense of kinship, albeit fictive, with the patron; (3) *inducement,* such as a dowry for the client's daughter, seed for his fields, or a daily ration of bread or money;[62] and (4) *influence,* passing on a favorable word to the client's creditor or putting the client in touch with the right person to solve the client's problems. As Malina has shown, God is regularly understood as the patron-

60. Note the features of patron-client relations as described in anthropological literature: (1) patron-client relations are particularistic; (2) patron-client interaction involves the exchange of a whole range of generalized symbolic media: power, influence, inducement, and commitment; (3) the exchange entails a package deal, so that the generalized symbolic media cannot be given separately (i.e., concretely useful goods must go along with loyalty, solidarity); (4) solidarity here entails a strong element of unconditionality and long-range social credit; (5) hence, patron-client relations involve a strong element of personal obligation, ranging from high to low salience, even if relations are often ambivalent; (6) these relations are not fully legal or contractual, but very strongly binding, i.e., they are informal and often opposed to official laws of the country; (7) in principle, patron-client relations entered into voluntarily can be abandonded voluntarily, although always proclaimed to be lifelong, long-range, forever, etc.; (8) patron-client relations are vertical and dyadic (between individuals or networks of individuals), and thus they undermine the horizontal group organization and solidarity of clients and other patrons; (9) patron-client relations are based on strong inequality and difference between patrons and clients. Patrons monopolize certain positions of crucial importance to clients, especially access to means of production, major markets, and centers of society (Malina, "Patron and Client," 3-4).

61. Malina, "Patron and Client," 4.

62. Duncan Cloud ("The Patron-Client Relationship: Emblem and Reality in Juvenal's First Book," in *Patronage in Ancient Society,* 210) notes that Pliny, Martial, and Perseus all describe Roman patrons bestowing twenty-five asses on each client at the morning *salutatio.*

benefactor who bestows "grace" or favor,[63] that is, altruistic benefaction. God's patronage, similar to that of earthly patrons, consists of first-order goods: (1) *power:* ability to create; to defeat Egyptian, Assyrian, and Seleucid armies; and to subdue the heavenly spirits who attack God's clients; (2) *commitment:* pledges of eternal loyalty and fidelity in a covenant of steadfast love with Abraham, David, and their descendants; (3) *inducement:* bestowal of rain and sunshine for crops, increase of herds, and many children; (4) *influence:* knowledge of God's law and prophetic information of God's plans. Clients, as we saw above, cannot give *power* to this patron, for God is omnipotent, or provide God with *information,* for God is omniscient. But clients can bring *inducement,* a material gift, such as a sacrifice, and offer *commitment,* public praise of and loyalty to him.

Second, although we identified earlier four distinct symbolic media of exchange, the patron-client relationship does not seem to function in a one-for-one exchange: i.e., clients petition for *inducement* to pay taxes, in return for which they offer *commitment.* Rather, the symbolic media are exchanged as a package. With *commitment* from God the Patron come *power* and *inducement.* In prayer, however, it becomes clear that the pray-er best brings God only *commitment;* for, as many biblical instances note, sacrifices and holocausts do not move the Deity, but rather faithfulness, obedience, and loyalty, i.e., commitment.[64]

Third, anthropologists describe the relation between patron and client as particularistic, in that the patron does not treat all real or potential clients the same. Some individuals or groups are "chosen" favorites, singled out from the rest, and most favored.[65] Thus favoritism, so offensive to

63. In a lengthy note, Malina ("Patron and Client," 171-72) describes the various meanings of χάρις, χαρίζομαι, and χάρισμα, which express patronage.

64. The more notable examples are 1 Sam 15:22; Pss 40:6-8; 50:8-15; 51:16, 17; Isa 1:10-17; 58:6-7; Jer 7:21-26; Hos 6:6; Amos 5:21-24.

65. Mary, the mother of Jesus, is declared "favored" by God (Luke 1:28, 30), a favoritism that forms part of her canticle (1:47-49). In ancient Israel, David, his successors in his dynasty, and also the people Israel are all declared "chosen" or "elected" by God. The psalmist prays, "But know that the LORD has set apart the faithful for himself" (Ps 4:3); and in another place, "You are the glory of their strength; / by your favor our horn is exalted" (Ps 89:17); "He brought his people out with joy, / his chosen ones with singing" (Ps 105:43). In the Christian Scriptures Jesus himself is "a living stone, though rejected by mortals yet chosen and precious in God's sight" (1 Pet 2:4); and the followers of Jesus are called "a chosen race, a royal priesthood, a holy nation, God's own people" (1 Pet 2:9). On this theme of favoritism, see G. Quell, "ἐκλέγομαι," in *TDNT* 4:145-68.

modern democratic ears and their notions of egalitarianism, thrives in a patron-client world. The Bible knows of many favorites of God:[66] Abraham (Gen 12:1-3; 15:13-16), David (2 Sam 7:8-16), and Israel: "The LORD your God has chosen you out of all the peoples on earth to be his people, his treasured possession. It was not because you were more numerous than any other people that the LORD set his heart on you and chose you — for you were the fewest of all peoples" (Deut 7:6-7).

Fourth, patron-client relations purport to endure for a long time, either for the lifetime of the patron and client or, in the case of God's covenant with Israel, forever. An important corollary of this suggests that the virtues of loyalty and faithfulness, which are parts of the virtue of justice, will then become important in prayer relationships with the Deity.[67] As Deuteronomy says above about God's covenant with Israel, the Deity "keeps covenant and steadfast love . . . to a thousand generations." Similarly, the promise to David came to be interpreted as the patron's pledge of an eternal dynasty: "Your house and your kingdom shall be made sure forever before me; your throne shall be established forever" (2 Sam 7:16). Mortal clients, on the other hand, may pledge the same undying loyalty but be unable to maintain the commitment. Nevertheless, mutual pledges are frequent characteristics of patron-client relations, especially in prayers. In this context we recall the Athenian benefaction proclamation to Hyrcanus, in which they made it painfully clear that the client's duty to acknowledge the patron's worth entirely depends on Hyrcanus's continued patronage to them. Ideally, then, faithfulness and loyalty are core elements of a patron-client relationship.

What do we know as a result of this? The ubiquitous and ancient pattern of benefactor and patron-client relations greatly aids our interpretation of prayer. First, in prayer God and the pray-er are hierarchically or vertically positioned. God, who is Sovereign, Father, Lord, and Savior, is

---

66. For example, it seems to be a pattern that God chooses the younger son over his older brother, a clear mark of favoritism: Abel over Cain, Isaac over Ishmael, Jacob over Esau, Joseph over his brothers. The same argument is used by Paul in his explanation of the choosing of the Gentiles (Rom 9:6-29).

67. Paul's "thanksgiving" prayer that opens 1 Corinthians contains an inventory of God's blessings past and future; it concludes appropriately with confession of God's faithfulness: "God is faithful (πιστός); by him you were called into the fellowship of his Son" (1:9; see 10:13). And the doxology that concludes 1 Thessalonians also expresses the same idea: "The one who calls you is faithful (πιστός), and he will do this" (5:24; see 2 Thess 3:3).

also the Most High and vastly removed in status from mortals; nevertheless, there is a personal relationship expressed in these patron-client relationships. Second, in terms of the commerce of this relationship, God possesses and bestows all four media of exchange; but mortals, always the recipients of patronage, have only their *commitment* with which to acknowledge divine benefaction, and frail commitment at that. Prayer, then, is not an exchange of heavenly patronage for clients' earthly gifts. Rather, divine patronage is honorably acknowledged (i.e., commitment) with the sense that nothing else is suitable to bring to God. Finally, favoritism emerges as a significant element in patron-client relationships. Only some individuals or some peoples enjoy the patron's attention.

Prayer and Ritual

Bruce Malina conveniently summarized for us the anthropological understanding of ritual, an essential element for appreciating the social dynamics called prayer. Gathering the insights of those who study ritual, Malina articulated a basic distinction between *status-transformation ritual* and *ceremony.*[68] By *status-transformation ritual* he means the process where persons assume a new role or status, hence a transformation of their status. For example, two people who marry move from single to exclusive status; and should the female in this marriage bear a child, she assumes a new role, namely, mother. Similarly, in the transformation that is baptism, people enter a Christian church, changing status from outsider to insider and from unclean to washed clean in the blood of the Lamb. Other status-transformation rituals include: birth and death (entering and leaving the land of the living), trial and imprisonment (unfitness for society), graduation (from unskilled or ignorant status to that of a skilled and trained professional), and the like. Conversely, *ceremonies* serve to confirm institu-

68. Malina, *Christian Origins,* 139-65. Victor Turner makes this distinction clear: "I consider the term 'ritual' to be more fittingly applied to forms of religious behavior associated with social *transitions,* while the term 'ceremony' has a closer bearing on religious behavior associated with religious *states.* . . . Ritual is transformative, ceremony confirmative" (*The Forest of Symbols: Aspects of Ndembu Ritual* [Ithaca, N.Y.: Cornell University Press, 1967], 95). See also Raymond Firth and John Skorupski, *Symbol and Theory: A Philosophical Study of Theories of Religion in Social Anthropology* (Cambridge: Cambridge University Press, 1976), 164.

Elements of a Ritual	Category	Elements of a Ceremony
(1) irregular pauses	Frequency	(1) regular pauses
(2) unpredictable, when needed	Schedule/Calendar	(2) predictable, planned
(3) present-to-future	Temporal Focus	(3) past-to-present
(4) professionals	Presided Over By	(4) officials
(5) change: status reversal or status transformation	Purpose/Function	(5) confirmation of roles and statuses in institutions

tions as well as roles and statuses within them. For example, a school or business or municipality may at a picnic or dinner host people employed by it or who are benefactors of it. The institution experiences confirmation of loyalty and support from those who attend the fete. Ceremonies include all memorials, anniversaries, and birthdays at which the roles and statuses of those honored are reburnished and thus confirmed. The entire liturgical calendar of the Christian church consists of a series of ceremonies.

The diagram above aims at sharpening the differences between status-transformation rituals and ceremonies so as to make salient the social functioning of each. (1) It is evident that transformation rituals are irregular, since no one plans to be ill or unclean or guilty or dead. Ceremonies such as meals, anniversaries, or festivals, on the other hand, occur regularly, either daily, weekly, monthly, or annually. (2) Thus transformation rituals, which focus on the change from sickness to health, sinfulness to holiness, or life to death, do not fit into a calendar or schedule, since they occur unpredictably. Yet ceremonies are anticipated and planned for: the civic calendar marks the founding of the city, the birthday of the emperor, and the feasts of the city's patron deities. (3) Transformation rituals all begin with the present, current situation (illness, sinfulness) and look to the future when that status will be changed. On the contrary, ceremonies look to some past event, historical or mythical, and affirm its significance in the present, as do national holidays such as July 4 and Memorial Day. (4) Transformation rituals are presided over by people deemed competent to deal with the situation; police deal with criminals, doctors treat the sick, firemen control blazes, ministers and priests counsel and forgive, and sanitation engineers dispose of our waste. On the other hand, the officials in our various national, state, or local political institutions conduct ceremonies such as anniversaries and memorials (politics), priests and ministers officiate at liturgies (church), and parents prepare daily as well as birthday festivities for their children (kinship). (5) Finally, rituals of transformation do just that: they ritualize either elevation or demotion in role and status. The person undergoing a transformation ritual experiences social change that is noted by a public: in marriage two people "become one flesh," a new social entity; in criminal proceedings the accused may be convicted and thus incarcerated or acquitted and set free; in illness the sick may either recover and return to family or worsen, die, and be buried. Ceremonies, however, function to confirm role and status in a given institution. Anniversaries and birthdays bring to mind the king's birthday (Mark 6:21) or deliverance from bondage (Exod 12) or the temple's purification (2 Macc 10:7-8; John 10:22). In the realm of sacrifice, those who participate in the consumption of the meat of the offering indicate their status as members of a clan or family or fictive family.[69] Thus Antipas's powerful status is acknowledged both by the feast he prepares and by the attendance of his courtiers.[70] Participation with Jesus at the Passover meal on the night before he died confirms for all time the identity and status of Jesus' select disciples (Luke 22:14-34).

When we interface this information on prayer as either status transformation or confirmation with the earlier classification of prayer as communication, we further appreciate the character of those seven types of prayers (see the diagram on page 59). Petitionary prayer, then, implies a status-transformation situation. Sinners beg for mercy so as to be changed into a state of blamelessness and holiness once more (Pss 38; 51); those overwhelmed by trials or attacked by enemies ask to be elevated from the current negative status to one of peace and harmony (Pss 56; 59). Regulatory prayers look to changes in status, either the rise in the pray-er's status or the lowering of someone else's. The other prayers ceremonially confirm

69. Nancy Jay, *Throughout Your Generations Forever* (Chicago: University of Chicago Press, 1992), 41-60; see Marcel Detienne, "Culinary Practices and the Spirit of Sacrifice," in *The Cuisine of Sacrifice among the Greeks*, ed. Marcel Detienne and Jean-Pierre Vernant (Chicago: University of Chicago Press, 1989), 4-14.

70. Matt 22:3-4 and Luke 14:17-20, 24. See Richard L. Rohrbaugh, "The Pre-Industrial City in Luke-Acts," in *The Social World of Luke-Acts*, 137-46.

Type of Communication	Status Transformation or Ceremony	Distinguishing Aim
1. petitionary	status transformation	petition for what is lacking
2. regulatory	status transformation	petition to change self or other
3. interactional	status transformation	petition to restore favored relationship
4. self-focused	ceremony	contentment with current status
5. heuristic	status transformation	seeking information that is currently lacking
6. imaginative	ceremony	maintaining relationship
7. acknowledgment	ceremony	confirmation of God's role and status

roles and statuses in the institution of the House of Israel. Those who pray Psalm 84 ("How lovely is your dwelling place") are members of the House of Israel who find contentment and fulfillment in the temple of Israel's God; and the deity addressed in this way is confirmed as the patron of the people. Far from asking for change, those praying express satisfaction with their current status and wish it to continue. Self-focused prayer confirms the status of the pray-er, who may even boast in his present situation. Heuristic prayer seeks a transformation from not knowing to knowing the mind and plans of God. Imaginative prayer, such as speaking in tongues, seems to have functioned at Corinth initially as a status transformation but subsequently as ceremony. Those speaking in tongues initially experienced a transformation from nonelite to elite status, but every subsequent prayer in tongues confirmed them as special elite members of the Corinthian church. The acknowledgment type of prayer would seem to reflect what was said about ceremonies; namely, it serves to confirm roles and statuses in a given institution. Hence prayers of praise, thanks, honor, and glory to God do not change the status of those praying or the deity so honored; on the contrary, such prayers confirm God's role and status as creator or patron, while at the same time confirming the status of those praying as clients of this heavenly patron and worshipers of this particular deity, all within the House of Israel. For example, the rubrics for Passover specify that Israel pray the Hillel psalms, Psalms 113–116, two after the third cup and the rest at the very end of the meal (Mark 14:26). Those praying these psalms confirm their membership in the people God rescued from slavery in Egypt. God, moreover, is confirmed as the deity who works mighty works for his chosen people. Finally, prayers and psalms that become attached to certain festivals serve to confirm the roles and statuses of those praying and the deity addressed; by commemorating a past event they bring the past into present consciousness, thus renewing and strengthening the relationship of the clients with their Patron.[71]

Summary and Conclusions

This social-science introduction to the scholarly conversation about biblical prayer provides new and profitable ways of interpreting it, and should take its place alongside of and in conversation with more conventional form-critical and history-of-religion studies of prayer. We do not find this approach in conflict with other methods of interpretation; rather it is a new player drafted onto the team. This chapter presented a systematic approach to understanding prayer in terms of cultural patterns that make up the social and political lives of those praying. It began with a taxonomy of prayer based on a communications model, followed by a model for uncovering the complex value systems of both pray-er and God. Then it brought into conversation cultural and rhetorical notions of honor and shame, highlighting how honor is acquired (virtue, prowess, benefaction, conflict) or ascribed and how this material relates to God as described in Israelite and Christian prayers. The system of exchange and modes of reciprocity served to clarify what pray-ers think they are offering and receiving from God. Most importantly, this material sharpened the ancient criticism of ritual and sacrifice, offering a coherent way of appreciating the frequent critique of formal reli-

71. Certain types of psalms are best classified as ceremonies: (1) royal psalms (Pss 2; 20; 21; 45; 72; 89; 101; 110; 132; 141); (2) songs of Zion (Pss [46]; 48; 76; 84; 87; 122; [132]); (3) festival psalms and liturgies (Pss 50; 81; 95).

gion by ancient reformers. Finally, the theory of ritual allowed us to examine more closely the process (transformation or confirmation) and players (prophet or priest) involved in the various types of prayers classified by the communications taxonomy. Thus we see that the various models used in this study overlap and often replicate one another.

The scope of this chapter allowed no space for a lengthy interpretation of this or that prayer to test the model so as to draw any conclusions about its suitability for study of ancient prayers. But such is the focus of the next two chapters, namely, to read some of the familiar and not-so-familiar prayers from the ancient world.

Further Questions

What other cultural models for interpreting prayers might be added to those developed here? The following four perspectives seem like fresh questions to ask about prayers.

1. The conversation on prayer would benefit by the use of the model of social stratification articulated by Lenski and Lenski.[72] This allows a reader to plot the pray-er as well as others mentioned in the psalm by social location and social status. Thus the pray-er may be immediately in communication with God or employing priests and liturgy as intermediaries. The pray-er may be asking God to turn the world upside down, raising the lowly and humbling the mighty. Hence, the presence and performance of mediating figures are at stake, as well as a petition for reform of the social order.

2. Many biblical prayers employ language reflecting both the vocabulary of purity and pollution and the social function of this language. Strong boundary making and identity confirming are often noticed by scholars, which can be brought into conversation with the treatment above concerning status-transformation rituals and ceremonies, which move people across social lines or confirm social lines in and around a group.

3. Models of ancient personality should be brought into the conversa-

---

72. Gerhard Lenski and Jean Lenski, *Human Societies: An Introduction to Macrosociology* (New York: McGraw-Hill, 1987). For excellent use of this model, see Dennis C. Duling, "Matthew's Plurisignificant 'Son of David' in Social Science Perspective: Kinship, Kingship, Magic and Miracle," *BTB* 22 (1992): 99-116; and Richard L. Rohrbaugh, "The Social Location of the Marcan Audience," *BTB* 23 (1993): 114-27.

tion on prayer.[73] For if the ancients are group-oriented persons, not individualists as modern Westerners are, then the ego of the pray-er must be assessed in terms of that construct, lest we engage in ethnocentrism. By group-oriented person we mean the type of individual Josephus describes: "Our sacrifices are not occasions for drunken self-indulgence — such practices are abhorrent to God — but for sobriety. At these sacrifices prayers offered for the welfare of the community take precedence of those for ourselves; for we are born for fellowship, and he who sets its claims above his private interests is especially acceptable to God" (*Against Apion* 2.195-96).

4. Finally, since so many psalms and prayers contain references to body parts — lifting of hands, falling to one's knees, God's right hand, eyes, ears, and heart — it would be worthwhile to bring this material into conversation with symbolic appreciation of the body in terms of honorable body parts. This model might be particularly useful in assessing the degree of personal involvement in sin and repentance or praise. Moreover, it provides a way of assessing the tension that might arise in prayer between the external rituals of some (hands and feet) and the internal processes of reformers (heart).

73. Bruce Malina and Jerome Neyrey, "First-Century Personality: Dyadic, Not Individual," in *The Social World of Luke-Acts*, 67-96; and Malina and Neyrey, *Portraits of Paul*.

CHAPTER THREE

Five New Testament Prayers, in Other Words

I t is time now to read prayers in the New Testament in terms of the focus of this book, prayers "in other words." Many are the articles and chapters that discuss the prayers below in terms of literary, linguistic, historical-critical, and redaction-critical points of view. But why reproduce those results here? Rather we intend to use the major categories presented in the last chapter to expose fresh and unrecognized meanings in the prayers that follow. This is by no means novelty for its own sake, but an effort to look through social and cultural categories at materials not written for Western modernity. In an effort to bridge the time difference and the cultural difference between the world of the New Testament and modern readers, we need reliable models of inquiry that are suited for the first-century Mediterranean world. The success of using these cultural materials lies in the fresh and meaningful insights they produce. Therefore, we will examine "in other words" the following prayers: the Our Father (Matt 6:9-13); the prayer of the church in Acts 4:24-30; the doxologies in Romans 16:25-27, Ephesians 3:20-21, Jude 24-25, and 1 Timothy 1:17; the Magnificat (Luke 1:46-55); and the final prayer of Jesus in John 17.

The Lord's Prayer

The Lord's Prayer is of course the most intensely examined, analyzed, and scrutinized prayer in modern biblical scholarship.[1] Interpreters have em-

---

1. Hans Dieter Betz, *The Sermon on the Mount* (Minneapolis: Fortress, 1995).

ployed various methods to understand the prayer, such as (1) synoptic comparison of the Gospel prayer with that found in the *Didache*;[2] (2) literary reading of it vis-à-vis a Gospel, Matthew in particular;[3] (3) comparison with Israelite prayers;[4] (4) general biblical background to the phrases in it;[5] and (5) inquiry into its early patristic interpreters.[6] Digests of this material are ready to hand, so we need not reproduce them here. But it will benefit us to sum up what the Our Father means in light of these ways of reading.

Traditional Reading of the Our Father: A Rapid Survey

Addressing God as "Father" is rooted in Israelite ways of naming God, although the interpretation by Jeremias that it means "Dear Father" has come under severe criticism.[7] The "hallowing" of God's name is not easy to determine, for while most scholars argue that God is the agent of this hallowing, some claim that mortals hallow God's name by their behavior. Still others see both God and mortals as agents: "[God's] decisive turning toward man and together with this, the thankful response: namely, the praising word and the act of loyalty."[8] God's kingdom is the natural extension of naming the deity "King" ("I will be king over you," Ezek 20:33; Isa 29:23). But opin-

2. S. J. Kistemaker, "The Lord's Prayer in the First Century," *JETS* 21 (1978): 323-28.

3. Mark Kiley, "The Lord's Prayer and Matthean Theology," in *The Lord's Prayer and Other Prayer Texts from the Greco-Roman Era,* ed. James Charlesworth (Valley Forge, Pa.: Trinity, 1994), 15-27.

4. J. Heinemann, "The Background of Jesus' Prayer in the Jewish Liturgical Tradition," in *The Lord's Prayer and Jewish Liturgy,* ed. J. J. Petuchowski and M. Brocke (New York: Seabury Press, 1978), 81-91.

5. B. Young, *The Jewish Background to the Lord's Prayer* (Austin, Tex.: Center for Judaic-Christian Studies, 1984); S. T. Lachs, "The Lord's Prayer," in his *A Rabbinic Commentary on the New Testament* (Hoboken, N.J.: Ktav, 1987), 117-24.

6. K. Froelich, "The Lord's Prayer in Patristic Literature," *PSB* Supp. 2 (1992): 71-87; F. E. Vokes, "The Lord's Prayer in the First Three Centuries," *StPat* 10 (= TU 107) (Berlin: Akademie-Verlag, 1970), 253-60.

7. Joachim Jeremias, *Abba* (Göttingen: Vandenhoeck & Ruprecht, 1966); but see James Barr, "Abba Isn't Daddy," *JTS* 37 (1988): 28-47.

8. R. Quere, "'Naming' God 'Father,'" *CurTM* 12 (1985): 5-14. See also J. Killinger, *The God Named Hallowed: The Lord's Prayer for Today* (Nashville: Abingdon, 1988). This appears to be the compromise of Hans D. Betz (*Sermon on the Mount,* 378), who argues that "it is humanity's obligation to sanctify God's name," yet "human failure to sanctify God's name is considered so hopeless that only God himself can help."

ion is divided over whether this "kingdom" is an eschatological one to be realized in the unspecified future or an actual kingdom that is now inaugurated in Jesus (Mark 1:15).[9] The reference to the "will of God" is judged not to belong to the earliest version of the prayer, although a Gospel such as Matthew makes much of "doing the will of God" (Matt 7:21; 18:14).[10] All interpreters describe the next items in the prayer as petitions. Those praying ask for "bread," either "daily," "tomorrow's," or mannalike (i.e., something given in the morning to be consumed later in the day).[11] This bread for some is real bread, but for others spiritual bread or "the bread of salvation."[12] "Debts" to some are earthly, financial encumbrances such as the "debts" discussed in Matthew 18:23-34, but others spiritualize the term to mean "sins."[13] "Temptation" enjoys no consensus. While for some it is spiritual (temptation to sin), most consider it a petition for constancy in the face of apostasy and others claim that it looks to the climax of the age, an eschatological trial such as found in Revelation 3:10.[14] It is not uncommon, de-

---

9. Raymond E. Brown, "The Pater Noster as an Eschatological Prayer," *TS* 22 (1961): 175-208; reprinted in his *New Testament Essays* (Garden City, N.Y.: Doubleday, 1968), 275-320; see also Philip B. Harner, *Understanding the Lord's Prayer* (Philadelphia: Fortress, 1975), 71-72. Betz adds a special twist to the present-future timing of the "kingdom coming" when he interprets it as a "promise that is still outstanding" (*Sermon on the Mount,* 379). T. W. Manson ("The Lord's Prayer," *BJRL* 38 [1956]: 439) splits the difference when he remarks, "There is one sense in which it (the kingdom) is eternal, the basic relationship of Creator to his creatures. It is simply there, and there is no sense in asking whether it is past, present, or future."

10. Raymond F. Collins, "'Thy Will Be Done on Earth as It Is in Heaven' — Matthew 6:10," *TBT* 1 (1964): 911-17.

11. D. Hill, "'Our Daily Bread' (Matt 6:11) in the History of Exegesis," *IBS* 5 (1983): 2-11; Bernard Orchard, "The Meaning of *ton epiousion* (Mt 6:11/Lk 11:3)," *BTB* 13 (1973): 274-82.

12. W. D. Davies and D. C. Allison (*Matthew 1–7* [London: T. & T. Clark, 1988], 609) manage to link all the various meanings of bread: "So one could easily think, especially in view of the eschatological orientation of the three preceding petitions and the circumstance that in Jesus' ministry table fellowship was an anticipation of the eschatological banquet (note Mt 8.11; Lk 22.28-30), that the material bread which God gives today transparently symbolizes and foreshadows and causes one to desire the spiritual, eschatological bread, which will bring lasting satisfaction."

13. Bruce Chilton, *Jesus' Prayer and Jesus' Eucharist: His Personal Practice of Spirituality* (Valley Forge, Pa.: Trinity, 1997), 41-44.

14. C. F. D. Moule, "An Unsolved Problem in the Temptation Clause in the Lord's Prayer," *RTR* 33 (1974): 65-76. Manson, "The Lord's Prayer," 444, advances the testing of an ordinary Israelite in Sir 2:1-5 as an explanatory parallel to this petition; Jeremias (*The Lord's Prayer* [Philadelphia: Fortress, 1964], 28-29) calls attention to *b. Ber* 60b for comparison:

spite what James 1:13 says about God *not* testing us, to appeal to Psalm 66:10, etc., to claim that this verse presumes that God indeed tests, so that the prayer petitions God *not* to test us. The popular interpretation of "deliverance from the Evil One" sees this as a reference to Satan, the Accuser.[15] In summary, the prayer tends to be understood as an eschatological prayer begging God's aid to escape the tribulations sure to come. As such, the contents tend to be rather spiritualized and removed from the peasant quality of Jesus' parables. What this composite interpretation lacks is a cultural reading: How would this have been understood by first-century peasants living a life of subsistence, awash in debt, awaiting the tax collector in fear? It is not enough to say that the Our Father embodies concepts and phrases from Israelite scripture and worship, because one must then ask what these concepts and phrases meant in that ancient culture. Let us, then, take resources learned in the previous chapter and bring them to bear on reading the Our Father "in other words."

Before beginning our cultural interpretation, several comments about the shape and rhetoric of the prayer are in order. All commentators consider the statements made in the Our Father as "petitions," although they differ in how many petitions, six or seven.[16] Moreover, the "petitions" to God are qualitatively different from the petitions made by mortals.[17] In a different vein, others point to the prayer's rhetorical excellence: (1) it balances three "You" addresses with "We" ones; (2) the first three remarks form a further unity,

---

Lead me not into the power of transgression,
and bring me not into the power of sin,
and not into the power of iniquity,
and not into the power of temptation,
and not into the power of anything shameful.

All five crises occur here in life, not in a future judgment.

15. Davies and Allison (*Matthew 1–7*, 614-15) cite a parallel from *b. Ber* 16b: "Rabbi, on concluding his prayer added the following: May it be thy will, O Lord our God . . . to deliver us from . . . the destructive Accuser." They then cite patristic commentators on this passage as referring to the Evil One.

16. Betz (*Sermon on the Mount*, 376) indicates that in the early church Origen and Gregory of Nyssa listed six petitions, whereas Augustine counted seven but changed his mind by combining the final two. The tradition of seven petitions gained canonical status with its endorsement by Luther.

17. Betz (*Sermon on the Mount*, 376) notes a tradition that tried to distinguish the first three addresses to God in terms of rhetoric, namely, as εὐχαί (prayer wishes), from the other petitions, which are labeled αἰτήματα (petitions). See also Chilton, *Jesus' Prayer*, 27.

some saying that together they "look to the *telos* of history . . . the culmination of God's salvific work,"[18] and others observing that they represent "different ways of asking God for the same thing."[19] Ayo's observation is worth seeing in full: "An analysis of the thou-petitions reveals that there is a remarkable parallel construction . . . in the Greek all the thou-petitions contain the same number of words, the same word order, and the same rhythms."[20]

The Our Father in Social and Cultural Perspective

Types of Prayers

Scholars regularly label all statements in the prayer as "petitions." They are, after all, cast in a polite form of imperative, the third-person aorist imperative. But we should note the difference between the first three, where God is petitioned, and the subsequent four where a more direct address is used. In the first part God is commanded/petitioned to attend to God's own business. The paraphrase of these petitions by Bruce Malina and Richard Rohrbaugh teases this out:

> "Hallowed be your name" is a *command form* in passive voice. Passive voice statements in Israel presume God is/will be the doer of the action. . . . Hallowing the name of God, the symbol of God's person, is thus to distinguish the status of God from all others. Here God is *commanded to present himself in terms of the status he really has.*

> "Your kingdom come" is a *command to God to rule as God,* to inaugurate the Israelite theocracy proclaimed by John the Baptizer and by Jesus and his faction members.

> "Your will be done" is a *command to God to finally do what pleases him,* and this "on earth as it is in heaven," everywhere. Again the request is that the will of God supersede all others.[21]

18. Davies and Allison, *Matthew 1–7*, 603. See also Harner, *Understanding the Lord's Prayer*, 75.
19. Nicholas Ayo, *The Lord's Prayer* (New York: Rowman and Littlefield, 1992), 51-52.
20. Ayo, *The Lord's Prayer*, 51.
21. Bruce J. Malina and Richard L. Rohrbaugh, *Social-Science Commentary on the Synoptic Gospels,* 2nd ed. (Minneapolis: Fortress, 2003), 48, emphasis added.

As we saw, some insist that God's servants on earth should beg God's assistance to effect these things;[22] others see God as the only person who can achieve these.[23] God can assist mortals with their business, but it seems dishonorable for mortals to volunteer to do God's job. Many note that the aorist passive imperatives in these petitions are "divine passives," that is, circumlocutions for actually using the divine name.[24] The main point we would make on the first three petitions/commands is that they are very respectful, honorable, and polite. They acknowledge God's name, kingdom, and will, even as they petition the display and realization of them.

Whereas the first three petitions command God to act for God's own sake, the four subsequent petition the heavenly Father-Patron for specific benefactions. Whereas bread, debt relief, defense when on trial, and protection from the Evil One are things of this world prized by disciples, the objects of the first three petitions are hardly objects as such, but aspects of God's self and honor.

The model of ritual transformation and confirmation can bring some clarity to the issue of types of prayers. Inasmuch as the petitioners command God to act, God will not experience a transformation ritual. God's honor may finally and fully be acknowledged, but this does not entail any change in God. Rather, by being acknowledged, God's full honor will be confirmed. Hence, the first three petitions are a ceremony wherein God fully manifests his divinity. The four petitions that follow are indeed status-transformation rituals. Change is petitioned on four fronts: change the hungry to full, change debtors to solvency, change those threatened with bankruptcy court to freedom, and change those menaced by the Evil One to salvation. We turn now to the ancient value of "honor" to examine the many ways that value is expressed in this prayer (title, name, being "set apart," epithets) and role (kingdom, patron-client relations, and patronage).

22. For example, Hans Dieter Betz (*Sermon on the Mount,* 378) says, "The first three petitions concern the needs of God . . . it is humanity's obligation to sanctify God's name."

23. For example, Davies and Allison (*Matthew 1–7,* 602) say, "the passive is probably divine," i.e., it belongs to God to bring these things about.

24. Joachim Jeremias, *New Testament Theology* (New York: Scribner, 1971), 9-14.

Honor: "Father"

As we saw noted earlier, "Abba Father" is not "Dear Daddy," but reflects the cultural world in which fathers were owed honor, respect, and obedience ("Honor your father and your mother"). The role of father in a patriarchal family encompassed a duty to rule and protect his offspring, as is reflected in the remark about the group's overseer: "He must manage his own household well, keeping his children submissive and respectful in every way" (1 Tim 3:4). A father's duty[25] included socializing his children into those roles and traditions he himself had learned (Prov 1:8; 4:1), which, we are told, may entail "beating [their] ribs."[26] A rebellious (Deut 21:18-21) or disobedient (Matt 21:28-31) son was a major social shame, dishonoring the father.[27] In that culture fathers were owed respect, not affection; theirs was a most honorable role, with sanctions to enforce proper performance. As James Barr has argued, "Your Abba is not your daddy," because the role of father in that culture demanded of him duties quite unlike those of modern paternal figures. Thus, as Oakman urges, "the prayer addresses [God] as *paterfamilias*, 'head of the household.'"[28] It honors God in his premier roles as father and patron, and so acknowledges the respect God's children owe him.

Tertullian's commentary on this opening address of the prayer reads it in terms of the cultural value of honor. He repeats Jesus' remark that we call no one else "Father" (Matt 23:9), thus honoring God with uniqueness, always a mark of honor. Tertullian notes that when we call God "Father," we act in obedience, which honors the Father even more. Tertullian proclaims that those who act honorably by "acknowledging the Father" are themselves honored (*On Prayer* 3). Moreover, both Cyprian and Tertullian contrast this "acknowledgment" of God with the willful choice of rebellious sons *not* to acknowledge God (Cyprian, *On*

---

25. We find it curious, even dishonorable, when Betz (*Sermon on the Mount*, 378) talks about the "needs of God": "For the Lord's Prayer, God is not a god without needs."

26. John J. Pilch, "'Beat His Ribs While He Is Young' (Sir 30:12): A Window on the Mediterranean World," *BTB* 23 (1993): 101-13.

27. One finds the motif of "the rebellious son" in Scripture (Deut 21:18-20) and rabbinic literature. The right relationship of sons and fathers, therefore, was a recurring, common problem throughout the life cycle (see Mark 7:10-12; Matt 21:28-29; Luke 15:11-13).

28. Douglas E. Oakman, "The Lord's Prayer in Social Perspective," in *Authenticating the Words of Jesus*, ed. Bruce Chilton and Craig Evans (Leiden: Brill, 1999), 156.

the Lord's Prayer 10; Tertullian, *On Prayer* 2). Finally Tertullian comments that when we say Father, "we are also naming God in a form of address which demonstrates both devotion and power" (*On Prayer* 2). "Devotion" translates *pietas,* the most honorable virtue, which essentially means (the duty of) "respect for authority." "Power" translates *potestas,* in this case *patria potestas,* the authority a Roman father had over his children, grandchildren, and other descendants. Thus the claims of the honorable Father are honorably acknowledged.

Honor: "Name"

The cultural value of honor continues as the prayer respects the "name" of God. Scholarship informs us of the rich background of this phrase in Scripture and worship, but more attention needs to be paid to the cultural meaning of a name, any name. One's "name" serves as a vehicle for one's reputation, worth, and respect. Iago told Othello: "Who steals my purse steals trash. 'Twas mine, 'tis his and has been slave to thousands. *But who filches from me my good name,* robs me of that which not enriches him, but makes me poor indeed" (*Othello* 3.3.157-61, emphasis added). Name equals honor, face, respect. This connection with the world of honor is commonly made in the Hebrew Scriptures in regard to God's name. Israel seems always in danger of "profaning my holy name," such that it becomes God's task to "hallow it" (Lev 22:32). This contextualization of the name of God in terms of honor and shame is common in Scripture, for example, in Ezekiel 36:23, where Israel is reproached because it had "profaned" God's name by its wickedness; yet God says he will "vindicate the holiness of my great name" (RSV). Similarly, the commandment not to "make wrongful use of the name of the LORD your God" (Exod 20:7) is intended to prevent any form of dishonoring God by manipulation of his name or taking it lightly. The Psalms sing of honor and respect for God's name: "Ascribe to the LORD the glory of his name" (Ps 29:2) and "Sing the glory of his name; / give to him glorious praise" (Ps 66:2). It would seem that humans can either profane God's name or honor that name; but God alone vindicates, i.e., God manifests himself, claims universal respect, and causes his name to be honored in the eyes of the world. This "name" of God is not devoid of content, but expresses power to save ("Save me, O God, by your name, / and vindicate me by your might," Ps 54:1) or power to defend ("The name of the God of Jacob protect you!" Ps 20:1). Power is always an honorable attribute, and the human reaction to God's name is one of praise and honor: "Praise the name of the LORD" (Ps 135:1); "Let them praise the name of the LORD" (Ps 148:5). But as the Our Father phrases it, God and God alone is called upon to set his name apart from all others and so to distinguish God's status from all others.[29]

Honor: "Hallowed"

This is a rare word in modern usage, and its unfamiliarity obscures its root meaning. "Hallowed" derives from "holy," as in "Holy, holy, holy" (Isa 6:3; Rev 4:8). "Holy" means "dedicated" or "set apart," that is, "separated" from what is ordinary, mortal, and profane. To address God as "holy" means to declare God's uniqueness and superiority, and to acknowledge God's deity as utterly separated and different from all that is mortal and sinful.[30] When mortals are acclaimed "holy," they are seen as belonging more to the world of God than to the world of humans (1 Thess 2:10), thus being "separated" to some degree from this world. Christians are exhorted to "Be holy as I am holy": "As he who called you is holy, be holy yourselves in all your conduct; for it is written, 'You shall be holy, for I am holy'" (1 Pet 1:15-16; Lev 11:44-45). As regards "hallowed be your name," we take to heart the suggestion of Nida and Louw to bring "hallowed" into the orbit of "reverence or honor":[31] "May your name be revered as holy." It is one thing for mortals to revere or honor God's name — we may indeed acknowledge the uniqueness of God — but God is called upon here to do what only God can do, "to distinguish the status of God from all other . . . to present him-

---

29. The interpretation of "name" as expressing "honor" should be juxtaposed to other claims that "name" (i.e., "Father") explains God's "nature" or "essential character"; see Harner, *Understanding the Lord's Prayer*, 61; Davies and Allison (*Matthew 1–7*, 603) state that "name" indicates "person."

30. Chilton, *Jesus' Prayer*, 33.

31. Johannes P. Louw and Eugene A. Nida, eds., *Greek-English Lexicon of the New Testament Based on Semantic Domains* (New York: United Bible Societies, 1988), 88.27. Commentators often connect this petition with the Kaddish prayer, which clearly expresses the honor quality of the remark: "Exalted and hallowed be his name in the world which he created according to his will. . . . Praised be his great name from eternity to eternity." See Davies and Allison, *Matthew 1–7*, 595.

self in terms of the status he really has."[32] It is out of the question for mortals to *make* that name known, respected, or honored,[33] because this would imply that God's honor is ascribed and that God can change in receiving more or less honor.

Honor: "Kingdom"

This term, likewise, should be appreciated in the context of honor. Israel acclaimed that "The LORD is king" (Ps 10:16) and that "The LORD is our king; he will save us" (Isa 33:22). Needless to say, this king is enthroned, either on the cherubim (1 Sam 4:4) or over the flood (Ps 29:10). His kingship, moreover, is forever (Ps 9:7). The role of king in antiquity was the most noble and honorable role imaginable; and when mortals attributed to the deity the role of king, they used the same honorable language to extol God, by exalting him above all others. For example, God will reign forever. Moreover, the honor of the heavenly King surpasses the greatness of the greatest earthly kings. Nebuchadnezzar may indeed be "king of kings" (Ezek 26:7; Dan 2:37), but the God of Israel is the "only Sovereign, the King of kings and Lord of lords" (1 Tim 6:15). God, who is king, casts down kings from their thrones, thus manifesting his power and so his honor. Thus those praying this prayer command God to rule, which will include kingly actions such as (1) judgment for sinners and justice for clients; (2) salvation, defense, and protection of his people; and (3) setting aright the ways of mortals on earth to produce an adequate living for all, free of slavery, taxes, debt, and the like.[34]

But "kingdom"? Is it a future, eschatological kingdom? A present-day kingdom?

32. Malina and Rohrbaugh, *Social-Science Commentary*, 48. Chilton (*Jesus' Prayer*, 36) puts it nicely by claiming that "hallowed be thy name" implies dynamic disclosure by God and appreciation by us.

33. Cyprian: "We say this not wishing that God should be made holy by our prayers, but asking the Lord that his name should be hallowed in us. Indeed how could God, who is himself the one who hallows, be hallowed?" (*On the Lord's Prayer* 12).

34. Philip B. Harner (*The Interpretation of the Lord's Prayer* [Philadelphia: Fortress, 1975], 71-72) relates this petition to Jesus' redefinition of the scope of the kingdom (who belongs), requirements for admission into it, and the time of its coming.

Excursus on Present and Future Time[35]

If New Testament scholars were polled on this question, the vast majority would vote for "eschatological" or future kingdom.[36] The problem with this viewpoint lies in the modern notion of time we impose on the ancients. Yes, they knew past and celebrated "today," but it is doubtful that they concerned themselves with "future," that is, with affairs unrelated to what was occurring, and knowledge of which was exclusively reserved to God and those God chose to reveal it to. If something happens nine months from now, that is not necessarily "future." A woman learns that she is pregnant and in nine months delivers a child: the end of those nine months is not "future" but the realization of a process that began "today." Similarly, the harvest that a farmer gathers in the summer after planting it in the winter or spring is not "future," but the result of an event begun a while ago. If a Christian prophet urges the Judean disciples to flee to Pella, the destruction of the city is not "future," but the result of present events. "Future," then, means for the ancients events disconnected from today, with no causal link to it. "About that day or hour no one knows, neither the angels in heaven, nor the Son" (Mark 13:32; Acts 1:6-7). It is a most shameful thing to try to learn this future, for it means poaching on God's turf, taking what is God's, and so dishonoring God. Is the Lord's Prayer, then, tinkering with the "future"? The honor acclamations not only acknowledge God's sovereignty and honor, but seem to urge God's action. The crux of "present" versus "future" lies in three issues: (1) in one's prior decision on whether Jesus was an eschatological prophet, (2) in how much disconnect there is between Jesus' proclamation of the kingdom and the Great Day, and (3) in trying to hold in tension the appreciation that the kingdom has begun and is here and that it will be fully realized hereafter.

Inasmuch as the other acknowledgments of God's honor look to present time, we are inclined to say that when God reigns as king, this takes place in the here and now. Kiley makes a key argument by showing how "kingdom" in the words of Jesus refers to a present relationship.[37] For ex-

---

35. This investigation of time draws heavily on the study of Bruce J. Malina, "Christ and Time: Swiss or Mediterranean?" *CBQ* 51 (1989): 1-31.

36. See Raymond E. Brown, "The Pater Noster as an Eschatological Prayer," *TS* 22 (1961): 175-208; Davies and Allison, *Matthew 1–7*, 603-5.

37. Kiley, "The Lord's Prayer," 16-17.

ample, a husband and wife lacking food and clothing are exhorted to "strive first for the kingdom of God" (Matt 6:33), which cannot mean that after they starve they shall find God's kingdom. Moreover, Malina urges us to see "king" and "kingdom" in terms of patronage, for sovereigns have at hand the goods and power to aid their clients.[38] Is there any place in Scripture where people petition that far in the unknown future some Patron would benefit them? But it is plausible that God's clients, who find on earth no patron who will not despoil and enslave them, expect that God's patronage in his kingdom will surely not favor the rich over the poor, the powerful over the weak. Moreover, patronage is needed immediately because people are hungry and starving and debts are swallowing up the land. God's kingdom will be just, unlike that of the Romans or the Jerusalem elites. But this is a cultural perspective, known only by the social-scientific mode of interpretation.

Honor: Obedient Children

While we often read how incumbent it is on God's faithful to "do the will of God," "Your will be done" is not the work of humans. Yes, "Whoever does the will of God is my brother and sister" (Mark 3:35) and "This is the will of God, your sanctification" (1 Thess 4:3), but this resembles the point made above, that human behavior correlates with the reputation of God. Good behavior brings credit to God, who authorized it: "That they may see your good works and give glory to your Father in heaven" (Matt 5:16; 1 Thess 2:12). The "will of God" is yet one more mark of honoring God. When Jesus prays to God to do "not what I want, but what you want" (Mark 14:36), he acknowledges the role of God, his status, and his right to command that Jesus obey. To obey is actually acknowledgment of the worth and standing of the one who commands; it is a virtue. Just as children honor their parents when they accept their discipline and instruction (Eph 6:1; Col 3:20), so do adults following the wishes of their earthly kings, chiefs, and sovereigns. To obey means to honor. But granted all this, the petition "Your will be done" is utterly different, because it does not envision that all the world will obey God's will. Rather

38. Bruce J. Malina, *The New Testament World: Insights from Cultural Anthropology*, 3rd ed. (Louisville: Westminster John Knox, 2001), 95-96.

it commands God "finally to do what pleases him . . . that the will of God supersede all others."[39]

Honor: "On Earth as in Heaven"

The scope of the reign of a monarch directly correlates to his power, respect, and honor. Hence, in Jesus' prayer in Matthew 11:25 he addresses God in a most honorable way: "I thank you, Father, Lord of heaven and earth . . ." (see Acts 17:24). He himself comes to enjoy maximum cosmic authority: "All authority in heaven and earth has been given me" (Matt 28:18). Moreover, it was not uncommon for Israelites to remark on the extent of God's sovereignty: "May it please thee, Eternal One, our God, to make peace in the family above and in the family below" (*b. Ber* 16b; Josephus, *Jewish Antiquities* 4.40). And in another place in the same tractate, we read: "Do thy will in heaven above, and give peace of spirit to those who fear thee below, and do what is good in thy eyes" (*b. Ber* 29b). More honorable than sovereignty over heaven and earth is God's command of land, sea, and sky: "Lord of all that is in the heaven and earth and sea. . . ."

Patron-Client Relationships

We take it as self-evident that the ancients readily assessed the relationship between God/Father and those praying as a patron-clients relationship. This ubiquitous model of social interaction in antiquity describes relationships that arise among people of unequal status and resources: landlord/vassal, aristocrat/peasant, king/subject, father/son, and God/Israel.[40] Moreover, patron-client relationships describe the vertical dimension of exchange between higher-status and lower-status persons. Building on our exposition of this native model in chapter 1, we now use it to illuminate important features of the Our Father.

The address to "Father," even if intended to one's biological parent, is

39. Malina and Rohrbaugh, *Social-Science Commentary*, 48.
40. See Jerome H. Neyrey, "God, Benefactor and Patron: The Major Cultural Model for Interpreting the Deity in Greco-Roman Antiquity," *JSNT* 27 (2005): 465-92.

still a distinctive way of naming a patron. Typical is the remark of Iamblichus: "Our parents alone are the first in benefaction, even before our birth, and ancestors are responsible for all the achievements of their descendants. We cannot go wrong if we show the gods that we do good to our parents before all others. The gods, we may suppose, will pardon those who honor their parents above all, for our parents taught us to honor the gods" (*Life of Pythagoras* 38). Parents, then, are the first benefactors (i.e., patrons) of their children. For their part, offspring honor their original patrons, as Iamblichus noted: "Divine favor rests on those who honor their parents because the parents taught them to honor the gods." It goes without saying that "honor your father and your mother" was a foremost law in Israel. The honoring of one's parents-patrons is the analogy that comes to describe the relationship of God, Father and Patron, and his earthly clients: "In like manner do the gods act, and especially the great King of Kings (βασιλεὺς βασιλέων), Zeus, who is the common protector and father (κηδεμὼν καὶ πατήρ) of men and gods" (Dio Chrysostom, *Oration* 2.75). And in another place Dio says: "Yet all these poets . . . call the first and greatest god Father of the whole rational family collectively. . . . what is more, some do not hesitate even to call him Father in their prayers" (*Oration* 36.35-36). God-Father, we are told, is named "because of universal beneficence" (Cicero, *Nature of the Gods* 1.64). "God" alone would indicate patronage, but more so "Father."

Patronage

What do patrons and fathers do when they play this role? In a polytheistic context, various deities were associated with specific benefactions, as Quintilian indicates. "In the case of Jupiter, we extol his power as manifested in the governance of all things, with Mars we praise his power in war, with Neptune his power over the sea; as regards inventions, we celebrate Minerva's discovery of the arts, Mercury's discovery of letters, Apollo's of medicine, Ceres' of the fruits of the earth, Bacchus' of wine" (*Institutio oratoria* 3.7.6-9). Thus, these Greco-Roman deities are perceived as patrons because of the benefaction they bestow — governance, power, arts, letters, medicine, and food. Because each deity does not bestow all benefactions, mortals found it prudent to form patron-client relations with many of them in view of their specialties. We know, moreover, that we can abstract and categorize these myriad benefactions into four comprehensive categories: power, commitment, inducement, and influence. Looking carefully at the Patron-Father in this prayer, we identify the following categories of patronage:

Power

"Father" implies the ability to make people do certain things, as earthly fathers can command their offspring; this Father presides over a kingdom, and will finally have his will done. Patron-Father is petitioned to protect and defend his clients.

Commitment

"Father" who is patron is also in a kinship relationship with the clients, the closest bond a human can have. The honor given to the Patron belongs here too, as it is the acknowledgment of the Patron-Father relationship. God does not need this honor, but it allows the clients to increase their relatedness to the Patron.

Inducement

Inasmuch as we consider "daily bread" to be food always in short supply for peasants, it is material benefaction. And since we also consider "debts" to be real problems that can be solved only by some material means, removal of debts, too, is material patronage.

Nothing explicitly states that the Father-Patron acts altruistically in bestowing benefaction, but we consider this self-evident for early Christian prayer. As we saw in chapter 2, thinking about patronage in a systematic way led many ancients to affirm that God is patron because it is the nature of God to give and to benefit. And since, say these thinkers, God needs nothing, God as patron does not act in terms of balanced reciprocity, expecting or demanding a return from his clients.

Bread

It greatly influences our interpretation of the "bread" petition if we put it in its proper cultural context, the agricultural world of subsistent peasants in antiquity.[41] Droughts and famines repeatedly caused acute hunger in the land (Josephus, *Jewish Antiquities* 15.299-316; 20.51-53; Acts 11:28).[42] Ruinous taxation was paid in kind, that is, in grain, wine, and other foodstuffs. Rates of taxation were excessively high, leading to a subsistence level of survival for peasants.[43] Unlike manna, there never was enough bread. One thinks of the feedings by Jesus at which 4,000 and 5,000 men "ate their fill," a very rare thing. In a peasant context "bread" is not Torah or bread for the age of salvation; it is literal food. It had always been the work of Israel's Patron to dispense food:

> These look to you
>   to give them their food in due season. (Ps 104:27)

Just as God gave manna in the early morning to be eaten later at the daily meal, so God is petitioned to give real bread for the daily meal.[44] Thus, knowing the cultural world of peasants and the actions of patrons to sustain their clients, we appreciate the immediacy of the petition and the honor given to the Patron for his benefaction, i.e., "bread."

Debts

Luke speaks of "sins" forgiven, but Matthew of "debts" remitted. In a peasant cultural context, debt-as-moneys-owed is the more likely meaning. Taxes in antiquity supported empires and their armies; and no monarch ever had so much wealth that he could relax taxes, unless as a favor in a patronage context. How much might peasants pay in taxes? Demetrius tells the Judeans that he will *not* collect the following annual taxes: "I now free you and exempt all the Jews from payment of tribute and salt tax and crown levies, and instead of collecting the third of the grain and the half of

---

41. Oakman, "The Lord's Prayer," 158-60; see also Manson, "The Lord's Prayer," 442.

42. See Peter Garnsey, *Famine and Food Supply in the Graeco-Roman World* (Cambridge: Cambridge University Press, 1988), 219-23.

43. John S. Kloppenborg, "Literary Convention, Self-Evidence and the Social History of the Q People," *Semeia* 55 (1991): 86-88.

44. Yet many urge that "bread" be interpreted in terms of the eschatological banquet, a symbol of the "kingdom" that is to come; see Harner, *Interpretation*, 97. Yet Betz, among others, argues for an interpretation that it is one of God's duties as creator and sustainer to provide for his creatures in this present time (*Sermon on the Mount*, 379).

the fruit of the trees that I should receive . . ." (1 Macc 10:29-30). But if he did collect taxes, he would receive at least a third of the grain and half the fruits. Tacitus states that in the reign of Tiberias, "The provinces of Syria and Judaea, exhausted by their burdens, were pressing for a diminution of the tribute" (*Annales* 2.42). And the result of this taxation? Debt!

Peasants in the best of times would have difficulty paying all the taxes demanded by the Romans; in a drought, the difficulty became an impossibility. Without recourse to a moneylender, debt became devouring.[45] Is there a single instance when an indebted peasant repaid it? The likely trajectory is debt and more debt and then foreclosure. We know of the rapid expansion of latifundia in the great plains of Galilee, which means that a rich person is acquiring more and more land from peasants drowning in debt. Very many were simply losing their land and being forced into a tenancy position of working for wages or becoming sharecroppers on the land they just forfeited.[46] Plausible? Josephus tells us that in the Roman war one of the earliest actions against the Jerusalem elites consisted of solving the debt problem: "[The rebels] next carried combustibles to the public archives, eager to destroy the money-lenders' bonds and to prevent the recovery of debts, in order to win over a host of grateful debtors and to cause a rising of the poor against the rich" (*Jewish War* 2.427).

Jesus often speaks of debts. He tells a parable of a man greatly indebted to a king, and of a lower-class person who is indebted to the first man (Matt 18:23-34). The king forgives the great debt, a thing utterly farfetched, foolish, and outrageous, because a king's honor would be seriously impugned if he absolved debts. All would take him for a fool, a weak person. Failure to repay debts could lead to imprisonment and torture until the clan coughed up the money (Matt 18:34; Luke 12:58). Peasants, then, petition their true Patron to assist them in their most acute problem: helping them out of debt.[47]

---

45. On taxation and debt, see Douglas E. Oakman, "Jesus and Agrarian Palestine: The Factor of Debt," in SBLSP (1985): 57-73.

46. In just a few pages Douglas Oakman summarizes the process of larger and larger estates for the elite and the consequent economic realities of debt, taxation, and oppression for the peasants ("The Countryside in Luke-Acts," in *The Social World of Luke-Acts: Models for Interpretation,* ed. Jerome H. Neyrey [Peabody, Mass.: Hendrickson, 1991], 162-64).

47. See Douglas E. Oakman, *Jesus and the Economic Questions of His Day* (Lewiston, N.Y.: Edwin Mellen Press, 1986), 57-80; and Oakman, "The Lord's Prayer," 164.

Value Model

In general, the ancients were acutely aware of their vertical relationship to those above and below them. This does not exclude the horizontal relations of kinship, for both coexisted. God, as Father-Patron, who has a kingdom and who can effect his will, stands vertically above his clients. The translation of Abba as "Dear Daddy" is both philologically incorrect and culturally strange: sons simply did not relate to their fathers as if on a horizontal rather than a vertical dimension. While they experience themselves as subject to all the earth's forces, mortals acknowledge God as having complete control of them. Of course, peasants were also in the power of tax collectors, tax judges, and landlords, all vertical relationships. As regards time, we argue that "today" is the main time indicator for these clients: "Today this scripture has been fulfilled in your hearing" (Luke 4:21); "I must stay at your house today" (Luke 19:5); "Today you will be with me in Paradise" (Luke 23:43); and "Today I have begotten you" (Acts 13:33; Ps 2:7). God's time seems to be different, at least in the first part of the prayer, for embedded in the Israelite understanding of God is "eternity," that is, no beginning and no end. Moreover, inasmuch as the future belongs exclusively to God, clients cannot know this time nor seek to discover it. Clients' principal mode of activity is "being," since they cannot of themselves effect what they petition; but God's mode of activity is "doing," since the Patron begins, sustains, and resolves all issues relative to the clients at all times. The Patron, moreover, alone can act.

As regards type of prayer, the Our Father is universally labeled as petitionary prayer. But there is considerable unease at simply calling the "Thou" words "petition." What is the alternative? There is much in the "Thou" words that expresses honor and praise, which the clients are quick to acknowledge, as in the prayer "Worthy are you . . ." (Rev 4:11). Earlier we attempted to link types of prayers with kinds of rituals, either status transformation or ceremony. The "Thou" words envision no change in God, but only the full acknowledgment of God's sovereignty. Thus God's role and status as Father and Patron are confirmed in the communication; God does not have to wait to assume full godliness. On the other hand, God's clients by virtue of their petitions are assuredly asking for a change of status, from starving to adequately fed, from indebtedness to solvency, and from threat to safety.

Acts 4:24-30

After Peter and John were released from custody, they went to their friends and reported what the chief priests and elders had said to them. Upon hearing this narrative, all began to pray as one (Acts 4:23-30).[48]

Types of Prayers

In terms of prayer types, 4:24-28 combines several kinds. Part of it is a prayer of acknowledgment that addresses God in terms of great honor and respect. God is "Sovereign" (Δεσπότης), who acts in faithfulness and in power. This type of prayer we label a ceremony, because God is in no way changed, but rather his role and status are confirmed. The second type of prayer, 4:29-30, petitions God to "grant to your servants to speak your word with all boldness." It also asks God to act boldly, by stretching out his hand to heal and work signs and wonders. Thus, it envisions some change, not in God, but in the praying group, that they will be emboldened to speak God's word and will experience God acting to protect them. The current state includes arrest, scrutiny, and threat by the group's enemies. Although they are not presented as in a state of weakness and fear, the petitioners ask that the relationship between the group and God move to a higher level, which means change for the petitioners.

The identification of two types of prayers in 4:24-30 is confirmed by a different type of analysis, namely, literary analysis with attention to the use of chiasm.[49] The first part of 4:24-30, the acknowledgment, is bracketed by declaration of God's absolute sovereignty, both in creation and current history ("Sovereign Lord, who made the heaven and the earth . . . grant to your servants to speak your word"). God's control of events is acknowledged by citation of Psalm 2, which is understood as a prophecy, which is now fulfilled. The prayer speaks of the "kings of the earth . . . the rulers . . . Herod and Pontius Pilate" challenging God by attacking God's "anointed . . . your holy servant Jesus." But all earthly plots are "vain," for God is ac-

48. The study of this prayer by Beverly Gaventa is of particular merit: "The Prayer in Acts 4:24-31," in *Spiritual Life in the Early Church*, ed. Bonnie Thurston (Minneapolis: Fortress, 1993), 55-65.

49. See Urban C. von Wahlde, "Acts 4:24-31: The Prayer of the Apostles in Response to the Persecution of Peter and John — and the Consequences," *Biblica* 77 (1996): 237-44.

knowledged as all-powerful, ever in control ("your plan had predestined to take place").

> A. "Sovereign Lord, who made the heaven and the earth and the sea and everything in them, who by the mouth of our father David, your servant, said by the Holy Spirit,
>> B. 'Why did the Gentiles rage, and the peoples imagine vain things?
>>> C. The kings of the earth set themselves in array, and the rulers were gathered together,
>>>> D. against the Lord and against his Anointed'
>>>> D'. for truly in this city there were gathered together against your holy servant Jesus, whom thou didst anoint,
>>> C'. both Herod and Pontius Pilate,
>> B'. with the Gentiles and the peoples of Israel,
> A'. to do whatever your hand and your plan had predestined to take place." (author's translation)

God, then, is acknowledged and honored as "Sovereign," whose will and whose plan take place because of his providential power.

The second part of the prayer is, as all agree, petitionary prayer. It too is expressed in a crafted literary way as a chiasm.

> "And now, Lord, look upon their threats,
> A. with all boldness
>> B. grant to your servants to speak your word,
>>> C. while you stretch out your hand to heal, and signs and wonders are performed
>>>> D. through the name of your holy servant Jesus."
>>> C'. And when they had prayed, the place in which they were gathered together was shaken
>> B'. and they were all filled with the Holy Spirit and spoke the word of God
> A'. with boldness. (author's translation)

Just as the prayer of acknowledgment began with an honorable form of address ("Sovereign Lord"), so too the petitionary prayer starts with a comparable address ("Lord"). The chiastic form includes not just the petition but also the demonstration that it was heard and granted, something occasionally observed in Israelite and Greco-Roman prayers.[50] This analysis, while it sharpens the difference between the two halves, also appreciates that the prayer in 4:24-30 is one prayer, albeit of two types.

Honor: God's Title

They acclaim God as "Sovereign," a term that describes the relation of master to slave (e.g., Philo, *On the Life of Moses* 1.201) and expresses above all power, and fear (see Philo, *Who Is the Heir?* 22-23). Like the prayer in Acts 4:24, Josephus was wont to address God as Sovereign and Creator: "Lord (δέσποτα) of all the ages and Creator of universal being . . . confirm these promises" (*Jewish Antiquities* 1.272; see also 4.40; 5.41). Philo reflects Greco-Roman usage of "Sovereign" when he speaks about reverence for the emperor as "Master and Benefactor and Saviour (δεσπότην καὶ εὐεργέτην καὶ σωτῆρα)" (*Against Flaccus* 126). "Sovereign," then, expresses power and supreme sway; a "Sovereign" or "Master" rules and has his way, all of which is most honorable and expresses honor. The power of the Sovereign looks back in time to when God created the heaven, the earth, the sea, and all that is in them (4:24) — power, to be sure, but also the widest possible scope of his authority (heavens, earth, and sea). God, moreover, knows and foresees the events concerning Jesus; so he is to be praised for his unique knowledge, which is also an extension of his power. Furthermore, the honor of God is expressed by his making his will come to pass: "whatever your hand and your plan had predestined to take place" (4:28). God's "hand" in 4:28 and 30, an anthropomorphism, to be sure, nevertheless embodies God's power, and all power is honorable.[51] The "Sovereign," then, receives all the honor that his subjects can express, especially power, might, and knowledge.

50. See Pieter W. Van der Horst, "Hellenistic Parallels to Acts (Chapters 3–4)," *JSNT* 35 (1989): 44-46.

51. Dennis Sweetland ("Hand," in *The College Pastoral Dictionary of Biblical Theology*, ed. Carroll Stuhlmueller [Collegeville, Minn.: Liturgical Press, 1996], 405] summarizes the relationship of "hand" to "honor": "While the hand appears in numerous biblical passages simply designating a part of the body, on many other occasions it is used metaphorically. In most of these instances hand occurs as a symbol of power . . . on many occasions the mention of right hand suggests a position of power or honor."

Patron and Patronage

"Sovereign" is not a common synonym for patron, but as we noted above, Philo casually linked "Sovereign" with "Benefactor and Savior." This Patron, moreover, is a patron's patron, inasmuch as he possesses the most *power,* the most *wisdom,* and the most *loyalty* for his clients. His power created the world — all the world ("who made the heaven and the earth, the sea," 4:24) — guided events, controlling Herod and Pontius Pilate ("whatever your hand and your plan predestined to take place," 4:28), and will defend and embolden the disciples. The disciples petition a share of this power to stand before their enemies with boldness. Similarly, this Sovereign manifests *commitment* to "your holy servant Jesus" and to those "servants" who are praying, who will perform signs and wonders "through the name of your holy servant Jesus" (4:30). The pray-ers acknowledge God's benefaction of *"influence"* when they appreciate that David's Psalm 2:1-2 refers to the death of Jesus, an understanding of the hidden, prophetic meaning in it. Those praying, then, are requesting the Patron to act once more as the altruistic giver of good gifts.

Value Map

The praying group is clearly operating in terms of a vertical relationship with God. It admits that chief priests and elders, also above them, are threatening them. But God, who sits upon a throne above even the cherubim, is "Sovereign" over all spaces, times, and peoples. They experience themselves as subject to harm from the authorities, which on their own they cannot escape. They petition in present time for immediate assistance; God, however, operates in two classifications of time: *past* (creation, David's prophecy, passion of Jesus) and *present* (power, strength, signs and wonders). Again, the mode of activity of humans is "being," whereas they petition God, whose mode is always "doing."

"Give God the Glory": Doxologies in the New Testament

Outside of the Scriptures, "glory" (δόξα) most frequently means "opinion," which then shades into "reputation." Within the Scriptures this term

84

joins other terms of respect, praise. and acclaim. "Glory" is often linked with "honor" and its synonyms, as we find commonly in doxologies: to "the only God, be honor and glory" (1 Tim 1:17), with "praise": "for the glory and praise of God" (Phil 1:11), and with both: "result in praise and glory and honor" (1 Pet 1:7). Both Israelites and Christians command the people to "give glory" to God according to a literary form called a doxology. It should be noted that doxologies abound, but the precise label "doxology" seems to gain currency only in the second century, not during the time of the New Testament.

Doxologies

Matthew Black concluded that doxologies are structured in two different ways. In his examination of the complex doxology in 1 Chronicles 29:10-11:[52] "Then David blessed the LORD in the presence of all the assembly; David said: 'Blessed are you, O LORD, the God of our ancestor Israel, forever and ever. Yours, O LORD, are the greatness, the power, the glory, the victory, and the majesty; for all that is in the heavens and on the earth is yours; yours is the kingdom, O LORD, and you are exalted as head above all," he concluded that one form begins with a *berakah*: Blessed are you, O Lord, the God of Israel, and another with a different formula: To you, O Lord, are greatness, power, and glory. The first form is found abundantly in psalms, in temple worship, and also in New Testament writings.

Blessed are you, O God, with every pure blessing. (Tob 8:15-17)

Blessed are you, O Savior of Israel, who crushed the attack of the mighty warrior. (1 Macc 4:30)

Blessed be the Lord God of Israel,
   for he has looked favorably on his people and redeemed them.
                                                                    (Luke 1:68)

---

52. Matthew Black, "The Doxology to the *Pater Noster* with a Note on Matthew 6:13b," in *A Tribute to Geza Vermes,* ed. Philip R. Davies and Richard T. White (Sheffield: JSOT Press, 1990), 327-28; Eric Werner, "The Doxology in Synagogue and Church: A Liturgico-Musical Study," *HUCA* 19 (1945-46): 275-351; Ernst Lohmeyer, *The Lord's Prayer* (London: Collins, 1965), 230-46.

Blessed be the God and Father of our Lord Jesus Christ. (2 Cor 1:3; see Eph 1:3-10)

The second form is commonly found in the letters of Paul (Rom 11:36; 16:25; Gal 1:5; Phil 4:20) and elsewhere.[53]

To him be glory forever. Amen. (Rom 11:36)

To him be the glory both now and to the day of eternity. Amen.
(2 Pet 3:18)

Blessing and glory and wisdom
and thanksgiving and honor
and power and might
be to our God forever and ever! Amen. (Rev 7:12)

To whom be the glory and majesty for ever and ever. Amen.
(*1 Clem* 20.12)

It is noteworthy that 1 Peter contains both forms, although not together: "Blessed be the God and Father of our Lord Jesus Christ!" (1:3) and "To him belong the glory and the power forever and ever. Amen" (4:11).

In this study of prayers in the New Testament, we will focus on only the second form and examine in synoptic fashion four examples of it.[54] In interpreting these doxologies in light of the social science models we have been using, notice of the parallel forms and contents will aid us in appreciating how common yet how rich these prayers are. But on our way to that, it benefits us to pay closer attention to the precise form of this second type of doxology.

The Form of a Doxology

Scholars point out that this type of doxology is typically structured of four elements: (1) an addressee (in the dative case); (2) honor ascribed; (3) du-

---

53. New Testament addresses to God that begin with εὐλογητός include: Luke 1:68; 2 Cor 1:3; 11:31; Rom 1:25; 1 Pet 1:3.

54. See Gerhard Delling, *Worship in the New Testament* (London: Darton, Longman and Todd, 1962), 62-69; and Reinhard Deichgräber, *Gotteshymnus und Christushymnus in der frühen Christenheit* (Göttingen: Vandenhoeck & Ruprecht, 1967), 24-107.

Rom 16:25-27 (RSV)	Eph 3:20-21 (RSV)	Jude 24-25 (RSV)	1 Tim 1:17 (RSV)
To him	To him	To him	To the King of ages,
who is able to strengthen you . . . the only wise God	who by the power at work within us is able to do far more abundantly than all that we can ask or think	who is able to keep you from falling and to present you without blemish before the presence of his glory with rejoicing	immortal, invisible, the only God,
be glory	be glory	be glory, majesty, dominion, and authority	be honor and glory
for evermore.	to all generations.	before all time and now and for ever.	for ever and ever.
Amen.[55]	Amen.	Amen.	Amen.

ration of the praise, usually "forever"; and (4) "Amen," which invites the hearers to affirm and acknowledge the praise. In the diagram above, we compare four samples of this doxology, Romans 16:25-27, Ephesians 3:20-21, Jude 24-25, and 1 Timothy 1:17.

Types of Prayers

As regards types of prayers, this form of the doxology is a classic prayer of acknowledgment. God is given glory always, but also honor and other acknowledgments of respect and worth. God in no way is changed by this prayer, but rather is confirmed as Lord, Patron, and Sovereign. It is as though God has standing and eternal claims to sovereignty, which claims are acknowledged. A doxology, therefore, is a ceremony that confirms God's role and status. God does not change. The relationship of clients to Patron is likewise confirmed, namely, that the clients belong to the household of God and are worshipers of this one and only God.

55. On "Amen," see Deichgräber, *Gotteshymnus und Christushymnus*, 25-40, 97-102. See also David E. Aune, *Revelation 1–5* (Dallas: Word, 1997), 43-46.

Honor

Except for the title "King of ages" in 1 Timothy 1:17, no special name for God is used here. The honor that is usually conveyed in titles such as "King of kings and Lord of lords" or "Creator" or "Sovereign" is transferred to God by phrases such as "only wise God," and especially by the acknowledgment of glory, majesty, might, honor, and authority. These markers of supremacy and power express the cultural value of honor. Individually and as a package they credit God with maximal ability and worthiness. What can we say about these? First, we should understand them more accurately, both as translated and especially as translated from an honor culture.

δύναμις: power, might, strength, force
εὐλογία: speaking in favorable terms, praise
ἰσχύς: capacity to function effectively, strength, power and might, ability
κράτος: ability to exhibit strength, might
μεγαλωσύνη: a state of greatness or preeminence, majesty
πλοῦτος: abundance, wealth
σοφία: practical wisdom, secrets, esoteric knowledge

Since we consider all of them as "honor" markers, we will interpret them in terms of the understanding of masculine gender in the ancient world. Males were expected to have and exercise power to defend their families (δύναμις; ἰσχύς; κράτος). They should have wisdom (σοφία), either cleverness or executive skill to plan and execute. Honorable men generally have an abundance of good things and even wealth (πλοῦτος), as the culture knows it. Honor is never honor unless displayed and acknowledged (εὐλογία; μεγαλωσύνη); hence display of any form of greatness or strength demands praise and respect. Earthly kings would embody to a very high degree all these masculine qualities, namely, power to subdue and defend, might to extend their will, strength to gain and maintain kingdoms, and wisdom to make laws, provide for the kingdom (1 Kings 4:22-28), and adjudicate suits (1 Kings 3:16-28). "Honor" thus is replicated: what makes a male honorable also makes a king honorable and serves as the basis for God's honor, who is both Father and King. In doxologies, then, the marks of distinction, respect, and status that warrant praise on earth are correspondingly acknowledged as most fitting for the Person who most has them.

With this cultural scenario as a guide, we note that in three of the doxologies in the synopsis above God is acknowledged as the "powerful" one: he "who is *able*" or has "the power" (δυναμένῳ). In Ephesians this capacity to act with power is duplicated in the phrase that God acts with power in the church: "by the power at work within us." Timothy, moreover, acknowledges God as "King of ages," a title that expresses royal majesty that, unlike the grandeur of Ozymandias, endures forever. Romans declares the praise of the "*only* wise God." As we note in the next chapter, "uniqueness" is always grounds for honor. Finally, although it may seem that worshipers "give" glory to God, they are doing no more than acknowledging the honor claims of God.

Patron and Patronage

None of these doxologies, we noted, addresses God by any name or title that we have come to appreciate as suggesting that God is patron to those praying. But a patron-client relationship may be presumed in a high-context society.[56] The prayers are most respectful, as befits speech to a patron, even as the topics of the prayers are likewise appropriate. Patrons bestow patronage, such as *power* and *commitment.* Although God is honored by being acknowledged as worthy of glory, majesty, might, power, and authority, those praying praise God's patronage of *power* that is actually effective in their lives: "God by the power at work within us is able to do far more abundantly than all that we can ask or think" (Eph 3:20); it is God "who is able to keep you from falling" (Jude 24) and God "who is able to strengthen you" (Rom 16:25). God-Patron also extends *commitment* to those who honor him. In addition to the fact that those praying would not be doing that unless God's favor and commitment had not already been extended to them, Jude's prayer explicitly honors God's commitment to those praying. God, he says, "is able to keep you from falling and to present

---

56. In low-context societies, such as modern Euro-America, nothing is presumed and all must be spelled out. Antiquity was just the opposite: most was presumed. The author who wrote "the time when kings go out to war" knew that his audience knew that he was speaking of the springtime after the late rains. Chariots and other war machines cannot travel in mud. One might pursue this in two ways, first through Bruce Malina, who has synopsized the work of Edward T. Hall (*The Social World of Jesus and the Gospels* [London: Routledge, 1996], 24-29), or from Edward T. Hall, *Beyond Culture* (New York: Doubleday, 1976), 91-116, and *The Dance of Death: The Other Dimension of Time* (New York: Doubleday, 1983), 59-77.

you without blemish before the presence of his glory with rejoicing" (Jude 24). People "keep" or defend what is dear to them. And those praying presume an unending time line for God's commitment to them. This surfaces another aspect of divine commitment, namely, faithfulness or steadfastness. Thus God's commitment extends to the time when those whom God keeps blameless will indeed rejoice in the presence of his glory.

Value Map

The relationships expressed here are vertical, as between a superior and inferiors. As regards time, those praying are totally focused on present time while they acknowledge that God's time is past-present-and-future time: "before all time and now and for ever," or simply eternity in the future: "for evermore . . . to all generations . . . for ever and ever." God's eternity is itself a singular mark of honor, since only deities have no beginning and no ending. Pray-ers are not doing anything by praising God; rather God is characterized by "doing," inasmuch as the exercise of power and wisdom is that for which mortals praise God.

The Magnificat

Types of Prayers

Although many contend that this prayer is better prayed by Elizabeth, the barren one who was lifted up, tradition finally ascribes it to Mary, the lowly virgin made fruitful. Using traditional classifications of psalms, scholars classify it as a "hymn of praise," which typically consists of three parts: (1) praise of God, (2) followed by motives for praise, either God's deeds or his attributes, and (3) conclusion. We prefer to classify it in terms of types of communications, and thus we find two types of prayers in it, mostly "informative" prayer that is praise of God and a "self-focused" prayer. Mary begins the prayer with praise, although with an uncommon verb: "My soul *magnifies* the Lord,"[57] which is followed by warrant for this praise. "Magnify" or "extol," found only here in the New Testament, ap-

---

57. The wording of the Magnificat comes from the Revised Standard Version.

pears in the Psalms (30:1; 69:30; 145:1), but rarely elsewhere. Honoring is expressed by "magnifying" God, "rejoicing in him" and celebrating God's might and holy name. In addition, Mary states that "all generations will call me blessed," which is spoken to God in the same prayer, for which reason we consider it a different type of prayer, namely, self-focused prayer. It is *not* addressed to future generations, but only to God. As such, it is a prayer. Mary acknowledges that she is the object of extraordinary benefaction ("he who is mighty has done great things for me," 1:49), the fame of which will be a sort of eternal glory: "All generations will call me blessed." Because the Magnificat is a prayer of acknowledgment, we understand it as a ceremony in which God is recognized and confirmed in his role as Savior to Mary, Israel, and Abraham. God is in no way changed, but is confirmed in his greatness, acknowledged as the faithful one par excellence, praise of whom recognizes his claims to respect and honor. Mary, however, experienced as the context for this prayer a status transformation from virgin to pregnant woman; her praise is the completion of the transformation begun with Gabriel's message, then acknowledged by Elizabeth ("the mother of my Lord"), and now expressed by Mary herself.

Honor

As a prayer of acknowledgment, we readily identify many aspects of the value of honor in it. The verbs themselves express honor and praise: "magnify" and "rejoices in." Not only are the names and titles of God honorific, "Lord" and "Savior," so are attributes credited to him, such as "mighty." But honor is best expressed in the verbs describing God's power, a constant element of honor: "he has shown strength . . . scattered the proud . . . put down the mighty . . . sent [the rich] empty away." But honor is also expressed in patronage, to which we now turn.

Patron-Client Relations

Patrons bestow patronage, which best describes the actions of God in this prayer. It is fair to say that God has shown Mary favoritism, a common feature of patron-client relationships. God's messenger addresses her as "highly favoured" (1:28 KJV) and informs her that "you have found favor with God"

(1:30). "Favor" (from *charis*) is one of the typical terms used to express that a patron is bestowing patronage on someone.[58] Moreover, Mary is an unlikely client because of "her low estate," and so when she says, "he who is mighty has done great things for me," she stands out as a "favorite" client. God's "mercy," a synonym of "favor," will lead to a kind of eternal glory: "all generations will call me blessed," that is, as God's favorite client. This Patron, she says, typically extends his "mercy"/patronage to "those who fear him," a reliable patronage that endures "from generation to generation." This patronage also has a history, beginning with Abraham and Israel, and including all those in need of favor. It might be argued that "favoritism" extends to those of low degree, the hungry, and those in need of help; conversely, God is not patron to the proud of heart, the mighty, and the rich.[59]

Patronage

Patrons and benefactors, who serve as the source of gifts and blessings, bestow patronage for various reasons. God's patronage appears to be altruistic, magnifying Mary and benefiting many others. Mary's "magnifying" of the Lord basically acknowledges God's favor; she is not "giving" thanks, nor is her prayer a return, however unbalanced, for favor received. It is polite to respond, but it is not duty that repays God's favor. What, then, does God give in patronage?

power	"Savior"
	he who is *mighty* has done great things
	shown *strength with his arm*
	scattered the proud
	put down the mighty
	the rich he has sent empty away

58. Bruce J. Malina ("Patron and Client: The Analogy behind Synoptic Theology," *Forum* 4, no. 1 [1988]: 5-6) explains: "Of course the vocabulary of 'grace' (*charizomai, charis, charisma*) belongs to the favoritism of patronage. I suggest *charizomai* refers to showing patronage, *charis* to willingness to be a patron, and *charisma* to the outcome of patronage. This is what Paul (and the rest of the New Testament) mean with this set of terms."

59. Taking a clue from Aristotle's περιπέτεια, John O. York (*The Last Shall Be First: The Rhetoric of Reversal in Luke* [Sheffield: Sheffield Academic Press, 1991], 44-54) describes in rhetorical terms what we refer to here in terms of favoritism in patron-client relations. The degree of favoritism is in direct proportion to the extent of the reversal of fortune.

	helped his servant Israel
commitment	*regarded* the low estate of his handmaiden
	done great things *for me*
	his *mercy* is on those who fear him,
	from generation to generation
	his *servant Israel,* in remembrance of his *mercy*
	spoke to *our fathers,* to *Abraham* and to *his posterity*
	for ever
inducement	Mary's child
	filled the hungry *with good things* ("rich")
	exalted those of *low degree* ("peasants")

Two categories of benefaction stand out: power and commitment. God's power is manifested in power to create a child in Mary; power to reverse the pattern of power, wealth, and privilege of the earth's elite; and power to help and lift up the lowly. God-who-is-Savior sends a savior to Israel (Jesus) to battle the spirits oppressing his people and to declare a kingdom utterly different from that of Rome. Second, Mary celebrates God's commitment to her and to Israel, which we should also understand in terms of patronal favoritism. God promised Abraham and his posterity, helped his servant Israel, and now favors Mary and her child. This favor is all the more significant because it extends to those without any of the marks of honor and status, hardly the people that culture would think of as worthy of notice. God's commitment, moreover, is utterly reliable, for his mercy is on those who fear him "from generation to generation." Finally, God's benefaction also includes "inducement," that is, the bestowal of the tangible goods of this world. God "fills" the hungry, not just feeds them; God exalts those of low degree, whom I understand as the peasant world of Jesus and his first followers. As we saw in the Our Father, peasants lived at subsistence levels; therefore, being "filled" with food was a rare and extraordinary event. And since peasants were universally oppressed by the mighty through taxes, debt, and land seizure, how blessed, then, if those who sit on thrones are cast down. Those of "low estate" may also refer to Israel as occupied by the Roman legions.

Value Map

Mary has both horizontal and vertical relationships. She is horizontally related to Elizabeth and to all generations who will come to know her blessing. But her honor resides in the vertical relationship she enjoys with the Savior, Lord, Mighty and Holy One; indeed, hers is a Patron-client relationship. As regards activity, Mary is the passive recipient of God's favor; hence, "being" characterizes her typical activity, although one might consider the growing of a child as "doing." God, however, is always "doing" something, such as making Mary with child, showing strength, scattering the proud, filling the hungry, and remembering his promise to Abraham. Mary thinks primarily in terms of present time, although she claims that her benefaction in present time will lead future generations to sing her praises. God, in contrast, operates in past, present, and future time. In the past, God made a promise to Abraham, which God is presently bringing to fulfillment and will continue to fulfill "from generation to generation." God shows current help to Mary, his favorite client, as well as to his client "servant Israel." The prayer, moreover, indicates that God has a timeless way of acting toward his clients: reversing their bad fortune and honoring them with his patronage, a pattern presently operative in the case of Mary. Indeed, God's constant patronage will continue indefinitely into the future, inasmuch as God's promises extend to Abraham "and to his posterity for ever." Thus, in the present time God has "regarded the low estate of his handmaiden," and in the future God will act favorably to his clients, "in remembrance of his mercy." Only God transcends this world ever in need of salvation. The world of mortals is subject to war, drought and famine, and injustice over which God has sovereignty to make it subject to his will. He does this in the prayer by reversing statuses: exalting those of low estate, pulling down the mighty from their thrones, filling the hungry, but sending the rich away empty. Thus, the value map invites us to a fresh and full consideration of God by virtue of his unique positioning vis-à-vis mortals.

Jesus' Prayer in John 17

Introductory Matters

Recognition that this prayer concludes the Farewell Address in John 14–17 aids us in appreciating it as part of Jesus' own testament to his disciples and as his last communication with God. From the fifth century, Christians have considered this a "priestly prayer," not because we have other prayers spoken by priests to compare it with, but for several other reasons. First, scholars connect the seamless character of Jesus' garment (19:23-24) with the high priest's robe described in Josephus (*Jewish Antiquities* 3.161) and Philo (*On Flight and Finding* 110-12). Second, the Letter to the Hebrews shaped Christian understanding of the crucified Jesus as high priest, which seems to have had considerable impact on the scholarly interpretation of John 17. Neither of these arguments carries much weight, especially since nothing in the Fourth Gospel corroborates these suggestions. "Priests" functioned as *mediators* and *brokers*, the social role by which we understand Jesus' dealings between God and the disciples in this Gospel. While all priests are brokers, not all brokers are priests. The only cogent historical evidence, then, is the seamless garment Jesus removed before his crucifixion — thin evidence for his identity as a priest.

Is John 17 a Johannine "Our Father"?

William O. Walker argued that John 17 strongly resembles the Our Father in the Synoptic Gospels. He claims that "the basic contents, to a somewhat lesser degree the overall structure, and occasionally at significant points the actual language of the High Priestly Prayer can best be understood as a reworking and expansion of the basic themes of the Lord's Prayer in terms of the specifically Johannine theology."[60] Let us examine this suggestion.

Father

The address to God as "Father" (17:1, 11, 21, 24, 25) constitutes the clearest link between the two prayers. But addressing God as "Father" is such a common feature of Jesus' Johannine prayers (11:41; 12:27-28) that dependency on the Our Father here is difficult to show.

Name

When Jesus mentions God's "name" four times (17:6, 11, 12, 26), he declares that he has faithfully manifested it; he is not praying that God's name be exalted, as in the Our Father.

60. W. O. Walker, "The Lord's Prayer in Matthew and John," *NTS* 28 (1982): 238.

Hallowed Name

Jesus declares that in the past he revealed the name only to disciples, and now petitions that God keep the disciples in it. This differs from the Our Father, which prays that God's name be acknowledged by all, both now and forever.

Kingdom

"Kingdom" appears but twice in this Gospel: (1) a status transformation is needed to enter the kingdom (3:3, 5); and (2) the "kingdom" of Jesus is not of this world (18:36). While we hear of God's "house" or "household" (14:2), these are not places, but relationships. "Kingdom" in the Our Father, then, does not match anything in the prayer in John 14–17.

Will Be Done

Jesus knows that God has a special "will" for him. His bread is to "do the will of him who sent me" (4:34). And God's will for the crowds and disciples is this, "that you believe in him whom he has sent" (6:29). Jesus acclaims that he has done God's will by "finishing the work that you gave me to do" (17:4). Hence, the prayer for God to achieve something is a celebration of Jesus' current attention to the affairs of God.

Daily Bread

The disciples were instructed to practice petitionary prayer, asking in the name of Jesus for whatever they needed. We have no evidence that their "asking" would be for material benefactions such as food or healing. More likely, these petitions are for knowledge, revelation, and the like. Yet the Our Father unabashedly requests food for subsistence peasants.

Forgive Trespasses

Although the Gospel tells us of terrible violence and hostility toward the disciples, they are never instructed to offer forgiveness for personal affronts. This important feature of the Our Father is utterly absent from the Fourth Gospel.

Lead Not into Temptation

Jesus declares that he himself has "guarded them, and not one of them was lost except . . ." (17:12); he petitions God "to protect them from the evil one" (17:15). Like Jesus, the disciples are aliens in an alien land, which seeks their ruin. Unlike Jesus, however, they do not leave this world, but remain in it in all its hostility (17:9, 11, 14-16). Jesus, then, might be said to be petitioning God for this.

Therefore, although we cannot decide whether the Fourth Gospel is consciously redacting the Our Father, there seem to be some verbal parallels. But they radically differ in terms of the logic and dynamic of both prayers. In John 17 Jesus does *not* teach the disciples to pray, as he does in the Synoptics. Rather they hear *his* own unique prayer, which no disciple could ever imagine praying. Moreover, in keeping with the self-focused nature of this prayer, Jesus is as much the center of the prayer as God is; Jesus declares that *he* manifests "the name"; *he* seeks glory from God; *he* declares that he has accomplished God's will. The Our Father is totally focused on God in both the "you" and "we" petitions. Rather, we think of John 17 as an extraordinary compendium of Johannine Christology.

Types of Prayers

How strange it is to find scholars hesitant to classify Jesus' communication to God in John 17 as a prayer. But using our definition of prayer as communication, we will examine it precisely as a combination of several types of prayers.[61]

Petitionary Prayer

Jesus not only instructed the disciples to pray petitionary prayer,[62] but he himself prayed the same type of prayer:

61. We would be remiss if we did not attend to Jesus' remark: "This is eternal life, that they may know you, the only true God . . ." (17:3). This should be classified as a prayer of acknowledgment, that is, a prayer of respect and praise.

62. Scholars regularly note Jesus' repetitive instructions in John 14–16 about "asking" the Father for some benefit. The verbs used here (αἰτέω, ἐρωτάω) differ from the more com-

Glorify your Son so that the Son may glorify you (v 1).

Glorify me in your own presence with the glory that I had in your presence before the world existed (v 5).

I am asking on their behalf; I am not asking on behalf of the world, but on behalf of those whom you gave me (v 9).

Protect them in your name that you have given me, so that they may be one, as we are one (v 11).

I am not asking you to take them out of the world, but I ask you to protect them from the evil one (v 15).

Sanctify them in the truth (v 17).

I ask not only on behalf of these, but also on behalf of those who will believe in me through their word, that they may all be one. As you, Father, are in me and I am in you, may they also be in us (vv 20-21).

Father, I desire that those also, whom you have given me, may be with me where I am, to see my glory, which you have given me because you loved me before the foundation of the world (v 24).

When petitioning, Jesus asks favors both for himself and for his disciples. In the Synoptics we find Jesus petitioning for himself during his prayer in the garden: "Abba, Father . . . remove this cup from me" (Mark 14:36), the beginning of his passion. Here, on the contrary, he asks for glory. God should glorify Jesus now, returning him to the glory that was his from eternity. Alternately, he prays for the disciples as their broker with their Father Patron, and he prays only for them. We will consider these petitions in more detail when we examine John 17 in terms of Patron-Broker-client relations.

mon ones such as δέομαι and προσεύχω. Except for Martha's remark that Jesus could petition God for Lazarus (11:22), the other eleven instances of petition occur in the Farewell Address, which thus constitute a distinct body of materials on prayer.

14:13-14 "I will do whatever you *ask* in my name. . . . If in my name you *ask* me for anything, I will do it."

14:16 "I will *ask* the Father, and he will give you another Advocate."

15:7 "If you abide in me, and my words abide in you, *ask* for whatever you wish. . . ."

15:16 "The Father will give you whatever you *ask* him in my name."

16:23-24 "On that day you will *ask* nothing of me. . . . If you *ask* anything of the Father . . ."

16:26 "On that day you will *ask* in my name. . . ."

Self-Focused Prayer

Jesus says much more to God in this extensive communication, but not for
the purpose of petitioning God. In the first chapter we identified a type of
prayer labeled "self-focused" prayer. The "I" addresses God, announcing
what the "I" has done in relationship to God. It is not a matter of praising
God for allowing the one praying to have done good, but rather a confession of self-worth, obedience, or piety. Take, for example, the opening of
Psalm 131:

> O Lord, my heart is not lifted up,
>   my eyes are not raised too high;
> I do not occupy myself with things
>   too great and too marvelous for me.
> But I have calmed and quieted my soul. (Ps 131:1-2; see also Ps 62:1-7)

The speaker knows his place; he does not seek more than he already has
and is (petitionary prayer). The omniscient God of course knows his place
or status. But the one praying communicates this in all innocence (self-
focused prayer). Some self-focused prayer seems arrogant and so dishon-
ors God (Luke 18:11-12), but as Downing's article indicates, not all self-
focused prayer is egoistical.[63] As we noted in the first chapter, Jeremias
identified a self-focused prayer that minimally proves that people did in
fact pray this type of prayer, a suggestion that this is sanctioned speech: "I
thank you, O Lord my God, that you have given me my lot with those who
sit in the seat of learning, and not with those who sit at the street corners; I
am early to work on the words of the Torah, and they are early to work on
things of no moment. I weary myself and they weary themselves; I weary
myself and profit by it, while they weary themselves to no profit. I run, and
they run; I run toward the life of the Age to Come, and they run towards
the pit of destruction."[64] The speaker repeatedly identifies himself in the
prayer: "I am early to work . . . I weary myself . . . I run." Evidently the
speaker gives warrants to God for honoring him. Here and in Luke 18:11-12
a contrast is made between those who confess their worth to God and

63. F. Gerald Downing, "The Ambiguity of 'The Pharisee and the Toll-Collector' (Luke
18:9-14) in the Greco-Roman World of Late Antiquity," *CBQ* 54 (1992): 80-99.
64. Joachim Jeremias, *The Parables of Jesus*, rev. ed. (New York: Scribner, 1963), 142;
b. Ber 28b.

those who have no respect. The speaker asks God to confirm his relationship with the deity and so honor him.

In the case of Jesus in John 17, we identify the following verses as illustrations of self-focused prayer:

> I glorified you on earth (v 4).
> I have made your name known (vv 6, 26).
> The words that you gave to me I have given to them (vv 8, 14).
> I protected them in your name (v 12a).
> I guarded them (v 12b).
> I have sent them into the world (v 18).
> I sanctify myself (v 19).
> The glory that you have given me I have given them (v 22).
> I know you (v 25).

In addressing God, Jesus seems to be claiming that he has fulfilled the role of agent whom God sent into the world. In other words, he declares his faithfulness to his Sender, obedience to his will, and completion of his task. In fact, a central element of his role as apostle was to honor God: glorifying him on earth (v 4), manifesting God's name (vv 6, 26), conveying God's words (vv 8, 14), and knowing (acknowledging) God. As Jesus said: "I glorified you on earth by finishing the work that you gave me to do" (v 4). While Jesus acknowledges his role and commission, he informs God that he has been an obedient son and a loyal agent. Honor rests only with God; Jesus' confession celebrates this honor. But Jesus' task extended to God's clients, a task he claims to have fulfilled. He gave them revelation (vv 8, 14), kept and guarded them (v 12), sent them (v 18), and gave them the glory God had given him (v 22). There is no boast here, because Jesus has done all and only what God sent him to do. Nor is he in any way enlarging himself or making vain claims, because all that he did was the fulfillment of his role as apostle, the one whom God sent.

Transformations and Ceremonies

After identifying the types of prayers in John 17, let us view these materials in the light of the model of status-transformation rituals and ceremonies. Petitionary prayer is uttered by Jesus, both for himself and for the clients.

He petitions his Father to "glorify me" (vv 1, 5) and to protect the clients: "protect them" (v 11), "sanctify them" (v 17), "that they may all be one" (v 21), and "I desire that [they] . . . may be with me . . . to see my glory" (v 24). Jesus prays to be transformed back into the glory he once enjoyed but does not now have; his transformation will reverse his current status by restoring him to his previous one. In contrast, the clients do not now have nor have they previously enjoyed the benefits Jesus petitions for them. Their transformation will not be a restoration to former status, but an elevation to a new status. The self-focused prayers in John 17 have nothing to do with change and transformation. Jesus speaks to the Father-Patron in ways that confirm his role and relationship with God. In the litany of his services to God, Jesus speaks in terms of his role as agent/apostle, and announces that he has indeed fulfilled that role — a confirmation of it. All that he does, says, and gives the clients, he does because he was authorized to do so. He proved to be a most dutiful and obedient son and a competent and faithful broker. There is no change here, no transformation. Of course, the Father-Patron is not changed; rather, his authority is fully acknowledged by Jesus, and his role as Patron confirmed by the services of the perfect Broker.

Patron

Looking at John 17 in terms of patron-client relations requires an elaboration of that model because a "broker" is functioning between patron and client. The Patron is overwhelmingly addressed as "Father" and "holy Father" (17:1, 5, 11, 21, 24, 25); and he is "the only true God." This Patron has the most valuable goods to give as patronage: "authority over all people," "eternal life," "glory" both before the world began and even now, manifestation of God's name, "words," "sanctification," and "love." The clients are the narrow group of Jesus' disciples, to whom alone God's patronage comes. Moreover, these unique clients enjoy favoritism because they are those special few whom God gave Jesus "out of the world"; they alone received God's "words." These clients are "not of this world," and must be "kept" and "guarded." They are, then, favorite clients who depend on their Patron for protection.

Jesus as Broker[65]

But there is a broker here, Jesus, who mediates God's benefaction to the clients and their needs to the Patron. Where do brokers fit? What do they do? Petitioners employed the services of persons well placed in the circles of power (i.e., Pliny). A "priest" in Rome was called a "pontifex," that is, a bridge-maker, for he bridged the interests and needs of gods-patrons and mortals-clients. A broker, then, is a mediator, a bridge, a go-between, an ambassador, etc.

Moses, Israel's Traditional Broker

Of Israel's many mediators, two stand out, Abraham (Gen 18:22-33) and Moses. Moses served as Israel's broker with God both at its arrival at Sinai (Exod 20:18-20) and on the occasion of the golden calf (Exod 32:11-14). At Sinai the clients feared to have God speaking directly to them, so a broker/mediator was needed, which Philo described: "This fear made us address to one of those mediators (μεσιτῶν) the entreaty 'Speak to us and let not God speak to us, lest we die' (Exod 20:19). For if He, without ministers (ὑπηρέταις), holds out to us . . . benefits unmixed and exceeding great, we are incapable of receiving them" (*On Dreams* 1.143; see *On the Posterity of Cain* 143). Then when God told Moses that Israel was worshiping a golden calf, Moses "took the part of mediator (μεσίτης) and reconciler (διαλλακτής) and did not hurry away at once, but first made prayers and supplications, begging that their sins might be forgiven. Then, when this protector (κηδεμών) and intercessor (παραιτητής) had softened the wrath of the Ruler, he wended his way back in mingled joy and dejection" (Philo, *On the Life of Moses* 2.166). Moreover, because he serves both Patron and clients, Moses the mediator is a two-way mediator, bringing God's words to Israel and petitioning God on Israel's behalf. Brokers/mediators, then, were known and appreciated in Israel.

---

65. The New Testament labels Jesus as "mediator" (1 Tim 2:5) or "mediator of a new covenant" (Heb 9:15; cf. 8:6). Indeed, many prayers to God are made "through Christ our Lord," identifying Jesus' intermediate role (Rom 1:8; 5:1; 7:25; 1 Cor 8:6; 2 Cor 5:18; 1 Thess 5:9; Jude 25). Note especially the final prayer in Heb 13:20-21: "Now may the God of peace . . . make you complete in everything good . . . working among us that which is pleasing in his sight, through Jesus Christ, to whom be the glory forever and ever. Amen."

Israel's New Broker

Granted that brokers/mediators were well-known in antiquity, we need to know more about this role to appreciate Jesus in John 17. Three questions need be asked: How does a broker become a broker? What makes for a successful broker? What does he broker? First, Jesus is broker because he is "sent" by the Patron: "They have believed that you sent me" (see 17:3, 5, 8, 18, 21, 23, 25) — undoubtedly an important emphasis in confirming Jesus' role as broker. Second, brokers are successful for two reasons: (1) they belong to the worlds of both patron and clients, and so represent fairly the interests of both, and (2) they maintain loyal and faithful relationships with both. Jesus the Broker clearly belongs to the world of the Father Patron. We are told that he was at home in the heavenly world as a favored person and desired to return to that same world in glory: "Glorify me in your own presence with the glory that I had in your presence before the world existed" (17:5; see 1:1-18 and 13:1-3). We learn that he who had come from God was returning to God (16:5, 17; 14:28). No doubt, Jesus the Broker belongs to the world of the Patron.

Jesus belongs equally and fully in the world of the clients. For, the Word "became flesh and lived among us" (1:14). Like them, he hungers (4:8, 31-34), thirsts (4:7), grows weary (4:6), and is disturbed in spirit (12:27-28). Moreover, he performs signs on ill, dying, and dead persons in a gesture that expresses his solidarity with those of this earthly world. Moreover, the relationship of broker and clients is a qualitatively rich relationship, not a fickle one (15:9-17).

A successful broker belongs to both worlds *at the same time* by virtue of his relationships. "In my Father's house there are many dwelling places. . . . And if I go and prepare a place for you, I will come again and will take you to myself, so that where I am, there you may be also" (14:2-3). The relationship of the Patron-Father and his Broker-Son is secure, and so is that of the Broker and his clients. He secures relationships for the clients in God's household, and he comes back to the clients and takes them to himself. This, moreover, is a relationship the clients may rely on: "Do you not believe that I am in the Father and the Father in me? . . . The Father who dwells in me does his works. Believe me that I am in the Father and the Father is in me; but if you do not, then believe me because of the works themselves" (14:10-11). This relationship must be highly significant for it to be repeated many, many times (14:20, 23;

17:21, 23). Not only does he belong to both worlds, he bridges them in his own person.

A successful broker must maintain his relationships with patron and clients. In short, he should have a lasting bond of reliability, loyalty, and faithfulness between himself and both of them.

Patron and Broker

The author tells us that the Patron Father "loves" the Son, indicating just such a reliable relationship: "The Father loves the Son and has placed all things in his hands" (3:35). For his part, the Broker Son shows loyalty to his Patron Father by obeying his commands. "I seek to do not my own will but the will of him who sent me" (5:30; 6:38; 4:34). The absolute loyalty of the Broker to his Patron-Father constitutes the topic of John 17 where Jesus gives an audit of his actions prior to his death, in the self-focused prayer noted above (17:4, 6, 8, 12, 14, 19, 22, 26).

The Broker and Clients

The Broker maintains bonds of loyalty with his clients by "loving" them. This bond of loyalty is never more important than when Jesus "goes away" or enters into the events of his death. The Book of Glory begins with the note that "having loved his own who were in the world, he loved them to the end" (13:1). I follow Bruce Malina in interpreting "love" in this context as loyalty or faithfulness.[66] In fact, upon departure Jesus gives a commandment that replicates the "love" between him and the clients in the new relationship of client with client: "I give you a new commandment, that you love one another. Just as I have loved you, you also should love one another" (13:34). "Solidarity" between broker and clients is also highlighted. In that same chapter 17, Jesus speaks more broadly of his relationship to his disciple-clients. He tells the Father that he has "protected them in your name . . . and not one of them was lost . . ." (17:12), and petitions the Patron also to "protect them" (17:15).

66. Bruce J. Malina, "Faith/Faithfulness," in *Handbook of Biblical Social Values,* ed. John J. Pilch and Bruce J. Malina (Peabody, Mass.: Hendrickson, 1998), 72-75.

Patron, Broker, and Clients

The three figures, moreover, are glued together in an utterly reliable relationship, as the following citations indicate.

> They who have my commandments and keep them are those who love me; and those who love me will be loved by my Father. (14:21; see 14:23)

> I in them and you in me, that they may become completely one, so that the world may know that you have sent me and have loved them even as you have loved me. (17:23)

"Love," then, is the mark of reliability in these relationships: the Patron with the Broker, the Broker with the clients, and the Patron and Broker with the clients.

What Does the Broker Broker?

Well, everything: "the Father had given all things into his hands" (13:3), which is just what Jesus told the disciples: "All that the Father has is mine" (16:15). But "all" is too unspecified; what, in fact, does this broker broker? For an answer we return to the model of the four general symbolic media to classify accurately what of the Patron's bounty he mediates. The catalogue that follows is not focused on John 17, but attempts to be as comprehensive and specific as possible. Since the notion of Jesus as agent/apostle/broker arises from the beginning of the narrative, a canvass of Jesus' brokerage should be comprehensive.

Power

1. Power = signs, seven traditional miracles.
2. Power = miracles as credentials: "a teacher who has come from God ... no one can do these signs that you do apart from the presence of God" (3:2); "Never since the world began has it been heard that anyone opened the eyes of a person born blind. If this man were not from God, he could do nothing" (9:32-33).

3. Power = two powers[67] of God: creative (1:1-3; 5:19-20) and eschatological (5:21-29):
eschatological power:
   - "as the Father raises the dead and gives them life, so also the Son gives life" (5:21).
   - "the Father . . . has given all judgment to the Son" (5:22, 27).
   - "as the Father has life in himself, so he has granted the Son also to have life in himself" (5:26).
   - "the dead will hear the voice of the Son . . . those who hear it will live" (5:25, 28-29).
4. Power = over death: I will "raise it up at the last day" (6:39, 44, 54); no snatching by the Angel of Death (10:28-29); "Lazarus, come out!" (11:43); I have power "to lay down my life in order to take it up again" (10:17-18); "You have given him authority over all people, to give eternal life to all whom you have given him" (17:2).

Commitment

1. Kinship and Fictive Kinship:[68] relationship of Father and Son, which parlays into relationships between Patron and clients (15:1-2) and Broker and clients (15:15): "To all who received him, who believed in his name, he gave power to become children of God" (1:12); Jesus' fictive kin: "Woman, here is your son." "Here is your mother" (19:26-27).
2. Relationships: Father in Jesus, Jesus in the disciples, and Father and Jesus in them:
   - "I go to prepare a place for you[.] And if I go and prepare a place for you, I will come again and will take you to myself, so that where I am, there you may be also" (14:2-3); "We will come to them and make our home with them" (14:23).
3. Doing the Will of the Father:
   - the will (θέλημα): "I seek to do not my own will but the will of him who sent me" (5:30; 6:38; 4:34); "This is the will of him who sent me, that I should lose nothing of all that he has given me, but raise

67. See Jerome H. Neyrey, *An Ideology of Revolt: John's Christology in Social-Science Perspective* (Philadelphia: Fortress, 1988), 25-29, 34.
68. See J. G. van der Watt's *Family of the King: Dynamics of Metaphor in the Gospel according to John* (Leiden: Brill, 2000) and Sjef van Tilborg's *Imaginative Love in John* (Leiden: Brill, 1993).

it up on the last day. This is indeed the will of my Father, that all who see the Son and believe in him may have eternal life" (6:39-40).
- command (ἐντολή): "I have power to lay it down, and I have power to take it up again. I have received this command from my Father" (10:18); "They who have my commandments and keep them are those who love me; and those who love me will be loved by my Father, and I will love them and reveal myself to them" (14:21).

4. Love: love of Father for Son, Son for his disciples, and their love for one another:
   - "As the Father has loved me, so I have loved you; abide in my love. If you keep my commandments, you will abide in my love, just as I have kept my Father's commandments and abide in his love" (15:9-10); ". . . that the love with which you [Father] have loved me may be in them, and I in them" (17:26); "This is my commandment, that you love one another as I have loved you. No one has greater love than this, to lay down one's life for one's friends" (15:12-13).

5. Name: the all-important, unique name of God given to Jesus and manifested to them:
   - "I have made your name known to those whom you gave me from the world" (17:6); "I made your name known to them, and I will make it known" (17:26); "Protect them in your name that you have given me. . . . I protected them in your name that you have given me" (17:11-12).

Inducement

1. Abundant wine (2:7-10), water (4:14), bread (6:1-13), water and light (7:37-38; 8:12).
2. Everything . . . anything (14:14).

Influence

1. Jesus is Word: "In the beginning was the Word, and the Word was with God" (1:1-2).
2. Jesus bears witness to his relationship with God: "He testifies to what he has seen and heard" (3:32); "I testify on my own behalf, and the Father who sent me testifies on my behalf" (8:18; 3:34).
3. Teaching from God: "My teaching is not mine but his who sent me.

Anyone who resolves to do the will of God will know whether the teaching is from God or whether I am speaking on my own" (7:16-17); "I do nothing on my own, but I speak these things as the Father instructed me" (8:28).

4. Jesus the Teacher:
   - teacher in synagogue (6:59; 18:20) and temple: "Jesus went up into the temple and began to teach" (7:14; see 7:28; 8:20).
   - called "Teacher" (διδάσκαλος): "a teacher who has come from God" (3:2; see 11:28; 13:13); and rabbi: "Rabbi, you are the Son of God!" (1:49; see 1:38; 4:31; 6:25; 9:2; 11:8; 20:16).
5. Speaks the words of God: he whom God has sent utters the words of God (12:49); "The word that you hear is not mine, but is from the Father who sent me" (14:24); "I have given them your word" (17:14).
6. Sees and reveals God: "Not that anyone has seen the Father except the one who is from God; he has seen the Father" (6:46) and "No one has ever seen God. It is God the only Son, who is close to the Father's heart, who has made him known" (1:18).
7. Paraclete will make Jesus known: "the Advocate, the Holy Spirit . . . will teach you everything, and remind you of all that I have said to you" (14:26; 15:26).

Therefore, throughout the narrative, but especially in John 17, Jesus is best interpreted as acting in the role of unique and necessary broker (Acts 4:12). Authorized by the Patron of patrons, he functions as a superior broker. He not only belongs to the respective worlds of Patron and clients, but he serves their interests assiduously, loyal to both parties but especially faithful to the Patron. Like Moses, he is a two-way broker who mediates the favor of the Patron to the clients and brokers their prayers to the Patron. He should be acknowledged as a successful broker because he mediates all categories of benefaction: power, commitment, inducement, and influence, and brokers them most generously.

This is just what we have seen in John 17. We learn of the relationship of Patron to Broker when Jesus speaks about being "sent" and "finishing the work that you gave me to do" (v 4).

Jesus Christ whom you have *sent* (v 3)
. . . know in truth that I came from you; and . . . that you *sent* me (v 8)
As you have *sent* me into the world . . . (v 18)

... that the world may believe that you have sent me (vv 21 and 23)

To whom was this agent and apostle sent? To the favorite clients whom the Patron has "given" to Jesus. "I have made your name known to those whom *you gave me* from the world. They were yours, and *you gave them* to me. . . . Now they know that everything *you have given* me is from you. . . . I am not asking on behalf of the world, but on behalf of those whom *you gave me*, because they are yours" (vv 6-9; see 24). God, moreover, invested his broker with valuable goods for distribution, such as "authority over all people" (v 2), the words of God (vv 6, 8, 14), "glory" (v 22), and that the "love with which you have loved . . . be in them" (v 26). It is precisely the self-focused prayer that makes evident that Jesus has "finish[ed] the work that you gave me to do" (v 4). In short, he is an excellent broker.

Value Map

The value variations of activity, relationships, time, etc., provide still another important window into this prayer. The characteristic activity of God-Patron and Jesus-Broker is that of "doing," whereas "being" describes the clients. Jesus and Father are constantly active, sending the Son as agent and the Son laboring to do the tasks assigned him. On the contrary, the disciples are passive, people acted upon and in need of benefaction. All figures, God, Jesus, and the disciples, exist in a vertical relationship, but in different positions in it. God, who is Father and Patron, is the "only true God" (v 3), and so, the topmost figure who issues commands and bestows favors. Jesus the mediator of God's benefactions and the agent of his will is positioned under the Patron but superior to the clients. The disciples, then, are the lowest level in this relationship, yet those upon whom God's favor rests and on whose behalf Jesus labors. As regards time, the prayer identifies God as "eternal": in the past, before the creation of the world, God glorified Jesus. This too characterizes Jesus, who has a past history (vv 5, 22, 24). In the prayer Jesus announces his past services to the clients: he "made your name known" (v 6), he gave them God's words (vv 8, 14), he "protected them" (v 12), and so forth. The petitionary prayer is prayed in the present, which seems to be the focal time for all parties in John 17. The glorification of Jesus is forthcoming, not in the future; the petitions for the clients indicate a present and ongoing relationship. Nothing is spoken here about a distant future, rather the process of Jesus' glorification is even now under way ("Now the Son of Man has been glorified . . . ," 13:31). According to the calendar used by the author, two or three days are in view, no more.

The present-time orientation of John 17 is evident in terms of "one" and "in." Jesus petitions God about the current and future disciples, "that they may all be one" (17:21), which refers to abiding unity or relationship, a constant theme in John 17. This unity, first expressed as "one" (vv 11, 23), is amplified by reference to "in": the Father "in" Jesus, Jesus "in" God, and the disciples "in" Father and Son (vv 21, 23) — more abiding relationships. These abiding relationships take four forms in the Farewell Address: (1) making a home in them (14:23); (2) abiding in them (15:3-8); (3) God's words abiding in the disciples (15:7); (4) keeping them "in" God's name (17:11). "Home," not a physical building, is a metaphor for a household and its relationships.[69] The disciples never go to the "many rooms" in the Father's house; rather God and Jesus "make [their] home" in the disciples (14:23). "Abide" or "remain" metaphorically refers to the attachment of branches to the vine, and also to adherence to Jesus, his words, and the group's ideology about him. "Words" can abide, not necessarily on parchment, but in mind and heart; if disciples remain in the word, the word is surely "in" them. Therefore, "one" and "in" speak to the unique relationship disciples have with Jesus and through him with God. And all such relationships are current, present-time bonds.

What Do We Know If We Know This?

First of all, we simply know more about the dynamics and contents of these prayers than we can gain from typical interpretations by means of the historical-critical method. The new knowledge, moreover, is hardly trivial, for it matters what kind of prayer is prayed, how the honor of God is expressed, what specifically is prayed for (four symbolic media), and the formal but ordinary relationship of Patron and client. It benefits us to be able to assess God's values juxtaposed to those of creatures: God "action" is in contrast to human's "being"; God's time is eternal (past, present, and future), whereas mortals primarily understand their time as "present"; God

69. See James McCaffrey, *The House with Many Rooms: The Temple Theme of Jn. 14,2-3* (Rome: Pontifical Biblical Institute, 1988), 49-64.

is in no way subject to the powers, persons, and forces that afflict mortals; God, of course, sits on his throne atop the ladder of created things, at the bottom of which are creatures.

The use of social science materials, moreover, makes a strong claim to unveil the cultural world of the authors and those who prayed their prayers. None of the items mentioned above should be strange to readers familiar with the ancient documents, for when they are examined in formal terms ("honor," "patron-client," etc.), they explicitly relate to and echo similar materials in the literature of the Greco-Roman world. The models, then, are most appropriate to the ancient cultural world.

These models, moreover, do what models are supposed to do. A good model alerts a reader or observer to see data because there is a conceptual place for them in the reader's scheme of things. As we all know, there are simply no "immaculate perceptions," that is, naked understandings of what is observed; all must be put into an interpretative framework, which is formed in an ongoing manner as concept related to object. Besides surfacing data, a good model is able to indicate relationships between discrete blocks of data, relationships most unlikely to be made without a guiding model. The use of models, then, urges the interpreter to think more about individual items and reach for an appropriate scenario to explain the data. We judge that the various cultural models employed here are not only valid ones, but productive and necessary as well. This experience is not unlike that of people who go to formal gardens, arboretums, zoos, and museums: the thing observed is familiar, but until one reads its label or explanatory classification or biographical note, one lacks important information.

CHAPTER FOUR

Praise of God's Uniqueness,
Who Is "First," "Only," and "No One Else"

You alone are the Holy One,
You alone are the Lord,
You alone are the Most High.[1]

O ne type of prayer deserves further attention, namely, the prayer that praises, honors, glorifies, and celebrates God. In their hymns at worship, Christians are wont to sing to God: "Sing Praise to the Lord," "All Creatures of Our God and King, Lift Up Your Voice and with Us Sing," and the ubiquitous "Alleluia." In worship services Christians frequently say to God *"Kyrie, eleison,"* "It is right to give God thanks and praise," and "All honor and glory is yours, almighty Father." Many churches read a responsorial psalm between the Scriptures, such as "Bless the Lord, O My Soul" and "Make a joyful noise to God; sing the glory of his name." Indisputably, praise, glory, and honor are a ubiquitous and significant way of communicating to God for the purpose of maintaining a relationship.

This chapter will examine a particular type of prayer, the doxology, and view it in terms of a distinctive way of voicing praise and honor. All doxologies address God in formal terms of great respect, in addition to

1. There are two doxologies in the early church, the Great Doxology ("Glory to God in the highest . . .") and the Lesser Doxology ("Glory be to the Father, the Son and the Holy Spirit . . ."); the citation above is taken from the end of the Great Doxology. Its shape, history, and provenance are accessible in Joseph A. Jungmann, *The Mass of the Roman Rite: Its Origins and Development* (New York: Benziger Brothers, 1951), 1:346-59.

which they render to God "glory and honor" (δόξα καὶ τιμή).[2] But the particular focus here is the way glory and honor are amplified by noting that they are "unique." For example, significant actions metamorphose into grants of honor because the actor is the "first" or "only" or "one of a few" or "the one who most" performed them. Alcibiades' chariots won first, second, and fourth places in a celebrated race: he was the "first" and "only" man ever to do this.[3]

Praise of humans by humans, however, is not our aim here, but rather the praise of God. The way to discovering how to praise God's uniqueness begins in the ancient rhetorical sources that instructed orators in the art of augmenting a person's praise according to its uniqueness. With this knowledge we aim to study carefully the two doxologies in 1 Timothy, simply because they are the richest texts for our study. Readers are referred back to chapter 3 for discussion of a doxology. Thus, this chapter contains two parts: (1) an investigation about uniqueness in rhetorical literature, illustrated by Greek and Israelite examples of praise, and (2) a consideration of New Testament use of uniqueness, particularly in the doxologies in 1 Timothy.

We necessarily begin with a survey of the terminology of uniqueness as it appears in the rhetorical handbooks of antiquity, in particular, in the third type of rhetoric, praise and blame. The database contains Aristotle's *Rhetoric, Rhetoric to Herennius,* Cicero's *De inventione rhetorica* and *De oratore,* Quintilian's *Institutio oratoria,* as well as progymnastic authors such as Aelius Theon and Menander Rhetor. Next we examine examples of the rhetorical theory as expressed in actual oratorical writings for a fuller sense of the cultural importance of the category of "uniqueness" in the ancient world. Finally, we focus on the uniqueness first in the Old Testament and then in the LXX. To what extent have the translators of the Scriptures employed Greek rhetoric in their expressions of praise and glory?

---

2. H. Hegermann ("δόξα," in *TDNT* 1:344-48) comments on how frequently in the New Testament "glory" "is used synonymously with τιμή: with the meaning *esteem, honor*" (1:345). Similarly, G. Kittel ("δόξα," in *TDNT* 2:232-37) says of glory, "[W]ith the Homeric κλέος and later τιμή: [glory] achieves central significance for the Greeks. Supreme and ideal worth is summed up in the term. A man's worth is measured by his repute" (2:235).

3. "He [Alcibiades] entered chariots in a larger number than the leading cities could match and of such quality that he came in first and second and fourth" (Isocrates, *On the Team of Horses* 34).

Rhetorical Theory

Aristotle's *Rhetoric* contains the earliest extant exposition of rhetorical theory in antiquity. Although Greek orators before Aristotle employ many instances of the formulae of uniqueness that we are studying, we begin with Aristotle simply because he was the first consciously to classify them, systematize them, and situate them within a complete theory of rhetoric. In short, he consciously tells us what he and others meant by the criteria of uniqueness. Aristotle divided rhetoric into three classes, forensic, deliberative, and epideictic, each distinguished by its own purpose and aim. In his exposition of epideictic rhetoric, he gives instructions on how to "amplify" praise. How might one elaborate on the praiseworthy deeds of someone? What strategies are likely to convince us that so-and-so deserves our respect? It is here that Aristotle articulates the principle of "uniqueness": "In epideictic one should also use many kinds of amplification, for example if the subject of praise is the *only* (μόνος) one or the *first* (πρῶτος) or *one of a few* (μετ᾽ ὀλίγων) or the one who *most* (μάλιστα) has done something; for all these things are honorable" (*Rhetoric* 1.9.38, emphasis added). Four amplifications of praise are mentioned, all of which stress some form of uniqueness. As we shall see, being the *first* and being the *only* person to achieve something became the most common forms of amplification in Greek literature.

Cicero's articulation of the principle of uniqueness, four centuries later, provides us with an important Roman witness to the tradition we are tracing. Speaking about what deserves an orator's praise, he cites virtue, beneficent deeds, endurance of misfortune, and then unique deeds: "And one must select achievements that are of outstanding importance (*magnitudine praestabiles*) or unprecedented (*novitate primae*) or unparalleled in their actual character (*genere singulares*); for small achievements or those that are not unusual or out of the ordinary are not as a rule felt to be specifically admirable or to deserve praise at all" (*De oratore* 2.85.347, emphasis added). "Unprecedented" sounds like "first" in Aristotle's catalogue; thus an unprecedented deed, which has never before been done, is unique. "Unparalleled" suggests "only," in the sense that this person alone has ever done such and such. Although Cicero's tag "of outstanding importance" does not automatically signal "unique" or "exclusive," it serves to set an action apart from what is "*not* unusual . . . *not* out of the ordinary." And so, it might be said that an action, if not done by this man alone, was rare and done by "one of a few."

Quintilian's rhetorical treatise contains remarks on uniqueness in line with those found in Aristotle and Cicero, establishing that "uniqueness" was a commonplace way of amplifying praise: "[W]hat most pleases an audience is the celebration of deeds which our hero was *first (primus)* or *only (solus)* man or at any rate *one of the very few (cum paucis)* to perform: and to these we must add any other achievements which *surpassed* hope or expectation *(super spem aut expectationem)*" (*Institutio oratoria* 3.7.16, emphasis added). In keeping with rhetorical tradition, Quintilian repeats the formula: "only," "first," "one of a few," or "surpassing expectation."

If Quintilian articulates the criteria for praise among the Roman elite, Aelius Theon represents this same epideictic tradition in regard to the standardized education of other peoples who learned to write Greek. His *progymnasmata* contain formal instructions for writing an encomium, which rules domesticate the descriptions of epideictic rhetoric for school purposes. Theon's importance for us consists in the fact that: (1) he represents a rhetorical tradition that is truly ancient and consistent over time; and (2) his rules for an encomium indicate that knowledge of and practice in the art of praise were truly widespread and conventional. His contribution is as follows: "Praiseworthy actions are also those occurring in a timely manner, and if one . . . is the *only* (μόνος) one [who acted] or the *first* (πρῶτος) or *one of a few* (μετ᾽ ὀλίγων) or the one who *most* (μάλιστα) or when *no one acted* (οὐδείς), or *more than others* (μᾶλλον τῶν ἄλλων), or with a *few* (μετ᾽ ὀλίγων), or *beyond one's age* (ὑπὲρ ἡλικίαν)" (Theon 9.35-38, emphasis added).[4] In summary, all the marked terms indicate what Theon and his tradition understand as grounds for praise, what we are calling the criteria of uniqueness and which may be expressed in a variety of ways. It may refer to what is absolutely unique, such as when one acted alone, or first, or with a few. Great praise is also warranted for those who set new personal standards, such as acting "beyond one's age" or "exceeding expectations." The synopsis of the remarks of rhetoricians in the chart on page 116 serves as a simple indicator of the contents and duration of the tradition of uniqueness in epideictic rhetoric. We give considerable weight to criteria for praise such as these because they represent the conscious, continuous articulation of the formal rhetorical tradition. A writer such as Aristotle may be primarily codifying the practice of his day; nonetheless,

---

4. James R. Butts, "The 'Progymnasmata' of Theon: A New Text with Translation and Commentary" (Ph.D. diss., Claremont Graduate School, 1987), 470-71.

Synopsis of Rhetorical Criteria for Uniqueness

Aristotle Rhetoric 1.9.38	Aristotle Rhetoric 2.7.2	Rhetorica ad Herennium	Cicero De inventione rhetorica 1.54.103	Cicero De oratore 2.85.347	Quintilian Institutio oratoria 3.7.16	Aelius Theon 9.35-38	Menander Rhetor 1.362.4-20
only	only	singular / unheard of	not ordinary / unheard of among savages / not committed even by the worst	unparalleled	only	only	only/alone
first	first	—		unprecedented	first	first	first
one of few	—			outstanding importance	one of very few	one of very few	with few
most done	most done						more than others
—	—				surpassed expectations	surpassed in hope and expectation	exceeded expectations
—	—				—	—	most easily and quickly

he makes formal the general principle that is only intuitively grasped from instances occurring in actual literary and forensic practice. The evidence for the criterion of uniqueness from Roman rhetoricians indicates that knowledge and practice of it were alive and well during the time the New Testament was written.

Rhetorical Practice

Athenian funeral speeches constitute a distinctive body of Greek rhetoric of praise, some of which Aristotle actually mentions in his treatise. We briefly visit some funeral speeches to examine their use of the principle of uniqueness. Together with the formal theory cited above, these examples attest that the principle of uniqueness existed as a constant literary tradition that extends from the golden age of Athens down to the age of the *progymnasmata*.

In his funeral oration, Lysias (459-380 B.C.E.) follows a convention whereby people were praised in terms of geography, generation, and gender.[5] Thus he celebrates Athens as the polis of the deceased, and by doing so he implies that the dead soldiers he eulogizes share in the virtues of the city. His encomium for the fallen is based on praise of their geographical mother, Athens, and their generational ancestors who ennobled the city. "It was natural to our ancestors . . . to fight the battles of justice, for the very beginning of their life was just. . . . They were the *first and only* (πρῶτοι καὶ μόνοι) people in that time to drive out the ruling classes . . . and establish a democracy" (*Funeral Oration* 17-18, emphasis added).[6] The fallen soldiers are eulogized by association with their ancestors, who are exalted because of their uniqueness: they were the first and only to fight (23). No Greeks elsewhere (οὐδείς) would dare to attempt the deliverance of others. Nowhere else in Greece could one find a government such as Athens had; no other peoples enjoyed such freedom; no one else lived in a democracy. About those who died recently in battle, Lysias continued, "it was one thing for them to share their death with many, but prowess with a

5. See Bruce J. Malina and Jerome Neyrey, *Portraits of Paul: An Archaeology of Ancient Personality* (Louisville: Westminster John Knox, 1996), 3-4, 113-25.
6. Several other remarks by Lysias are worthy of note: "They *alone* fought for all Greece against many thousands of barbarians" (26). "They *alone* should be considered the leaders of the Greeks" (57).

few" (24). Thus men of Athens past and present are honored as the "first and only," "one of a few," and achievers of what "no one else" had done.

Thucydides (455-400 B.C.E.) likewise praises Athens as the geographical source of nobility of those commemorated in his funeral oration (2.35). In praising those who fell recently in the Peloponnesian War, he again celebrates their greatness by extolling the greatness of Athens. She is the mother of heroes because she is a uniquely noble city. He states: "Athenians *alone* regard the man who takes no part in public affairs, not as one who minds his own business, but as good for nothing" (2.40.2). He continues, "we *alone* confer benefits without fear of consequences, not upon a calculation of the advantage we shall gain, but with confidence in the spirit of liberality which activates us" (2.40.5). And finally, he states: "For Athens *alone* (μόνη) among her contemporaries . . . is *superior* (κρείσσων) to the report of her, and she *alone* (μόνη) neither affords to the enemy who comes against her cause for irritation at the character of the foe by whom he is defeated, nor to her subjects cause for complaint that their masters are unworthy" (2.41.3, emphasis added). Whereas we have been examining the principle of uniqueness expressed as "the first and only," clearly we have a variant form of it in the praise Thucydides heaps on Athens as the "only" one to act nobly in civic life and military campaigns.

Plato's (429-347 B.C.E.) *Menexenus* also attests to the currency of the principle of uniqueness. Socrates delivers to Menexenus a funeral oration composed by Aspasia, which contains all the conventions of the day. As with Lysias, a person's geography provides one sources of honor, in this case, Athens once more. Socrates lists a host of reasons for Athens's honor, and in particular, this instance of its uniqueness: "[Our country] was the *only and first* (μόνη . . . πρώτη) in that time to produce human nourishment" (*Menexenus* 237e; see Demosthenes, *Funeral Oration* 60.5). The soldiers of Athens, moreover, "by the victory which they gained over the barbarians *first* taught other men that the power of the Persians was not invincible" (*Menexenus* 240d). Noble soldiers, moreover, died in the battle of Oenophyta, thus becoming "the *first* to be buried by the city in this tomb" (242b). Uniqueness, then, rests in being the "first" and "only" to do something.[7] We are warranted in concluding that the criteria of unique-

7. Isocrates (436-338 B.C.E.) amplifies the praise of a person with claims to his uniqueness: "You, Nicocles, are the *first* and the *only* (πρῶτος καὶ μόνος) one of those who possess royal power, wealth, and luxury who has undertaken to pursue the study of philosophy"

ness became and remained a regular part of the rhetoric of praise from the Athens of Thucydides and Aristotle down to the time of the Christian writers.[8]

Greek Hymns and Prayers

Greek hymns and prayers also contain the criterion of uniqueness, and so they provide examples of its use in praise of the gods. Greek prayers, we are told, tend to have a tripartite structure: (1) *invocation* (deity addressed by means of name, surname, epithets, and descriptive predicates); (2) *discourse* (pray-ers explain why they call on this particular god); and (3) *petition* (content of the address).[9] In this structure we expect to find uniqueness primarily in the prayer's invocation. Consider the address in Cleanthes' "Hymn to Zeus":

Most glorious of immortals	κύδιστ' ἀθανάτων
honored under many names,	πολυώνυμε
O Zeus, first cause of nature	φύσεως ἀρχηγέ
guiding all things through law.	νόμου μέτα πάντα κυβερνῶν.[10]

Clearly the poet acknowledges Zeus as unique, for he is "most glorious" even among the immortals, hence the apex of an already elite group. Dio

---

(*Evagoras* 78); likewise Demosthenes (384-322 B.C.E.) about fallen soldiers: "These men were the *first* to foresee danger to the Greeks" (*Funeral Oration* 18); speaking of the fallen, "They *alone* receive the words of universal praise" (33).

8. Augustus Caesar claimed that he should be treated with the utmost honor because of his unique benefactions. As evidence, he listed in detail his substantial benefactions, in particular lands given to his soldiers for which he paid 860 million sesterces. "I was the first and only one *(primus atque solus omnium)* to do this of all those who up to my time settled colonies of soldiers in Italy or in the provinces" (*Res gestae* 16); see Plutarch, *Old Men in Public Affairs* 788E.

9. H. S. Versnel, "Religious Mentality in Ancient Prayer," in *Faith, Hope and Worship: Aspects of Religious Mentality in the Ancient World*, ed. H. S. Versnel (Leiden: Brill, 1981), 2. See also Larry Alderink and Luther Martin, "Prayer in Greco-Roman Religions," in *Prayer from Alexander to Constantine: A Critical Anthology*, ed. Mark Kiley (London: Routledge, 1997), 123-27.

10. The text is that of A. C. Pearson, *The Fragments of Zeno and Cleanthes* (New York: Arno Press, 1973), 274-75; it may also be found in von Arnim, *Stoicorum veterum fragmenta*, 1:121-22, frag. 537.

Chrysostom provides an apt illustration of Zeus being "many named": "The titles by which Zeus is known: he alone of the gods is entitled 'Father and King,' 'Protector of Cities,' 'God of Friendship,' 'God of Comradeship,' and also 'Protector of Suppliants,' 'God of Hospitality,' 'Giver of Increase'" (*Oration* 12.75). Being "many named," then, Zeus is honored as the distinctive and exclusive deity of Cleanthes and the Stoics.[11] By addressing Zeus as "first cause of nature," the hymn honors him as the unique giver of reason and rationality that make the world accessible to human minds. And finally, Zeus serves as master and guide over "all things," indicating his unique sovereignty and power. Thus Cleanthes amplifies Zeus's honorable and unique status even among the gods ("first"), his many names ("most"), and his exclusive and preeminent role in making and governing the universe ("only").

An aretalogy of Isis offers claims for her uniqueness. Although spoken by the goddess and thus not a prayer, the hymn invites its audience to honor Isis for the items listed.

> I am Isis, queen of every land,
> who was taught by Hermes,
> and whatever laws I have ordained,
> these no one can abrogate.
> I am the oldest daughter of the youngest god, Kronos.
> I am wife and sister of king Osiris.
> I am the first one to discover corn for humans.
> I am mother of the king Horus. (Diodor of Sicily 1.27.4)

Various elite roles of very high status belong to Isis: queen, oldest daughter, wife-sister, and mother. One or two might warrant praise, but the variety of kinship roles and their connection to the important Egyptian gods are grounds for unique honor. Her sovereignty, moreover, extends over "every land"; she is not a local goddess. She was taught by the best of teachers, Hermes. Her law — in a world where male, not female, rulers were the norm — is unique, and "no one" can abrogate it. Moreover, she is the

---

11. In a Hellenistic poem little Artemis sat on her father's lap and asked for a special gift that would put her on a par with her brother: "Give me many-namedness (πολυωνυμίην)." Cited by J. M. Bremer, "Greek Hymns," in *Faith, Hope, and Worship*, 194-95. See also the cultural study of names by Jerome H. Neyrey, *Honor and Shame in the Gospel of Matthew* (Louisville: Westminster John Knox, 1998), 55-60.

"first" to discover corn, and as we know, being the first to achieve anything sets that person above all others in that category.

As a third example of Greek hymns we present a summary of the eighty-seven Orphic Hymns.[12] The following survey was made with an eye to the rhetoric of uniqueness, both the items noted in epideictic rhetoric and other materials found in the hymns that function in the same way. While "first" is rarely used (38.6; 40.8),[13] "only/alone" occurs quite frequently.[14] Use of superlatives to emphasize a god's uniqueness is present but not common.[15] More frequent are the titles and epithets not found in rhetoric: rare is the deity who is not king of this or queen of that;[16] some deities are acclaimed as sovereign over "all," such as "father of all" (4.1; 6.3; 13.1; 20.5), "mother of all" (10.1; 9.5), "lord of all" (12.4), and "master of all" (45.2).[17] Often one finds mention of the extent of the domain of this or that god: Helios begets both dawn and night (8.4); Zeus presides over earth, sea, and sky (15.4-5). Thus the gods are honored in terms of their unique roles and statuses as well as for their exclusive sovereignty over their domains. As befits only gods, their eternity[18] and deathlessness are proclaimed: Ouranos, eternal cosmic element, is primeval as well as "beginning of all and end of all" (4.1-2); Zeus, too, is "father of all and beginning and end of all" (15.7). The deities are often called "blessed" (μάκαρ, μακάριος), which distinguishes their blissful lot from the turmoil of mortals.[19]

The epithets of the deities are easily grouped into categories: those using negative predicates to distinguish gods from mortals and those using

12. The text and translation used here is that of Apostolos N. Athanassakis, *The Orphic Hymns: Text, Translation, and Notes* (Missoula: Scholars, 1977). See also M. L. West, *The Orphic Poems* (Oxford: Clarendon, 1983).

13. Variations of "first" include "oldest of all" (10.2) and "first born" (10.5).

14. Hymns 33.2; 58.8; 61.1; 64.8; 68.11; 74.6; 75.7; 85.3; 87.8. Persephone and Athena are the "only-begotten" (μονογένεια) offspring of Demeter and Zeus respectively (29.2; 32.1).

15. Adonis is called "best god" (ἄριστε, 56.1); Okeanos, "highest divine purifier" (μέγιστον, 83.6); Dream, "greatest prophet to mortals" (μέγιστε, 86.2).

16. For example, moon is "divine queen" (9.1); Pan is "queen of all" (11.2); Zeus, of course, is "king" (15:2) in one place and "begetter of all and great king" (20.5); Hera, "queen of all" and consort of Zeus (16.2).

17. For example, "πολυώνυμε" in 2.1; 10.13; 11.10; 36.1; 40; 41.1; 42.2; 45.2; 50.2; 56.1; 59.2.

18. Variations of "eternity" include "self-born" (8.3) or "self-fathered" (10.10); "end that has no end" (10.8); as well as note of a god's "everlasting life" (10.27; 11.3).

19. For example, 4.4, 8; 6.3, 10; 8.1; 9.11; 12.14; 13.1; 16.2; 22.10; 28.6; 32.3; 33.9; 34.1; 45.1; 52.1.

some form of πᾶν. Examples of the former include: "unconquerable" (ἀδάμαστε, 4.7; 12.2; 65.2), "ineffable" (ἄρρητος, 12.4; 19.11), "untiring" (ἀκάμας, 8.3), "unconquerable" (ἄφθιτος, 15.1), "unbreakable" (ἄρρηκτος, 65.1), and "invincible" (ἀνίκητον, 19.9). Such labels distinguish the deities from mortals who are subject to the very things from which the gods are immune, thus identifying the gods as belonging to an exclusive group of persons, the "only" ones or "one of a few." Epithets employing some form of πᾶν include: "all-seeing" (πανδερκές, 4.8; 9.7), "all-conquering" (πανδαμάτωρ, 10.3), and "all-mighty" (παντοκράτειρα, 10.4).

Therefore, while labels of uniqueness such as "first," "only," and "one of a few" occur, the hymns declare the uniqueness and exclusivity of the gods in terms of *role* (king, queen), *status* (mistress of all), *domain* under their unique control (earth, sea, sky), *benefactions* tied exclusively to them, and *duration*. Negative predication immediately distinguishes the gods from mortals.

Uniqueness in the Hebrew Bible[20]

In 1966 Labuschagne published a study on the incomparability of God in the Scriptures,[21] in which he identified a number of ways in which uniqueness was claimed for God. The most common expression of incomparability he found in declarative statements such as "There is none like *x*." For example, Hannah prays:

> There is no Holy One like the LORD,
>   no one besides you;
>   there is no Rock like our God.

(1 Sam 2:2; see also Exod 8:10;
Ps 86:8; Deut 33:26; 2 Chron 20:6)

20. Unfortunately this brief study cannot do justice to the topic of uniqueness in the Hebrew Scripture; one of the most important motifs not covered is henotheism/monotheism. But see Walter Strolz, "The Unique One: The Uniqueness of God according to Deutero-Isaiah," in *Standing before God: Studies on Prayer in Scriptures and in Tradition with Essays*, ed. Asher Finkel and Lawrence Frizzell (New York: Ktav, 1981), 257-66.

21. C. J. Labuschagne, *The Incomparability of Yahweh in the Old Testament* (Leiden: Brill, 1966).

Biblical authors used this same formula to praise mortals as well as God: Solomon (1 Kings 3:12, 13; Neh 13:26), Hezekiah (2 Kings 18:5), Josiah (2 Kings 23:25), and Job (Job 1:8; 2:3). Moreover, incomparability was expressed by rhetorical questions: "Who is like *x*? No One!" For example,

> Ps 35:10   O LORD, who is like you?
>
> Ps 89:8   O LORD God of hosts, / who is as mighty as you, O LORD?
>
> Exod 15:11   Who is like you, O LORD, among the gods?[22]

No one, of course, because God is unique in what God does.

Another study of the incomparability formula focused on the praise accorded select monarchs who found favor in the eyes of the writer.[23] Of Solomon, the editor says: "I give you also what you have not asked, both riches and honor all your life; no other king shall compare with you" (1 Kings 3:13; cf. 10:23). Of Hezekiah we read: "He trusted in the LORD the God of Israel; so that there was no one like him among all the kings of Judah after him, or among those who were before him" (2 Kings 18:5). And of Josiah we are told: "Before him there was no king like him, who turned to the LORD with all his heart, with all his soul, and with all his might, according to all the law of Moses; nor did any like him arise after him" (2 Kings 23:25). The uniqueness expressed in this formula claims that these monarchs are the best of David's line; no king before or after them matched them.

Labuschagne and Knoppers provide us with clear examples of what uniqueness looks like in the Hebrew Bible, namely, "incomparability." Yet Morton Smith argued years ago that there was a "common theology" in the ancient Near East that applied as well to God in Israel's literature. He noted that "prayer and praise are usually directed to one god at a time,"[24] with the result that the god is made unique, at least for the moment. Smith labels this "flattery": "Though a god may occupy a minor position in the preserved mythological works, yet in worship addressed to him he is regularly represented as greater than all other gods. He created not just the world, but other gods. He is, then, the only true god."[25] Smith argued that

---

22. See also Pss 71:19 and 113:5; see Labuschagne, *Incomparability of Yahweh*, 16-22.

23. Gary N. Knoppers, "'There Was None Like Him': Incomparability in the Books of Kings," *CBQ* 54 (1992): 411-31.

24. Morton Smith, "The Common Theology of the Ancient Near East," *JBL* 71 (1952): 137.

25. Smith, "Common Theology," 139.

Israel's religious language was itself not unique, but rather belonged to a larger cultural area that can be said to have a "common" theology.

Uniqueness in the LXX

It is indubitable that rhetoric influenced the way Israel began to praise God in Greek. Most of the aspects of incomparability just observed were simply translated into Greek, although they do not appear as the Greek rhetorical buzzwords for uniqueness. (1) Commonly we read negations that God has any peer or rival, such as ". . . that you may know that there is not another such as I in all the earth (οὐκ ἔστιν ὡς ἐγὼ ἐν πάσῃ τῇ γῇ)" (Exod 9:14). (2) We find rhetorical questions, such as: "O Lord, who is like you (κύριε τίς ὅμοιός σοι)?" (Ps 35:10) or "What God is there in heaven or on earth (τίς γάρ ἐστιν θεὸς ἐν τῷ οὐρανῷ ἢ ἐπὶ τῆς γῆς) who will do as you have done?" (Deut 3:24). (3) Other expressions of incomparability contain the frequently appearing formula "no other besides you," such as: "To you it was shown, that you might know that the Lord is God; there is no other besides him (οὐκ ἔστιν ἔτι πλὴν αὐτοῦ)" (Deut 4:35).[26] (4) Finally, we find God's uniqueness articulated by the claim that God "alone" (μόνος) is Lord (or virtuous, mighty, etc.). In some cases "alone" or "only" (μόνος) is part of a monotheistic confession, as in Hezekiah's prayer, that embodies the henotheistic worship praised by the Deuteronomic writer: "You are the only God (σὺ εἶ ὁ θεὸς μόνος) in all the kingdoms of the earth" (2 Kings 19:15).[27] Labeling God as "only" (μόνος) is a convenient blend of Israelite henotheistic tradition and Greek rhetoric of praise. Four names, "Lord," "God," "Creator," and "King," indicate unique status and role. Moreover, titles such as "almighty" (παντοκράτωρ) and abstract predicates such as "eternal" (αἰώνιος) are appropriations of Hellenistic god-talk. The concept of uniqueness is present, even if the distinctive expressions of it are not.

---

26. For example, Deut 4:39; 1 Sam 2:2; 1 Kings 8:23; 2 Kings 5:15; Isa 43:10-13; 45:5-6, 14, 18, 21-22; Dan 3:29; Sir 36:5; Joel 2:27.

27. See also, Deut 6:13; 10:20; Judg 10:16; 1 Sam 7:3; 1 Kings 18:37; Neh 9:6; Pss 71:16; 72:18; 83:18; Isa 37:16.

Miscellaneous Instances of Uniqueness in the New Testament

As we approach the doxologies in 1 Timothy, it is worth our while to notice how the principle of uniqueness occurs in New Testament narrative and prayer.

Only (*μόνος*)

Christian authors generally declare God's uniqueness with some form of "only" or "alone" (σὺ εἶ ὁ θεὸς μόνος). In his temptations Jesus affirms exclusive loyalty to God: "You shall worship the Lord your God and him *only* shall you serve" (Matt 4:10 RSV//Luke 4:8; Deut 6:13). Service of God excludes that of all others. Similarly, Jesus rebukes his audience for seeking the approval of its peers and not seeking "the glory that comes from the *only* God" (John 5:44 RSV; 17:3). Jesus makes a striking confession about the secrecy of the coming of the end time: "But about that day and hour *no one* (οὐδείς) knows, neither the angels of heaven, nor the Son, but *only* the Father" (Matt 24:36). Thus God alone enjoys unique knowledge and does not share it with either his heavenly messengers or his earthly messiah. Hence "no one" knows.[28] Yet God knows, for which Paul honors him: "to the *only* wise God (μόνῳ σοφῷ) . . . be the glory forever! Amen" (Rom 16:27).[29] God's unique wisdom is the thrust of the doxology: "revelation of the mystery that was kept secret for long ages but is now disclosed" (16:25-26). Thus to "the only wise God" is glory due for the uniqueness of "wisdom" now revealed. Critics accuse Jesus of poaching on God's unique prerogatives: "Who can forgive sins but God *alone?*" (εἰ μὴ εἷς ὁ θεός) (Mark 2:7) or "Who can forgive sins but God *only?*" (εἰ μὴ μόνος ὁ θεός) (Luke 5:21 RSV).

28. In this prayer God is thrice honored as "only": "the only High One (μόνον ὕψιστον) . . . the only finder (μόνον εὑρέτην) . . . the only God (ὁ θεὸς μόνος)" (1 Clem 59.3).

29. For an excellent study of Rom 16:25-27, see Jacques Dupont, "Μόνῳ Σοφῷ Θεῷ," *ETL* 22 (1964): 362-75. See also Eduard Norden, *Agnostos Theos* (Darmstadt: Wissenschaftliche Buchgesellschaft, 1956), 240-51.

One (εἷς)

Apropos of God's uniqueness, Jesus endorses the monotheistic faith of Israel (Mark 12:29-30), which is a confession of God's uniqueness. He cites the Shema (Deut 6:4-5 RSV): "Hear, O Israel: The LORD our God is *one* (εἷς θεός)." Echoing this, his interlocutor repeats Jesus' words, confessing that "he [God] is *one* (εἷς)" and adding that "there is *no other* (οὐκ ἔστιν ἄλλος πλὴν αὐτοῦ)" (Mark 12:32). Similarly, when honored with the compliment "Good teacher," Jesus deflected it to God: "No one is good but God *alone*" (Mark 10:18).

No One (οὐδείς)

This rhetorical form of uniqueness is used most frequently of Jesus himself. For example, Jesus informs his disciples: "All things have been handed over to me by my Father; and *no one* (οὐδείς) knows the Son except the Father, and *no one* knows the Father except the Son and anyone to whom the Son chooses to reveal him" (Matt 11:27//Luke 10:22). Note the claims to uniqueness: (1) "all things" have been given him by his Father-God; (2) knowledge of him rests exclusively with God; and (3) knowledge of God belongs exclusively to Jesus. The claim made here credits both Father and Son with uniqueness, exclusive knowledge shared only by the two of them. We find, moreover, honor claims made by Jesus and on his own behalf that rest upon his uniqueness, which "no one" else has. For example:

No one (οὐδείς) has ever seen God; the only (μονογενής)[30] Son . . . has made him known. (John 1:18 RSV)

No one (οὐδείς) has ascended into heaven except the one who descended from heaven. (John 3:13)

30. The term μονογενής is generally translated as "only" or "single"; see Paul Winter, "Μονογενὴς Παρὰ Πατρός," *ZRGG* 5 (1953): 335-65; Gerard Pendrick, "Μονογενής," *NTS* 41 (1995): 587-600, whose data overwhelmingly indicate that its proper translation is "the only one of its kind" or "unique." But see also J. V. Dahms, "The Johannine Use of *Monogenes* Reconsidered," *NTS* 29 (1983): 222-32.

No one (οὐδείς) takes it from me, but I lay it down of my own accord. (John 10:18)

No one (οὐδείς) comes to the Father except through me. (John 14:6)[31]

John 1:18 and 3:13 declare Jesus' uniqueness because of the unique benefit of seeing the invisible God and descending from heaven. Certainly, no mortal on earth could make such claims. The remark in John 14:6 declares the uniqueness of Jesus as the only way to come to the Father, positioning him as the exclusive mediator or broker of God,[32] which uniqueness warrants great honor and respect for him. These examples are rhetorically crafted to exclude all other claimants while affirming the uniqueness and exclusivity of Jesus' mediation.

This survey of the principle of uniqueness has identified in the Gospels the same rhetorical terms from Greek rhetoric that also are used to amplify the honor of God. As we turn to Israelite and Christian prayers, the language of praise and honor becomes quite formal and standardized; and the principle of uniqueness continues to have a special place as a way to augment praise and honor.

God's Uniqueness in Christian Doxologies

The Doxology in 1 Timothy 1:17

The form of this doxology consists of four elements: (1) *addressee,* in the dative case; (2) *honor proclaimed,* either "glory" or "honor" or comparable terms; (3) *duration of praise,* usually "forever"; and (4) *"Amen,"* an invitation to hearers to affirm the praise. This directs our attention to the first two elements as the likely places to observe the rhetoric of uniqueness. In what does God's uniqueness rest?

31. Consider the absoluteness ascribed to Jesus: "There is salvation in no one else (ἐν ἄλλῳ οὐδενί), for there is no (οὐδέ) other name under heaven . . . by which we must be saved" (Acts 4:12).

32. Bruce J. Malina and Richard L. Rohrbaugh, *Social-Science Commentary on the Gospel of John* (Minneapolis: Fortress, 1998), 230-31.

King

This title, rarely applied to God in the New Testament, was common in the Hebrew Bible[33] and infrequent in the Greek Orphic Hymns.[34] But here God is the "King of the ages," which stresses God's eternity, an attribute unique to a deity.[35] Thus God is acclaimed unique in terms of both the power he exercises and the endless duration of his sovereignty. It became, moreover, a commonplace among commentators on the Pastorals to claim that the Christian author wishes to counter the claims of the divinized Roman emperor by acclaiming God as "king" and "eternally reigning." If we could be more certain of this, the comparison itself would deserve to be taken as an instance of uniqueness in the sense that God is the *first* God and the *only* God. No mere mortal man, emperor or not, *can match God.*

Imperishable

Next the author ascribes to God three predicates that merit close consideration: "imperishable" (ἀφθάρτῳ), "invisible" (ἀοράτῳ), and "only" (μόνῳ) God. In regard to "imperishable," Greco-Roman authors constructed a topos for a true deity, which claimed that a genuine god has no beginning in the past and is imperishable in the future.[36] For example, when Diodor of Sicily contrasts true gods with mortals made gods after death, he names as the distinguishing characteristic of a true god eternity of existence, both in the past and in the future. "Men of ancient times have handed down two different conceptions of the gods. Certain of the gods are eternal and imperishable; for each of these genesis and duration are from everlasting to everlasting" (6.1.2). Such a claim became a commonplace in Greco-Roman philosophical circles; Sextus Empiricus declared: "God is eternal (ἀΐδιον) and imperishable (ἄφθαρτον) and perfect in happiness" (*Against the Phys-*

---

33. In fact, only 1 Tim 6:15; Rev 15:3, but commonly in the Old Testament: Isa 6:5; Jer 10:10; Ps 74:12; and Sir 51:1.

34. For example, Zeus is "king" (15.3) and Korybas too (39.1); the hymns acknowledge many female gods as "queen": Moon (9.1), Artemis (36.1), Semele (44.1), Nemesis (61.1), Hygeia (68.1), and Hestia (84.1).

35. See Ceslas Spicq, *Les Épitres Pastorales* (Paris: Gabalda, 1969), 346-47. See also Tob 13:7, 11; Sir 36:17.

36. See Charles H. Talbert, *What Is a Gospel? The Genre of the Canonical Gospels* (Philadelphia: Fortress, 1977); and Jerome H. Neyrey, "'Without Beginning of Days or End of Life' (Hebrews 7:3): Topos for a True Deity," *CBQ* 53 (1991): 441-44.

icists 1.45). Plutarch repeats this unique distinction: "Now we hear the theologians affirming and reciting . . . that the god is imperishable (ἄφθαρτος) and eternal (αἴδιος) in his nature" (*E Delphi* 388F). Thus true deities are distinguished from heroic mortals by their temporal uniqueness. This topos, insofar as it compares true gods with heroized mortals, asserts something that is rare and in the possession of the very few, the only divine ones, and hence unique. It acclaims an immortal god as uniquely superior to all mortals who are born and die.

Invisible

Although the thought expressed here can be found in the Hebrew Bible, where it is claimed that God cannot be seen even by Israel's most celebrated prophet Moses (Exod 33:20), the precise term "unseen" comes from the Greco-Roman world. When Philo[37] and Josephus[38] use this term, their usage reflects Greek god-talk. It is not used of God in the LXX, although Christian writers as early as Paul used this Greek expression to claim that God is unseeable or unseen (Rom 1:20; Col 1:15; Heb 11:27).[39]

Both "imperishable "and "invisible" require us to enter the world of negative predication of god in the Greco-Roman world.[40] In reaction to crass anthropomorphisms in Greek piety, some philosophers developed a special god-talk that avoided such excesses on the one hand, and on the other produced a refined way to celebrate the uniqueness and excellence of god. Negative predication concerning god resulted from this process

37. Philo notes that the unseen God sees even the most secret of things (*On the Special Laws* 4.30; *On the Creation of the World* 69); in another place he contrasts the wonders of the nature of the mind with "the honor given to the Immaterial (ἀειδοῦς), the Invisible (ἀόρατου), the apprehended by the understanding alone" (*On the Special Laws* 1.20).

38. When speaking of the human soul, Josephus uses most of the unique epithets we are examining in 1 Tim 1:17: "The soul . . . enjoys a blessed energy . . . like God Himself, invisible (ἀοράτος) to human eyes . . . itself of a nature one and incorruptible (ἄφθαρτον), but a cause of change in the body" (*Jewish War* 7.346-47). See A. T. Hanson, *The Pastoral Epistles* (Cambridge: Cambridge University Press, 1966), 29.

39. See Wilhelm Michaelis, "ὁρατός, ἀόρατος," in *TDNT* 5:368-70. See also 2 *Clem* 20.5; Diognetus 7.2; Ignatius, *To the Magnesians* 3.2; and Ignatius, *To Polycarp* 3.2.

40. H. A. Wolfson, "Albinus and Plotinus on Divine Attributes," *HTR* 45 (1952): 115-30; Wolfson, "Negative Attributes in the Church Fathers and the Gnostic Basilides," *HTR* 50 (1957): 145-56; John Whittaker, "Neopythagoreanism and Negative Theology," *Symbolae Osloenses* 44 (1969): 125.

(e.g., some form of alpha -). Epithets prefaced by a negative deny imperfection in god and acclaim him superior to all things of this material world, mortals included. Although it is not a prayer, Theophilus's remark provides a particularly excellent example of negative predication: "The appearance of God is ineffable (ἄρρητον) and indescribable (ἀνέκφρα-στον) and cannot be seen by eyes of flesh. In glory God is incomprehensible (ἀχώρητος), in greatness unfathomable (ἀκατάληπτος), in height inconceivable (ἀπερινόντος), in power incomparable (ἀσύγκριτος), in wisdom unrivaled (ἀσυμβίβαστος), in goodness inimitable (ἀμίμητος), in kindness unutterable (ἀνεκδιήγητος)" (*To Autolycus* 1.3).[41] Theophilus begins by claiming that God cannot be verbalized or seen; hence God belongs not to our material world, but to a higher one. In terms of virtues that warrant praise and glory, God surpasses mortal standards. Although rhetorical tags such as "first," "only," and "one who has done *x* the most" are not here, the negative predicates attest God's uniqueness in the universe. To God alone exclusively belong glory, greatness, height, wisdom, goodness, and kindness.

Alone/Only

Past attention to this term distinguishes three usages: (1) the superlative expression of polytheistic piety, (2) the statement of philosophers, and (3) the predication of monotheistic religion. In the exposition of god-talk in the Orphic Hymns above, we observed that various gods were credited with unique tasks, an example of Delling's first category:

> Eros: you *alone* (μόνος) govern the course of all these (ether, land, and Tartarus, 58.8).
> Nomos: he *alone* (μόνος) steers the course of everything that breathes (64.8).
> Leukothea: you *alone* (μόνη) save men from wretched death at sea (74.6).
> Palaimon: you *alone* (μόνος) appear incarnate to save men (75.7).
> Sleep: you *alone* (μόνος) are master of us all (85.3).

---

41. The text of Theophilus is that of Miroslav Markovich, *Theophili Antiocheni ad Autolycum* (Berlin: De Gruyter, 1995), 18.

In this polytheistic context it is possible for one or another deity to be unique in one function, situation, or domain. As regards Delling's second use of "only," scholars generally ascribe it to the purification of the notion of god by the philosophers in a movement from anthropomorphism to apophatic theology.[42] Nothing more needs be said about it, as it was adequately illustrated above. Finally, Israelite and Christian monotheism constitutes Delling's third use of "only." We recall the examples of this in the New Testament discussion of "only" and "one," to which we add two important verses from Deuteronomy, 4:35 and 6:4 (see also Isa 44–45). The "only" God is unique because there is only one deity, and there is no other beside him.[43] Thus, returning to 1 Timothy 1:17, we recognize here Delling's third classification of "only," Christian monotheism. In itself it identifies God as unique, the "one" and "only" deity.[44]

Glory and Honor

The doxology in 1 Timothy 1:17 contains other traditional parts of the form, the giving of glory, its duration, usually "forever," and the people's response, "Amen." As one would expect, God is given glory and honor, synonyms because both connote esteem, reputation, praise, worth, and the like. We remember Kittel's argument that the Greek understanding of "glory" (δόξα) expresses the sense of "opinion," that is, "good opinion,"

---

42. Frances Young, "The God of the Greeks and the Nature of Religious Language," in *Early Christian Literature and the Classical Intellectual Tradition*, ed. William R. Schoedel and Robert L. Wilken (Paris: Beauchesne, 1979), 48-53; See Robert M. Grant, *Gods and the One God* (Philadelphia: Westminster, 1986), 75-83.

43. In the LXX there are several dominant patterns that express monotheistic faith: (1) *"who is like you? [No one]"* (τίς ὅμοιός σοι ἐν θεοῖς κύριε τίς ὅμοιός σοι) (Exod 15:11; 1 Sam 2:2; 2 Sam 22:32; Pss 35:10; 71:19; 89:7-8; 113:5; Mic 7:18); (2) *"there is no other besides you"* (ὅτι κύριος ὁ θεός σου οὗτος θεός ἐστιν καὶ οὐκ ἔστιν ἔτι πλὴν σοῦ) (Deut 4:35, 39; 6:4; 32:39; 2 Sam 7:22; 1 Kings 8:23; 2 Kings 5:15; Isa 43:10-13; 45:5-6, 14, 18, 21-22); (3) *"you are the only God in all the kingdoms"* (σὺ εἶ ὁ θεὸς μόνος ἐν πάσαις ταῖς βασιλείαις) (2 Kings 19:15; Neh 9:6). Evidently μόνος was hardly the sole way of expressing God's uniqueness.

44. For comparison's sake, we note the use of μόνος in other doxologies: "the only (μόνος) unbegotten and unruled . . . the only (μόνος) true, the only (μόνος) wise, the one who alone (μόνος) is most high . . . the only (μόνος) good and incomparable" (*Apostolic Constitutions* 8.5.1, in David A. Fiensy, *Prayers Alleged to Be Jewish: An Examination of the "Constitutiones Apostolorum"* [Chico, Calif.: Scholars, 1985], 90-91); see also David Fiensy and D. R. Darnell, "Hellenistic Synagogal Prayers," in *OTP*, 687.

"reputation," "worth," and "repute." The other term, "honor" (τιμή), expresses the value or worth of something or someone; thus it may express praise and admiration for a person's achievement, role and status, and reputation. Looking solely at doxologies in the New Testament, we observe that most of them give only "glory" to God (Rom 11:36; 16:27; Gal 1:5; Eph 3:21; 2 Tim 4:18; Heb 13:21); several give "glory" and "dominion" (1 Tim 6:16; 1 Pet 4:11; Rev 1:6); still others declare "glory" and "honor" (1 Tim 1:17; Rev 4:11 and 5:13).[45] Jude ascribes to God "glory, majesty, power, and authority" (v 25). This indicates the rhetorical function of ascribing piling-up statements of God's worth and distinction.

Forever and Ever

In his article on the doxology in synagogue and early church, Eric Werner seems embarrassed that his analysis of this form contained only two elements: (1) proclamation of God's praise (2) *coupled with an affirmation of his infinity in time.*[46] It is easily observable that New Testament doxologies contain such affirmations of God's infinity, although in a wide variety of expressions: (1) the simple formula: "forever" (Rom 11:36; 16:27); (2) a more elaborate statement, such as we see in 1 Timothy 1:17: "forever and ever" (Gal 1:5; Phil 4:20; 2 Tim 4:18; 1 Pet 4:11); and (3) a very elaborate form: "before all time and now and forever" (Jude 25). This represents a Judean mode of expression, although there are Greco-Roman parallels. Some Greco-Roman deities were acclaimed as "beginning of all and end of all" (Orphic Hymns 4.2; 15.7); others were said to have no beginning (10.10) and no end (10.8).[47] Still others were declared "imperishable"

45. H. Hegermann ("δόξα," *DIT* 1.345) notes that occasionally "glory" (δόξα) and "honor" (τιμή) are used synonymously (Rom 2:7, 10), and the same with "glory" and "praise" (Phil 1:11; 1 Pet 1:7). Marshall (*The Pastoral Epistles*, ICC [Edinburgh: T. & T. Clark, 1999], 405-6) considers "glory" and "honor" as synonyms, but claims that they "go back to the LXX translation of the Hebrew *kabod*," which seems excessively narrow in the light of Greek rhetoric of praise.

46. Eric Werner, "The Doxology in Synagogue and Church: A Liturgico-Musical Study," *HUCA* 19 (1945-46): 275-351, emphasis Werner's.

47. Cicero recorded: "Suppose we allow that the gods are made of atoms: then it follows that they are not eternal. For what is made of atoms came into being at some time; and if gods came into being, before they came into existence there were no gods; and if the gods had a beginning they must also have an end" (*De natura deorum* 1.24.68). Tertullian reflects traditional god-talk when he speaks of the eternity of the true God: "I give that definition

(ἄφθαρτος) or "deathless" (ἀθάνατος). And as was noted in the topos for true deities, they are "without beginning and without end."[48] The Hellenistic expression, we have seen, emerges in the philosophical refinement of the concept of god. But there is no question that the infinity of God expressed by the doxologies speaks to God's uniqueness, for no one else can boast of such timelessness. God is the only one who by virtue of God's person will continue to exist forever.

The Doxology in 1 Timothy 6:15-16

Like many doxologies, this one builds on the declarative statement made in 6:15 and flowers into its own address to God in 6:16. Compared with 1 Timothy 1:17, it contains a richer series of names, titles, and predicates, which deserve extended comment.

Blessed

Although some claim that this attribute of God is "common in Hellenistic Judaism,"[49] others note that "God is not called 'blessed' (μακάριος) in the Bible," with the exception of 1 Timothy 1:11 and 6:15, the texts under discussion here. Moreover, we recall that in the Greek Orphic hymns discussed above, most of the gods were acclaimed "blessed"; thus we find considerable evidence indicating that "blessed" was a common attribute of Greco-Roman gods[50] and now of the Christian God. God's "blessedness" constitutes a recurring theme in Philo's discussion of God. For example, "But the nature of God is without grief (ἄλυπος) or fear (ἄφοβος), and wholly exempt

---

(of God) which all men's common sense will accept, that God is supremely great, firmly established in eternity, unbegotten, uncreated, without beginning and without end *(sine initio, sine fine)*" *(Adversus Marcionem* 1.3; see *Adversus Hermogenem* 5). Theophilus, listing the attributes of God, states that the deity is "without beginning because He is unbegotten; and he is unchangeable, because he is immortal" *(To Autolycus* 1.4).

48. Neyrey, "Without Beginning," 440-47, esp. 444.

49. J. N. D. Kelly, *A Commentary on the Pastoral Epistles* (New York: Harper and Row, 1963), 46.

50. The strongest proponents for calling god "blessed" were the Epicureans, whose theology might be summarized in the confession that god was "blessed and eternal": "First believe that God is a living being imperishable and blessed (ἄφθαρτον καὶ μακάριον)" (Diogenes Laertius 10.123).

(ἀμέτοχος) from passion of any kind, and alone (μόνης) partakes of perfect happiness (μακαριότητος παντελοῦς) and bliss" (*On the Life of Abraham* 202; see *That God Is Unchangeable* 26). This statement and many more found in Philo derive from a philosophical tradition that talked about God in negative predicates and acclaimed God's unique blessedness.[51] Moreover, in Epicurean philosophical traditions god was acclaimed both "blessed" and "imperishable": "A blessed and eternal being has no trouble himself and brings no trouble upon other beings."[52] Uniqueness is contained in the attribute "blessed," in that it distinguishes god from mortals who labor, suffer, and die, implying that god alone knows blessedness and is not subject to changing fortunes. And so it represents a quality unique to a deity.

Only Sovereign

This term is used of god both in Greek and Israelite literature. It comes from the term used to describe "any official in government, as, for example, a prince or king,"[53] and thus it speaks to the role and status of someone with power, especially supreme power, a most honorable quality in antiquity. Commentators have long suggested that the phrase "only Sovereign" rhetorically asserts the Christian deity's superiority over all other deities, especially Roman imperial claims. Yet, we add, in the study of the rhetoric of praise, μόνος served as a successful claim for uniqueness by labeling the one being honored as the "first" or "only" or "one of a few." Here God alone is sovereign of all.

King of Kings

It is generally accepted that, while this sort of predicate is found within Israelite traditions, it was also extensively used to describe monarchs in the

51. For example, "Separate, my soul, all that is created, mortal, mutable, profane from thy conception of God the uncreated (ἀγενήτου), unchangeable (ἀτρέπτου), the imperishable (ἀφθάρτου), the holy and solely blessed (μόνου μακαρίου)" (*On the Sacrifices of Cain and Abel* 101); see also *Sacrifices* 95; *On Dreams* 1.95; *On the Special Laws* 1.329; 2.53; 3.178.

52. This Epicurean slogan about God's nature was widely known and cited; see Cicero, *Nature of the Gods* 1.45-49, 68, 85, 106-7; Lucretius, *Nature of Things* 1.44-49; 2.651; Plutarch, *Stoic Self-Contradictions* 1051E and *Common Conceptions* 1075E.

53. Daniel Arichea and Howard Hatton, *A Handbook on Paul's Letters to Timothy and to Titus* (New York: United Bible Societies, 1995), 158.

ancient East.[54] In all these instances, the ruler was uniquely sovereign of his empire and made vassals of conquered kings. It became a common way of addressing God in the Old Testament, and on occasion was linked with "God of gods" (Deut 10:17; Ps 136:2; 3 Macc 5:35). Nevertheless, the king of all other kings is unique in power: he alone rules.

Lord of Lords

This phrase, found in Philo, *On the Cherubim* 99, is occasionally linked with "God of gods" (Deut 10:17; Ps 136:2-3). The three expressions "King of kings," "Lord of lords," and "God of gods" belong to the vocabulary of praise and honor for several reasons. First, "king," "lord," and "god" indicate roles of the highest status in both earthly and heavenly realms, and by this very fact warrant respect and praise.[55] Moreover, all three expressions claim uniqueness for God simply by being cast in the superlative mode. As we saw in the list of grounds for praise, those who "only" or "most" do something deserve respect and glory. Here God "most" acts like king, lord, and god; or God is the ultimate or unique sovereign. Finally, it was part of the ancient grammar of honor to exalt the name of someone, just as it was shaming to have one's name slandered. Studies of the doxologies and benedictions in Paul's letters all point out how praise of the name of God was a significant feature in the Old Testament and synagogue Judaism. In comparison with synagogal and other Jewish prayers, New Testament doxologies are quite modest in celebrating the name of God and attributing to God many titles and functions. 1 Timothy 6:15-16 is unusual among NT doxologies precisely for its expansiveness in regard to the names of God.[56]

---

54. Diodor of Sicily relates how the following was written on a stele: "This land the King of Kings (βασιλεὺς βασιλέων) and Lord of Lords (δεσπότης δεσπότων), Sesoöris, subdued with his own arms" (1.55.7); Dio Cassius tells how Anthony commanded that Cleopatra be called "Queen of Kings" (βασιλίδα βασιλέων) and Ptolemy, whom he named Caesarion, "King of Kings" (βασιλεὺς βασιλέων) (*Roman History* 49.41.1); Dio also reports that Pompey demoted a man who was generally called "King of Kings" (βασιλεὺς βασιλέων) to a simple "King" (37.6.1-2); see also Dio Chrysostom, *Oration* 2.75. Israelite parallels include: Ezra 7:12; Ezek 26:7; Dan 2:37; 2 Macc 13:4. Similarly, G. K. Beale, "The Origin of the Title 'King of Kings and Lord of Lords' in Rev. 17.14," *NTS* 31 (1985): 618-20.

55. Remarking on "king of kings" and "lord of lords," Arichea and Hatton (*Handbook*, 158) state: "Alternative ways to translate these two phrases are 'The Greatest Ruler, the Mightiest King,' 'The Lord and King of All,' or 'The Most Powerful Ruler and Highest Chief of All.'"

56. For comparison's sake, we note how full the address to God is in *1 Enoch*: "Blessed is

Alone Has Imperishability

In 1:17 the author praises God as "imperishable" (ἄφθαρτος), whereas here God is said to "have immortality." Since we consider "immortal" and "to have immortality" to be virtually the same predication of God, we ask readers to return to the comments on ἄφθαρτος. As we saw, Epicurean theology regularly paired "imperishable" and "blessed" as the defining qualities of the philosopher's god, thus distinguishing deathless deities from mortals. Hence we assess God's immortality in 1:17 and 6:16 as a singular uniqueness, because God "alone" enjoys this extraordinary quality.

Dwelling in Inaccessible Light

We focus here on the sense of exclusivity contained in the term "inaccessible." Ancient monarchs were notorious for limiting and denying access to their presence as a mark of worth and high status; hence, the more inaccessible, the more honorable. As we saw above, philosophical god-talk regularly spoke of the deity by way of "negative theology,"[57] instances of which we observed earlier ("imperishable," "invisible"), to which we add "inaccessible." These indicate uniqueness in quite different ways. Imperishability serves to maximize the essential superiority of god over mortals, which is reflected in negative predicates such as "unoriginated" (ἀγένητον), "impassible" (ἄπειρον), "unchanging" (ἀναλλοίτον), and "without end" (ἀτελεύτητον). But predicates such as "invisible" and "inaccessible" have to do with god's unknowability, indicating that the most noble faculty of humans cannot approach, much less comprehend, the deity. If mortals cannot obtain access to god, much less can they see or know god.[58]

---

the Lord of the Spirits — the Lord of kings, the Lord of rulers, and the Master of the rich — the Lord of glory and the Lord of wisdom" (63:2).

57. See H. A. Wolfson, "The Knowability and Describability of God in Plato and Aristotle," *HSCP* (1947): 233-47.

58. Philo's anti-anthropomorphism is linked to Num 23:19, "God is not a human being." From this it follows, as Wolfson says, "that God could be described only by terms which state directly His unlikeness to other beings, such, for instance, as unborn (ἀγένητος, *Mos.* 2.171), unbribable (ἀδέκαστος, *Cher.* 17), incomprehensible (ἀκατάληπτος, *Det.* 89), unnamable (ἀκατανομάστος, *Somn.* 1.67), invisible (ἀόρατος, *Cher.* 101), uncircumscribable (ἀπερίγραφος, *Sac.* 59), ineffable (ἄρρητος, *Somn.* 1.67), and incomparable (ἀσύγκριτος, *Fug.* 141), all of which are used by Philo himself" (*Philo: Foundations of Religion Philosophy in Judaism, Christianity, and Islam* [Cambridge: Harvard University Press, 1947], 2:126-27).

Whom No Mortal Has Ever Seen or Can See

This last criterion for God's praise reflects the negative predication of God as invisible or beyond mortal sight. Thus God's "inaccessibility" and "invisibility" (1 Tim 1:17; 6:16) speak to the superiority of God to humans, especially in terms of their greatest power, mind. In regard to the rhetorical way this superiority is expressed, namely, by the formula "no one (οὐδείς) has ever . . . ," this expression serves to praise someone because he alone achieved something, and "no one else" has or can. In this mode Isocrates praises Evagoras because "*no one* (οὐδείς) whether mortal, demigod, or immortal, will be found to have obtained his throne more nobly, more splendidly, or more piously" (*Evagoras* 39). Thus, in theory and in practice the formula "no one . . ." claims praise and honor for some unique quality or achievement. The doxology in 6:16 employs the same rhetorical formula to underscore that God is the unique superior to mortals, for not only is God inaccessible, but in fact "no one" has seen or can see God.

In conclusion, we have observed the traditional doxological form in 1:17 and 6:15-16. Although we have researched the background of names, titles, and predicates ascribed to God, as have commentators, our investigation did not merely present parallels, but tried to assess their meanings in terms of the rhetorical principle of uniqueness. This focus, then, highlights fresh aspects of the terminology in the doxology. First, we find two of the rhetorical tags for uniqueness in evidence: the term "only" or "alone" (μόνος) qualifying God and his attributes, and "no one" (οὐδείς) who is able to see the invisible God. Since the doxologies are monotheistic, it is not surprising that other tags of uniqueness are absent. For, if God is the "only" deity, then it makes no sense to claim that God is "first" or "most" (in comparison with other gods) or "one of a few." In addition to the rhetoric of uniqueness, we gave attention to the philosophers' defense of god that purified god-talk of anthropomorphisms. This resulted in emphasis on god's eternity, no beginning and no end; also, god could be talked about only in ways that declared that god is utterly different from mortals, hence the cascade of negative predication. But this development of negative predicates likewise honors god because it sets god apart from us, celebrates his superiority over us, and testifies to the inability of the human mind to grasp or circumscribe him. God, then, is one of a kind, unique, exclusive, superior, etc.

The "Only" God of 2 Maccabees 1:24-25

For purposes of illustration, we consider only the invocation of a petitionary prayer found in a document that definitely was composed by an Israelite for Israelites. It addresses God as follows: "O Lord, Lord God, creator of all things, you are awe-inspiring and strong and just and merciful, you alone (μόνος) are king and are kind, you alone (μόνος) are bountiful, you alone (μόνος) are just and almighty and eternal" (2 Macc 1:24-25). The most salient feature of this prayer is the celebration of God's uniqueness by thrice honoring the deity for being the *only* One who rules with mercy, benefaction, and power that never ends. On one hand, his uniqueness is because he *alone* among persons has such powers. Yet the benefactions by which God alone is praised are not unique, but expected of every wise and just king. Here God's uniqueness is not expressed by some philosophical or abstract concept, but is linked with relationships with those praying who are the favorite clients of God's benefaction.

Embedded in this prayer are two typical concepts of the God of Israel, his attributes and his powers. In addressing God as "just and merciful," the author draws upon the unique revelation to Moses in Exodus 34:6-7:

> a God merciful and gracious,
> slow to anger, . . .
> yet by no means clearing the guilty,
> but visiting the iniquity of the parents
> upon the children
> and the children's children.

These paired attributes of mercy and judgment are abundantly attested in the Hebrew Bible, the Christian Scriptures, and later Jewish writings. We chose this example because of its explicitness: "Moses began to argue about God's decisions, and to criticize His ways. . . . Therefore the Attribute of Justice sought to punish Moses, but when God reflected that it was because of Israel's distress that Moses spoke thus, God dealt with him according to his Attribute of Mercy" (*Exodus Rabbah* 6:1-4). The best commentary on this is another explicit citation: "God says, 'If you cleanse your deeds before me, then I will arise from the throne of Judgment, and sit upon the throne of Mercy, and have mercy upon you, and the attribute of Judgment shall be changed for you into the attribute of Mercy'" (*Pesiqta of*

Rab Kahana 154a). Behind this prayer, moreover, is the notion of God's two powers, creative and executive, which are expressed in the address to God as "Creator" and then as "King." God first creates, but then exercises a king's power over what he created.

Like the two attributes, the two powers are found extensively in Israelite and Christian literature. For example, "For you, the creator of all things ('creative power') . . . , are a just Ruler ('executive power'), and you judge those who have done anything in insolence and arrogance" (3 Macc 2:3). Paul speaks of Abraham's faith "in the presence of the God . . . who gives life to the dead and calls into existence the things that do not exist" (Rom 4:17). Philo is the best exponent of these two divine powers: "I should myself say that they [the Cherubim] are allegorically representations of the two most August and highest powers of Him, that is, the creative and the kingly. His creative potency is called God *(theos),* because through it He placed and made and ordered this universe, and the kingly is called Lord *(kyrios),* being that with which He governs what has come into being and rules it steadfastly with justice" (*On the Life of Moses* 2.99). The powers are unique to God; no earthly monarch could possibly claim them. Uniqueness also is expressed in the acknowledgment that the God of Israel is "eternal," that is, endures forever, without end, without death, and without corruption.

A Synagogal Prayer

A second example provides more substance to the claim that negative predication is a form of uniqueness. The following is a piece of a synagogal prayer in which God's uniqueness is first acclaimed ("the only Mighty One"; "there is no god beside you alone; / there is no Holy one beside you"), after which follows a cascade of negative predicates declaring how God is "honored and exalted exceedingly."

> There is no god beside you alone;
> there is no Holy one beside you. . . .
> You are honored and exalted exceedingly:
> invisible by nature,
> inscrutable in judgments,
> whose life is in want of nothing,

whose continuity is unchangeable and unceasing,
whose activity is untiring,
whose majesty is not circumscribed,
whose beauty is everflowing,
whose habitation is inaccessible,
whose encamping is unmoving,
whose knowledge is without beginning,
whose truth is unchangeable,
whose work is without mediation,
whose might is not liable to attack,
whose monarchy is without successor,
whose kingdom is without end,
whose strength is irresistible.[59]

In the invocation, God's uniqueness is expressed in two ways: twice in the formula that "there is no god beside you" and once in the declaration that God is "alone" in aiding those praying. The author then utilizes a cascade of negative predications to separate the one God from every other being or person. Certain patterns may be discerned in the negatives. God is above and beyond human abilities to know: "invisible," "inscrutable," and "inaccessible." Moreover, God's chief and unique attribute is eternity, which extends back: "without beginning" but which consists of being incapable of coming to an end: "unchangeable/unchanging," "unceasing," "untiring," "everflowing," "unmoving," and a sovereignty that admits of no successor. There are still other negatives that speak to power and rule: "might" that has no opponent and "strength" that is unassailable. All of these celebrate God's uniqueness because they declare him to be now and forever incalculably superior.

Summary, Conclusions, and Further Questions

Our survey of the principle of uniqueness surfaced many forms of it, first and foremost the formula "first, only, one of a few. . . ." In Greek hymns the most frequent element of this formula was "alone/only"; but also in evidence were negative predicates that exalted a god with prefixes such as

59. *Apostolic Constitutions* 7.35.9; the text and translation is that of Fiensy, *Prayers*, 70-71; see also Fiensy and Darnell, "Hellenistic Synagogal Prayers," 681-82.

"all-" (all-powerful) and suffixes of "-all" (master-of-all). Before documents such as 2 Maccabees, Israelite formulae of uniqueness generally celebrate incomparability: "there is no one like you," "who is like you?" and "no one can compare with you." Finally, Greek philosophical discourse refined a language of uniqueness characterized by negative predication, which emphatically insisted on the incomparable distance between immortals and mortals. Within this discovery of the principle of uniqueness, we have focused on a conscious and consistent rhetorical tradition from Aristotle down to Theon and Menander Rhetor about uniqueness as expressed in the formula "first, only, one of a few," the chief amplification of praise.

In regard to 1 Timothy, we saw in the two doxologies that the author employed most of the modes of proclaiming uniqueness in epideictic rhetoric. God is (1) the "only" (μόνος) deity (1:17) and the "only" (μόνος) sovereign (6:15), who "alone" (μόνος) has immortality (6:16), whom "no one" (οὐδείς) can see. In addition, God's uniqueness is also articulated in two other ways: (2) by the use of superlatives such as "King of kings and Lord of lords" (6:15) that exalt God above all other rulers and (3) by the use of negative predicates such as "immortal," "invisible," "unapproachable," and the like. Shall we call this "one of a kind"? Although the names confessed of God are not strictly shaped by the principle of uniqueness, the piling up of names, titles, and predicates points to the exclusive sense that God "most of all" rules the cosmos: "God of the ages," "Sovereign," "King," "Lord," and "God." We recall, moreover, that in the Orphic Hymns gods were often called "many-named" (πολυώνυμος).

Second, commentators rightly claim that the New Testament doxology is not a Greco-Roman form, but an Israelite one, dependent upon an archetype found in 1 Chronicles 29:11 LXX. In the case of 1 Timothy 1:17 and 6:15-16, while the form derives from Israelite/synagogue practice, many of the names and nearly all the negative predicates of God are distinctively Greco-Roman modes of god-talk. Thus, the hands are the hands of Esau, but the voice is the voice of Jacob. While the doxological form remains constant down into the time of Theophilus and Justin, the negative predicates for God in them represent the traditions prevalent in Greek philosophy.

Third, doxologies normally contain some form of "glory"/δόξα, but need not. Eric Werner remarked that "not every passage where there is an affirmation of God's glory can be termed a doxology."[60] Thus 2 Corinthians

---

60. Werner, "Doxology," 277.

1:20 is not a doxology, although it contains δόξα and is in praise of God. Yet 1 Timothy 6:16, which does not contain δόξα, is a true doxology. We find τιμή instead of δόξα, which terms we argued earlier to be virtual synonyms.[61] Doxologies, moreover, may ascribe to God glory and honor, as well as "eternal dominion" (1 Tim 6:16), "majesty, power, and authority" (Jude 25), and "glory, honor, power and greatness and eternal dominion" (1 Clem 65.2), all of which express various aspects of or synonyms of honor. Thus praise, honor, and glory are given to God, which helps us situate doxologies under the umbrella of epideictic rhetoric, the rhetoric of praise.

Fourth, several other avenues for observing the principle of uniqueness are opened by this investigation. Other names of God might be traced, names with some form of "all"/παντ-, such as "all-creating (παντοκτίστης) God" (Diogenes Laertius 7.2), "all-seeing (πανεπόπτης) God" (1 Clem 64.1), and "Father of all (παγγενέτωρ)" (Orphic Hymns 4.1).[62] Similarly, the name παντοκράτωρ, which became quite common in the LXX as the translation for צבאות,[63] is a regular name of praise for God in Revelation 1:8, 4:8, and 11:17, where it is linked with profession of God's uncreated and imperishable character. Moreover, Greek gods were often praised with some form of "much or many"/πολυ- such as "Physis, resourceful (πολυ-μήχανε) mother of all (παμ-μήτειρα) . . . rich (πολύ-κτιτε) divinity" (Orphic Hymns 10.1-2); "Aphrodite, praised in many hymns" (πολύ-υμνη) (55.1); and "(Physis) many named (πολυώνυμε)" (10.13).[64]

---

61. In many doxologies we can observe a piling up of doxological words that, while not exactly true synonyms of glory (δόξα), belong to the same cultural value of "honor":

Jude 25 ". . . glory, majesty, power, and authority"
1 Clem 64.2 ". . . glory, majesty, might and honor"
1 Clem 65.2 ". . . glory, honor, power, greatness and eternal dominion"
Apostolic Constitutions 8.15.9 ". . . glory, praise, magnificence, reverence, worship"
Apostolic Constitutions 8.41.5 ". . . glory, honor, reverence, thanksgiving, worship"

62. The Orphic Hymns contain several striking examples of this: "Divine Earth, mother of men and the blessed gods, you nourish all (παντρόφη), you give all (πανδώτειρα) . . . you destroy all (παντολέτειρα)" (26.1-2); and "highest of all (πανυπέρτατε), all eating (παμφάγε), all taming (πανδαμάτωρ), and all consuming (παντοδίαιτε)" (66.5). See also 12.6.

63. See W. Michaelis, "παντοκράτωρ," in TDNT 3:914-15; H. W. Pleket, "Religious History as the History of Mentality: The Believer as Servant of the Deity in the Greek World," in Faith, Hope, and Worship, 171-73.

64. Other references from the Orphic Hymns include: 11.10; 36.1; 40.1; 41.1; 42.2; 45.2;

Finally, other superlative nouns might be traced, such as "Most High," for which there is now Greco-Roman as well as Israelite evidence.[65] These express uniqueness by claiming that god or God has absolute sway or power, or "most of all," or as "one of a few." In Christian doxologies, the monotheistic core would claim for God total and complete sovereignty.

We conclude with one more illustration of the uniqueness of God by means of negative predication, only we note that the negative is balanced with the positive.

> Recognize now that there is one God
> ... the Invisible (ἀόρατος) who sees (ὁρᾷ) all things;
> the Incomprehensible (ἀχώρητος) who comprehends (χωρεῖ) all
>   things;
> the One who needs nothing (ἀνεπιδεής),
>   of whom all things stand in need (ἐπιδεῖται),
> the Uncreated (ἀποιητός), who made (ἐποίησεν) all things by the
>   word of his power.[66]

Finally, this study of a particular way of honoring and praising the deity goes a long way in supplementing the typical prayers of acknowledgment found in psalms and the like. Prayers of acknowledgment may be much more than statements addressed to God that confirm God's glory, majesty, honor, and power, which may well be hymns of praise to conquering emperors. Uniqueness might well be said to be the perfect way to honor God, for it utterly and completely separates God from the mortals who may themselves be unique in some way, but never in the way God is unique.

50.2; 52.1; 56.1; 59.2. Irenaeus argues that although God has many names ("The Lord of Powers, The Father of all, God Almighty, The Most High, The Creator, the Maker"), these do not indicate different beings, but the one God (*Against Heresies* 2.35.3).

65. For example, "the most high god," although found in Luke 1:32, 35, 76; 6:35; Heb 7:1; Acts 7:48, is also attested to in Greek papyri and inscriptions; see Llewellyn, "Dedications to 'The Most High God,'" *NDIEC* 1 (1981), 25-29; and Arthur Darby Nock, "The Guild of Zeus Hypsistos," in *Essays on Religion and the Ancient World* (Cambridge: Harvard University Press, 1972), 1:414-43.

66. This text, part of the *Kerygma tou Petrou*, is found in Michael Cambre, *Kerygma Petri. Textus et Commentarius* (Turnhout: Brepols, 2003), 151. The translation used here is taken from Hennecke's *NTA* 2.99. A useful parallel appears in Plutarch's *Dinner of the Seven Wise Men;* speaking of the sun, Anacharsis said: "he solely (μόνος) or pre-eminently (μάλιστα) of all the gods is free and independent, and rules over all and is ruled by none" (155A).

CHAPTER FIVE

Worship, in Other Words:
Appropriate Cultural Models

M ost biblical scholars interested in this topic tend to describe worship, not define it. They favor itemizing its elements rather than considering them in terms of some social or liturgical theory. Hence, inventory of individual items in worship takes precedence over interpretation. The particular contribution to the topic of worship and prayer of this chapter is to propose appropriate models for analyzing and interpreting the data. And in many cases the models will help us surface data not previously noticed. Since there is an ongoing conversation on the topic of worship, we do well to consider some of its notable voices. Henton Davies offers this definition of Old Testament worship: "Worship is homage . . . the attitude and activity designed to recognize and describe the worth of the person or thing to which homage is addressed. Worship is thus synonymous with the whole of a reverent life, embracing piety as well as liturgy. The range of meaning therefore is very great."[1] Three elements are worth our notice: (1) object of worship = a worthy figure; (2) purpose of worship = to honor the deity ("to recognize and describe the worth of . . ."); (3) forms of worship = reverent life, piety as well as liturgy. This definition emphasizes the value of honor and its manifestations, although this

---

1. G. Henton Davies, "Worship in the Old Testament," in *IDB* 4:879; the corresponding article by C. C. Richardson ("Worship in New Testament Times, Christian," in *IDB* 4:883-94) omits any definition, but focuses on the sources and development of worship. Similarly, David Aune ("Worship, Early Christian," in *ABD* 6:973-89) takes a phenomenological approach to various elements of worship, although he notes that "not all of these activities [i.e., the list he compiles] can be characterized as the worship of God, though all are part of the distinctive Christian conception of divine service" (973).

is not without its critics: "It is clear that the heathen conception of the honour of God differs entirely from that in Christian circles. Perhaps that is the reason why the NT speaks so little of the τιμᾶν θεόν [honoring of God]: it knows that such an expression often means only lip-service. The heathen 'honours' the gods by his religious acts in sacrifices and prayers: but what he does remains of man's doing; it is his work, his merit."[2] Henton's definition, for all its fine points, totally excludes any notion of worship as communication by the Worthy One to the worshipers. Nor does it take up issues such as where and how worship is offered, as well as any differentiation in the shape of piety and liturgy. There is, then, much more to be done in understanding worship. Interpretation of texts is impossible without it.

Scholarly surveys[3] of early Christian worship agree that: (1) the early church borrowed heavily from synagogue worship both in form and content, especially prayer and the study of the Scripture; (2) its activities were not tied to particular places, but could be practiced virtually anywhere; and (3) the central forms of worship were verbal.[4]

All scholars ground their descriptions of worship in New Testament documents, such as Acts 2:42 ("they devoted themselves to the apostles' teaching and fellowship, to the breaking of bread and the prayers"), the letters of Paul (1 Cor 11:20ff.; 14:1-36), Pliny's letter to Trajan (*Epistle* 10.96), and reconstructions of early synagogue worship.[5] David Aune too depends on Acts, but he provides the description best representing current thinking on New Testament worship. "Christian worship had a primarily verbal character, and in this respect it was similar to synagogue Judaism. . . . Yet Christians did have religious gatherings where various types of rituals were practiced. Christians gathered to eat together, to baptize new mem-

2. Gerhard Delling, *Worship in the New Testament* (London: Darton, Longman and Todd, 1962), 2-3.

3. The sources consulted are: Oscar Cullmann, *Early Christian Worship* (London: SCM, 1953); Richardson, "Worship in New Testament Times, Christian"; Delling, *Worship in the New Testament*; Ralph P. Martin, *Worship in the Early Church* (London: Marshall, Morgan and Scott, 1964); Ferdinand Hahn, *The Worship of the Early Church* (Philadelphia: Fortress, 1973); Aune, "Worship, Early Christian."

4. Early Christianity differed from worship in the Greco-Roman world, in that it had no temples, no cult statues, and no regular sacrifices. Thus Aune stated: "Christian worship had a primarily verbal character, and in this respect it was similar to synagogue Judaism" ("Worship, Early Christian," 973).

5. See Martin, *Worship,* 18-27.

Aune	Cullmann	Martin
1. prayers	1. prayers	1. prayers
2. creeds and confessions	2. confessional prayers	2. creeds and confessions
3. doxologies	3. doxologies	3. doxologies
4. hymns, songs, psalms	4. hymns, songs, psalms	4. hymns and songs
5. prophecy	5. prophecy	5. prophecy
6. sermons and homilies	6. teaching and preaching	6. teaching and preaching
7. public reading of the Scripture	—	7. public reading of the Scriptures

bers, to read Scripture, to listen to God speaking through other Christians, to experience healing, to pray and sing hymns and thanksgivings to God. These activities were not tied to particular places, but could be practiced virtually anywhere."[6] The synopsis above aims to make salient the typical verbal forms of worship. The verbal communication goes in two directions: (1) address to the deity (prayer, confession, doxology, hymns) and (2) the deity's communication to worshipers (prophecies, Scripture, homilies). Cullmann urges us to add one more item to the catalogue of verbal forms of worship, namely, the transmission of the Jesus tradition. "The proclamation of the message of salvation had a fixed place not only in the early missionary preaching, but also in the worship services of the community. Intimately associated with it particularly in the assemblies of the community is the transmission of Jesus' words and narratives concerning him."[7] But the shape of worship includes more than verbal forms. Rites of transformation and ceremonies occur as part of the time of worshiping, and so should be considered parts or aspects of it. Some rituals pertain to

6. Aune, "Worship, Early Christian," 973.
7. Cullmann, *Early Christian Worship*, 48-49.

entering and leaving the holy group, others to change of status, as when healing rituals occur or when members of the group are dedicated to special service. The premier ceremony, of course, is the eucharistic meal, which confirms the identity of those eating as members of the body of Christ, whose body and blood they share. The importance of this material for our project lies in having the most complete index of typical elements of worship as we begin our reading of the New Testament.

At this point we know several important things: (1) worship is "primarily *verbal*"; (2) members not only speak to God in prayer, but also listen to God through the Scriptures, the words of Jesus, and Spirit-inspired utterances; and (3) these activities are *not* tied to *particular places*. But what is meant by "worship"?

Worship Defined

Definitions of worship are rare; even many social science dictionaries and encyclopedias do not include one (although they attempt to define "religion"). Bruce Malina proposed the social science model of communication theory for defining prayer, which we will adjust so as to be adequate for a definition of worship. The communications theory was originally proposed by David Berlo,[8] mediated to us by Everett M. Rogers and F. Floyd Shoemaker, and adapted by Malina. Of significance is the fact that the communication flows in both directions: A to B and B to A.[9] Malina's definition of prayer (he was not writing on worship) covers the A-to-B aspect, which when amplified accounts as well for the B-to-A direction. "Prayer is a socially meaningful symbolic act of communication, bearing directly upon persons perceived as somehow supporting, maintaining, and controlling the order of existence of the one praying, and performed with the purpose of getting results from or in the interaction of communication. *Likewise the one who controls the order of existence communicates with his or her devotees with the purpose of getting results from or in the interaction of worship.*"[10] This model contains five elements: *(1) a sender,* who sends a *(2) message (3)* by

8. David K. Berlo, *The Process of Communication* (New York: Holt, Rinehart and Winston, 1960), 30-71.

9. Everett M. Rogers and F. Floyd Shoemaker, *Communication of Innovations: A Cross-Cultural Approach* (New York: Free Press, 1971), 11, 18-19, 251-52.

10. Bruce Malina, "What Is Prayer?" *TBT* 18, no. 4 (1980): 215, emphasis Malina's.

means of some *channel* (4) to a *receiver* (5) for the *purpose* of having *some effect*. Malina's model explains how in prayer (1) worshipers *(senders)* (2) send a communication *(message)* (3) in language, gesture, sacrifice, libations, and the like *(channel)* (4) to God, the object of worship *(receiver)*, (5) in order to have some effect on the deity *(purpose)*. Similarly in worship, when God speaks to worshipers, we observe (1) God *(sender)* (2) sending a communication *(message)*, (3) using certain mediating figures (Jesus, Spirit, prophets, etc., as *channels*), (4) to bring a word to worshipers *(receivers)* (5) for the *purpose* of having an *effect* (to bless, inform, exhort, etc.). The two directional flows of worship, then, look like this:

	Worship as speaking to God	Worship as listening to God
sender	mortals	God
message	petitions, confessions, etc.	information, exhortation, rebuke, etc.
channel	voiced prayer; incense burned; sacrifice offered	Jesus or Holy Spirit or prophet
receiver	God	Christian group
effect	see many types of prayers below = effect	reform of behavior; inform; confirm; exhort

The relationships in view here are those of a subordinate to a superior. In the context of worship the superior person is God, who "supports, maintains and controls the order of existence" of the one worshiping and is expected to respond to praises and petitions with patronal generosity.

Classifying Worship in Terms of Communication Theory

Mortals Speaking to God

Speakers (group members) speak either to God (prayer) or to each other (creeds and hymns about Jesus). Human communication to God includes

the types of prayers discussed in the first chapter. Among these we emphasize acknowledgments and praise in the form of doxologies, creeds, confessions, and hymns.[11]

Group members also speak to God through Jesus. In many places the
prayer of the group *to God* is directed *through the mediation of Jesus.*

> To the only wise God be glory for evermore *through Jesus Christ!* (Rom
> 16:27 RSV)

> To the only God our Savior, *through Jesus Christ our Lord,* be glory, maj-
> esty, power, and authority, before all time and now and forever. (Jude 25)

> Thanks be to God *through our Lord Jesus Christ.* (Rom 7:25)

> Thanks be to God, who gives us the victory *through our Lord Jesus
> Christ.* (1 Cor 15:57)

Again all prayer is directed to God, but in these instances the role of Jesus
is acknowledged as "mediator" (1 Tim 2:5) or "priest" (Heb 7:26) or "apostle," or broker.

EXCURSUS: PRAYING *THROUGH* JESUS

Origen, in his tractate *On Prayer,* is one of the few ancient writers to give explicit instructions on whom to pray to and whom to pray through. He begins
by stating his thesis: "We should not pray to anyone begotten, not even to
Christ himself, but only to the God and Father of us all, to whom even the Savior himself prayed and to whom he taught us to pray" (15.1). Origen goes on to
describe the role of Jesus that we are currently examining, mediator, broker,
priest: (Jesus speaking to the rich young man) "Why do you pray to me? You
should pray only to the Father, to whom I myself pray. This is what you learn
from the Holy Scriptures, for you must not pray *to* the High Priest appointed
on your behalf by the Father (cf. Heb 8:3) or *to* the Advocate who is charged by
the Father with praying for you (cf. 1 John 2:1). Rather you must pray *through*
the High Priest and the Advocate. . . . You must pray only to the Father with
me and through me" (15.4).

11. Aune, "Worship, Early Christian," 981-82; Delling, *Worship,* 55-61; Martin, *Worship,*
28-52.

We do not, however, consider statements made *about* Jesus or *to* Jesus to be "prayers" in the formal sense, because it is doubtful that any disciples yet acclaimed Jesus as "God" and so prayed to him. Rather, seated at God's right hand, he functions as God's broker and mediator. Hence, New Testament prayers and praises are always addressed to God but through Jesus Christ.

In the New Testament we find speech about God that seems addressed to God as well as to the group itself. "Creeds" and "confessions," which are voiced during group worship, make boundaries, such that they differentiate insiders from outsiders (turn from idols to serve a living and true God — 1 Thess 1:9) and maintain them by group recitation of the same belief ("if you confess with your lips that Jesus is Lord and believe in your heart that God raised him from the dead," Rom 10:9). Speech about God, then, may have two functions, worship of God and group socialization. For example,

> Yet for us there is one God, the Father, from whom are all things and for whom we exist, and one Lord, Jesus Christ, through whom are all things and through whom we exist. (1 Cor 8:6)

> For there is one God, and there is one mediator between God and men, the man Christ Jesus, who gave himself as a ransom for all. (1 Tim 2:5-6 RSV)

In both, the senders (the Jesus group) send a message *about* God (and Jesus) both to God and to the group as receivers. The effect they intend by this speech is confirmation and support for their membership based on shared articulation of these group-specific statements as well as praise and acknowledgment of God. We know of, moreover, confessional acknowledgments of Jesus that are spoken *about* him but not addressed *to* him: "Jesus is Lord" (1 Cor 12:3).

God Speaking to the Jesus Group

Included here are hearing the Scriptures, the story of Jesus' words and deeds, a homily, an exhortation, and prophetic oracles of many types.

1. *Hearing the Scriptures.* In the course of a worship service, worshipers are addressed by God in many ways. For example, in Luke-Acts we find several instances where the Hebrew Scriptures are tweaked to speak prophetically of Jesus. Jesus himself does this with the disciples on their way to

Emmaus: "Beginning with Moses and all the prophets, he interpreted to them the things about himself in all the scriptures" (Luke 24:27); and in the company of the disciples, he "opened their minds to understand the scriptures" (Luke 24:45). Similarly in the process of bringing the eunuch to enlightenment, Philip explained Isaiah 53 to him as a prophecy about Jesus (Acts 8:30-38). In a more generic way, Timothy is charged to read the Scriptures publicly: "Give attention to the public reading of scripture" (1 Tim 4:13). It seems quite likely that a prophet in the group might claim a "word of the Lord" and interpret the Scripture.

2. *Hearing the Words of Jesus.* Cullmann was surely correct that a worship meeting would contain some study of the memory of Jesus, either a retelling of his words or a narrative about his deeds. In time this Jesus material was available in written Gospels. To be sure, in the beginning was the sermon. What circulated? The Q material in its various stages was available to many, especially the groups that eventually produced the Gospels of Matthew and Luke. It has long been the task of Pauline scholars to identify sayings of Jesus in the writings of Paul.[12] On occasion Paul claims to have "a word of the Lord" as the basis for an exhortation about: divorce (1 Cor 7:10), support for apostles (1 Cor 9:14), the Eucharist (1 Cor 11:23), and the fate of those already dead. Similarly, many find allusions to Gospel traditions in certain Pauline remarks: (1) Romans 12:14 = Matthew 5:44, (2) Romans 12:17 = Matthew 5:39, (3) Romans 13:7 = Mark 12:13-17, (4) Romans 13:8-9 = Mark 12:28-34, (5) Romans 14:14 = Mark 7:15, and (6) 1 Corinthians 13:2 = Mark 11:23. All these "words of the Lord" and allusions seem not to stand independently on their own, but to be used as proof of certain arguments or the basis of certain exhortations.

3. *Hearing the Deeds of Jesus.* But what about the deeds of Jesus? Until the writing of the Gospels, have we any mention of Jesus' deeds and miracles? Paul wrote to the Corinthians a remark that was once thought to claim that he had knowledge of the historical Jesus: "From now on, therefore, we regard no one from a human point of view; even though we once knew Christ from a human point of view, we know him no longer in that way" (2 Cor 5:16). But we find the arguments advanced by John W. Fraser to be very persuasive. Paul refers to the time when he was an enemy of

---

12. For a minimalist view, see David Dungan, *The Sayings of Jesus in the Churches of Paul* (Philadelphia: Fortress, 1971); for a maximalist view, see David M. Stanley, "Pauline Allusions to the Sayings of Jesus," *CBQ* 23 (1961): 26-39.

Christ and his followers ("we once knew Christ from a human point of view").[13] That knowledge was a judgment that Jesus was an abomination in Israel, a corruption; he does not claim historical knowledge, but expresses a bias against Jesus. Paul, however, assuredly knows that Jesus died, was raised, and will return, but this again is hardly "knowledge" of his life and career. These he constantly refers to, either individually or in sequence. But nothing prior to his death.

4. *Hearing Jesus Honored.* In various letters we find "hymns" about Jesus, which seem to be sung or recited by the group and have the same purpose as prayers that praise, glorify, and honor God. These "hymns," moreover, all focus on the death and vindication of Jesus, the core items that, when celebrated, serve to confirm group unity. The synopsis on page 153 lacks any sophistication in that it does not consider the complex scholarly issues of background, form, provenance, and the like. The aim is simply to point out that the authors and reciters of these "hymns" resemble Paul in that they know nothing about Jesus but his death, vindication (and enthronement), and return. None of the documents that include these "hymns" about Jesus tells us anything about his career prior to his arrest and death. But they know the Christ kernel: Christ has died, Christ is risen, (Christ will come again). Knowing the kernel, each author articulates it in a strikingly different way. Indeed he "died," although some express this as obedience unto death or manifested in the flesh or put to death in the flesh; moreover, they interpret his resurrection in quite different ways. Jesus is exalted beyond any role or status he previously enjoyed; he was raised in the spirit and vindicated in it; ultimately he was taken up in glory and enthroned. But in essence, he died and was raised. These hymns are genuine praise of Jesus, but they are hardly addressed to him, much less honoring him for anything more than his mediation and brokerage.

5. *Homilies to the Holy Ones.* It seems to matter if a "homily" was delivered in a synagogue or in a Greco-Roman church. Homilies/sermons in Israelite contexts tend to be concerned with exegesis or legal precision over what is proscribed or allowed. Two types have been identified — the "proem" and the *yelammedenu.*[14] The proem form takes its name from

13. John W. Fraser, "Paul's Knowledge of Jesus: II Corinthians V.16 Once More," *NTS* 17 (1971): 293-313.

14. J. W. Bowker, "Speeches in Acts: A Study in Proem and Yelammedenu Form," *NTS*

Phil 2:5-11	1 Pet 3:18-22	1 Tim 3:16	2 Tim 2:11-12
Who, though he was in the form of God, did not regard equality with God as something to be exploited, but emptied himself, taking the form of a slave, being born in human likeness.	For Christ also suffered for sins once for all, the righteous for the unrighteous, in order to bring you to God.		If we have died with him . . .
And being found in human form, he humbled himself and became obedient to the point of death — even death on a cross.	He was put to death in the flesh,	He was revealed in flesh,	If we endure . . .
Therefore God also highly exalted him and gave him the name that is above every name, so that at the name of Jesus every knee should bend, in heaven and on earth and under the earth, and every tongue should confess that Jesus Christ is Lord, to the glory of God the Father.	but made alive in the spirit, in which also he went and made a proclamation to the spirits in prison, who has gone into heaven and is at the right hand of God, with angels, authorities, and powers subject to him.	vindicated by the Spirit, seen by angels, proclaimed among Gentiles, believed in throughout the world, taken up in glory.	we will also live with him; we will also reign with him.

14 (1967): 96-111; J. Heinemann, "The Proem in the Aggadic Midrashim: A Form-Critical Study," *Studia Hierosolymitana* 22 (1971): 100-200; and William R. Stegner, "The Ancient Jewish Synagogue Homily," in *Greco-Roman Literature and the New Testament*, ed. David E. Aune (Atlanta: Scholars, 1988), 51-70.

proemium, or introduction of the speech.[15] It introduced the synagogue Scripture readings, which consisted of a passage from the Torah and then the Prophets. The proem was a verse chosen by the speaker, which was not found in either reading; as such, it was not an exegesis or explanation of either of them. Rather, the preacher chose the proem to be remote from the readings, but by his pursuit of some inner connection between this verse and the Pentateuchal reading he might suggest explanations and clarifications of it so that when the reading was finally read, hearers would have a taste for it, a hint of its hidden meanings, and an intellectual satisfaction. The second form, the *yelammedenu,* takes its name from the introductory formula of many sermons found in a collection of them named the *Tanchuma.* Each sermon begins with "Let our rabbis teach us [about] . . . ," *yelammedenu,* which is followed by an answer introduced by "Thus our rabbis taught us. . . ."[16] In general it might be said that these synagogue homilies tend to be instructions, teachings, and interpretations. They have more the flavor of school teaching than of exhortation to virtue.

Outside of an Israelite milieu, we turn to consider homilies written in Greek for a Greco-Roman audience. We build on the works of Lawrence Wills and C. Clifton Black, who have provided a fresh measure of clarity about the form and content of ancient sermons/homilies. Wills surveyed many New Testament and early Christian speeches and concluded that a homily typically contained three elements: "1. An indicative or exemplary section (exempla) in the form of scriptural quotations, authoritative examples from past and present, or reasoned exposition of theological points; 2. a conclusion, based on the exempla and indicating their significance to those addressed (often expressed with a participle and οὖν, διό, διά, τοῦτο, or some such particle or conjunction); and 3. an exhortation (usually in the imperative or hortatory subjunctive, often accompanied by οὖν)."[17] In Wills's parade piece, Acts 13:14-41, Paul begins with a reprise of

15. Peder Borgen (*Bread from Heaven* [Leiden: Brill, 1965]) examined John 6:31-59 in this fashion. He identified a "text" ("He gave them bread from heaven to eat," Exod 16:4, 15), which the author of the Fourth Gospel subsequently reinterpreted word by word and phrase by phrase to show that this text applies to Jesus, not to Moses. While this is not quite the "proem" described in our exposition, it represents how a text of Scripture (even the Pentateuch) was Christofied.

16. It would be interesting to examine the times that Jesus is challenged for breaking with tradition after which he gives a justification for his actions: Mark 7:1-22 and 10:1-12.

17. Lawrence Wills, "The Form of the Sermon in Hellenistic Judaism and Early Chris-

salvation history from the exodus to the conquest to the good news about Jesus (13:16-33), and concludes with a citation of Scripture that is interpreted to refer to Jesus (death, no corruption, raised from the dead, 13:33-37). After this the speaker draws a conclusion as though he were finishing a syllogism: "Therefore . . . through this man forgiveness of sins is proclaimed to you; by this Jesus everyone who believes is set free from all those sins from which you could not be freed by the law of Moses" (13:38-39). This conclusion about Jesus' mediation implies that the hearers should ally themselves with Jesus to share in his mediation. After urging acceptance, the author exhorts the audience not to fail to act, lest the dire prophecy of Habakkuk 1:5 be fulfilled (13:40-41).

C. Clifton Black basically endorses Wills's study, but considers it in terms of the types of classical rhetoric, especially deliberative rhetoric.[18] Wills's notion of deliberative rhetoric was narrowly focused on "arguments of policy usually before a governing body," which Black expanded to embrace "speeches that entail consideration of future action, a choice between two or more forms of conduct, based on self-interest or future benefit."[19] He is on the cusp of describing many exhortations to choose good or avoid evil as "deliberative," for example, Peter's speech in Acts 2:38-39: "Repent, and be baptized every one of you in the name of Jesus Christ so that your sins may be forgiven; and you will receive the gift of the Holy Spirit. For the promise is for you, for your children, and for all who are far away, everyone whom the Lord our God calls to him." Black then examines Acts 13:14-41 not only as deliberative rhetoric, but also in terms of the traditional parts of a speech. There is no *captatio benevolentiae* here, no speaker's attempt to win the good will of the audience. But one does find a *narratio* in the detailed recitation of God's saving acts to Israel (13:16-26), a *propositio* (13:26), followed by a *probatio*, or demonstration (13:27-37). By this the author demonstrates that "the significance of Jesus, formerly ignored by the inhabitants of Jerusalem, has been vindicated by the resurrection and corroborated by the Scriptures."[20] The speech ends with a classic

---

tianity," *HTR* 77 (1984): 278-80; C. Clifton Black, "The Rhetorical Form of the Hellenistic Jewish and Early Christian Sermon: A Response to Lawrence Wills," *HTR* 81 (1988): 1-18. See also David E. Aune, "Homily," in his *The Westminster Dictionary of New Testament and Early Christian Literature and Rhetoric* (Louisville: Westminster John Knox, 2003), 219-21.

18. Black, "The Rhetorical Form," 5, 8-10.

19. Black, "The Rhetorical Form," 5.

20. Black, "The Rhetorical Form," 8-9.

conclusio, or epilogue (13:38-41), which traditionally recapitulates the major points of the speech and excites the emotions: (1) recapitulation of the basic argument (13:38-39) and (2) arousal of emotions (13:40-41).

6. *Exhortations* (λόγοι παρακλήσεως). Black's attention to deliberative rhetoric might help us understand parts of the New Testament letters. Paul exhorted his disciples to "lead a life worthy of God" (1 Thess 2:12) or "lead a life worthy of [your] calling" (Eph 4:1). In addition, large sections of Paul's letters begin with some form of exhortation:

Romans 12:1	I appeal to you (παρακαλῶ)
Ephesians 4:1	I beg you (παρακαλῶ)
1 Thessalonians 4:1	We ask and urge you (ἐρωτῶμεν παρακαλοῦμεν)
1 Timothy 2:1	I urge that (παρακαλῶ)

The content of this brief exhortation includes some of the following: (1) lists of virtues (Gal 5:22-24; Eph 4:2-3; 1 Cor 9–10) and vices (Gal 5:19-21; Eph 5:3-6), (2) description of the two ways (Gal 5:16-25), (3) codes of household duties (Eph 5:21–6:9; Col 3:18–4:1), (4) stress on avoiding a certain vice, either treated singularly or in contrast (see 1 Thess 4:3-11; 5:1-9; Rom 12:12-13; 13:8-10; 1 Cor 13). These exhortations encourage steadfastness, courage in the face of the enemy, even putting on spiritual armor (Eph 6:13-17). It is not so much a question that this is a separate form, which as such can be compared with Black's outline of a classical speech, nor an instruction such as found in Israelite synagogue sermons. But exhortations such as these would seem to be part of a worship service nevertheless. Did group members have such exhortations except when letters were read to them at a worship service? The material in these exhortations is generally considered very traditional, and so the exhortation is less about the audience making a deliberation whether to pursue virtue and flee vice and more about confirming the patterns of behavior that have always been part of their membership and socialization. But exhortation it is, deliberative rhetoric.

Therefore, the NT contains many data that exhort group members to pursue certain behavior and eschew its opposite. In what sense might we consider it vertical speech from God? Inasmuch as Paul, Timothy, and Titus claim heavenly authorization to do what they do, they function as mediators for God and Christ, which means that their homilies and exhortations are God's speech to the group. When Paul introduces himself in the letter's address, he often states his authority to speak.

Paul, a servant of Jesus Christ, called to be an apostle, set apart for the gospel of God. (Rom 1:1)

Paul, called to be an apostle of Christ Jesus by the will of God, and our brother Sosthenes. (1 Cor 1:1)

Paul an apostle — sent neither by human commission nor from human authorities, but through Jesus Christ and God the Father, who raised him from the dead. (Gal 1:1)

Paul, an apostle of Christ Jesus by the command of God our Savior and of Christ Jesus our hope. (1 Tim 1:1)[21]

At the very least, his role depends entirely on God's authorization. His words, then, are God's speech. This is never clearer than when Paul claims in Galatians that he is superior to the Twelve of the Pillars who have a mediated commission, that is, through Jesus; he, in contrast, was immediately "set apart" by God in a role that strikes the reader as that of a prophet. His gospel, then, came immediately from God and so he did not need any mortal to inform him.[22] We find a similar description of Timothy: third-generation believer (2 Tim 1:5), scion of Paul, set aside because of "prophetic utterances" that pointed to him (1 Tim 1:18), when the "council of elders laid their hands upon you" (1 Tim 4:14 RSV; 2 Tim 1:6). These data persuade us that Paul and Timothy claimed and would be perceived as being authorized by God; their exhortations, then, are speech from God.

For what were they authorized? Paul identifies "gospel" as the subject of his speech ("proclaim," 1 Cor 1:17; "[steward] of God's mysteries," 1 Cor 4:1; praise and blame, 1 Cor 11:2, 17). In general, he teaches, instructs, trains, reveals mysteries, and the like. But we saw above that he also exhorts, corrects, rebukes, and teaches discipline. Timothy is authorized for similar speaking duties: "Put these instructions before the brothers and sisters" (1 Tim 4:6); "Command and teach these things" (1 Tim 4:11 RSV); "Give attention to the public reading of scripture, to exhorting, to teaching" (1 Tim 4:13); "Teach and urge these duties" (1 Tim 6:2). As is Titus: "Teach what is

21. While not the remark of the letter's addressee, this self-description is worth noting: "For this gospel I was appointed a herald and an apostle and a teacher, and for this reason I suffer as I do" (2 Tim 1:11-12); see Eph 3:1-13.

22. Bruce J. Malina and Jerome H. Neyrey, *Portraits of Paul: An Archaeology of Ancient Personality* (Louisville: Westminster John Knox, 1996), 39-41.

consistent with sound doctrine" (Titus 2:1), and "Declare these things; exhort and reprove with all authority" (2:15). We may not be able to describe a homily or exhortation in Paul's letters, but there is no doubt that he and Timothy were authorized to speak to the household of God for various purposes: (1) teaching and instructing and (2) exhorting, praising, and blaming. God is speaking through them as prophets, apostles, and mediators to the group.

7. *Prophecy.* From consideration of 1 Thessalonians 5:19-20 and 1 Corinthians 14, we learn that prophecy was spoken during the group assembly. First, what are we talking about? We find quite adequate the definition of prophecy from the 1973 SBL Seminar on Prophecy: "The early Christian prophet was an immediately-inspired spokesperson for God, the risen Jesus, or the Spirit who received intelligible oracles that he or she felt impelled to deliver to the Christian community, or representing the community, to the general public."[23] Where might we find illustrations of this? Agabus, surely at a group meeting, "predicted by the Spirit that there would be a severe famine over all the world" (Acts 11:28), as a result of which support was collected from the daughter churches to aid the mother church in Jerusalem. Although we do not know what these female prophetesses communicated, Paul attempts to impose some control over their dress and behavior at a group meeting (1 Cor 11:2-16).[24] Moving out of those shadows, we inquire what "prophecies" we find in Paul's letters. Paul claims to have a "word of the Lord" that is pertinent to three different occasions: (1) a word of encouragement to those who grieve the dead (1 Thess 4:15-17); (2) a word of revelation about the metamorphosis of believers as prerequisite to enter God's presence (1 Cor 15:51-52); and (3) a mystery of the hardening of Israel (Rom 11:25-26).[25] But in light of this more generalized study of prophecy in Christian worship, it seems better to turn from generalities to consider the purposes of prophetic speech. A sender sends a message to a receiver *to have an effect.* What effect? At the conclusion of Aune's examination of prophecy, he provides just such a list of purposes:

23. M. Eugene Boring, "Prophecy (Early Christian)," in *ABD* 5:496.
24. See Antoinette C. Wire, *The Corinthian Women Prophets: A Reconstruction through Paul's Rhetoric* (Minneapolis: Fortress, 1990); David E. Aune, *Prophecy in Early Christianity and the Ancient Mediterranean World* (Grand Rapids: Eerdmans, 1983), 199-208.
25. Aune, *Prophecy in Early Christianity,* 248-62.

Basic Forms of Prophetic Speech

1. Oracles of Assurance (2 Cor 12:9; see Acts 18:9; 23:11; 27:23-24)
2. Prescriptive Oracles (Gal 5:21; 1 Thess 4:2-6; Acts 13:2; 21:4)
3. Announcements of Salvation (Rev 14:13; 19:9; 22:7)
4. Announcements of Judgment (1 Cor 5:3-5; 14:37-38; Acts 13:9-11; Matt 3:7-10)
5. Legitimation Oracles (1 Cor 12:3; Rev 1:8, 17-20)[26]

Both the instances of prophecy in Paul and the broad classification of prophecy in terms of its aim and function indicate that prophetic oracles were spoken at the group assembly. A prophet is a person *through* whom God speaks, thus the speech is the communication of God-sender to group-receivers.

We consider, then, certain judgments on individuals as status-transformation rituals that may even occur during a worship service. The excommunication of the man in the incestuous marriage in 1 Corinthians 5:3-5 and the process described in Matthew 18:15-17 are indeed judgment oracles, not directed to distant cities ("Woe to you, Chorazin! Woe to you, Bethsaida!"), but directed immediately to people who were thought to be insiders. Because these oracles of judgment describe an actual process with severe results, the process involved in them seems more dramatic and more powerful than Paul's pronouncements of "anathema" (1 Cor 12:3; 16:22; Gal 1:8-9).

Classifying Worship in Terms of Transformation Rituals and Ceremonies

Classification of the verbal elements of a worship service according to communication theory proved very useful in that we can now discriminate between speech to God (prayer) and speech from God. But we can also examine the parts of worship in another way, that is, in terms of their ritual effect. Some produce change and transformation and others, confirmation.

Those who study prayer and worship in the New Testament regularly use the term "ritual" to classify its pieces. This term means many things to

---

26. Aune, *Prophecy in Early Christianity,* 320-25.

many persons, but most see some consistent elements such as: (1) structured patterns of bodily behavior, (2) affirmation of community unity, and (3) means by which collective beliefs and ideals are simultaneously generated, experienced, and affirmed as real by the community. Three elements surface: patterned behavior, expressing community beliefs, and affirming group solidarity.

Victor Turner, however, made a distinction in classifying rituals by noting the following differences: "I consider the term 'ritual' to be more fittingly applied to forms of religious behavior associated with social transitions, while the term 'ceremony' has a closer bearing on religious behavior associated with religious states. . . . Ritual is transformative, ceremony confirmatory."[27] He reserves the term "ritual" for transformative transitions, and "ceremony" for states.

The following diagram compares and contrasts the elements of status transformations and ceremonies that confirm status.[28] It is offered here as a reminder of the fuller treatment of transformation rituals and ceremonies in the first chapter.

		Elements of a Ritual	*Elements of a Ceremony*
1.	frequency	irregular pauses	regular pauses
2.	schedule/calendar	unpredictable	predictable
3.	temporal focus	present-to-future	past-to-present
4.	presided over by	professionals	officials
5.	purpose	change: reversal	confirmation of roles
		degradation, elevation	in certain institutions

1. Frequency: Both rituals and ceremonies represent pauses in life's rhythms. Certain pauses occur irregularly (sickness, uncleanness), which we call rituals, that is, pauses that allow us to assume new and different roles and statuses. Other pauses, which occur routinely in our lives, we call ceremonies (meals, festivals). These do not effect change of role or status, but confirm it.

27. Victor Turner, *The Forest of Symbols: Aspects of Ndembu Ritual* (Ithaca, N.Y.: Cornell University Press, 1967), 95. See also Raymond Firth and John Skorupski, *Symbol and Theory: A Philosophical Study of Theories of Religion in Social Anthropology* (Cambridge: Cambridge University Press, 1976), 164.

28. Bruce J. Malina, *Christian Origins and Cultural Anthropology: Practical Models for Biblical Interpretation* (Atlanta: John Knox, 1986).

2. Schedule/Calendar: Ritual pauses occur unpredictably; we undergo them when necessary. No one plans to be ill or unclean; but when sickness or pollution occurs, rituals for changing from those states are handy. Some rituals are unrepeatable status changes, such as birth, coronation, death, and the like. On the other hand, ceremonial pauses occur on fixed calendar dates, such as Sabbath and Passover. We anticipate and plan for them.

3. Temporal Focus: Ritual pauses take us from present needs to the future, as we change our current status and assume a new role in the future. Ceremonies, however, look to the past and celebrate its influence on the present. Past roles and statuses continue to exist in the present and influence present social dynamics.

4. Presided Over By: Different kinds of people preside over rituals and ceremonies. Professionals (physicians, prophets) preside over or direct status-transformation rituals. These are the "limit breakers" whom society allows to deal with marginal people as they cross fixed social lines. Officials (father at Passover meals, temple priests) preside over or direct the appropriate ceremonies in their institutions.

5. Purpose: Ceremonies leave in place the lines of the maps of society, because they function to confirm the values and structures of society and to celebrate the orderly classification of persons, places, and things in the cosmos. For example, birthdays, anniversaries, pilgrimage feasts, and the like confirm the roles and statuses of individuals in the group as well as the group's collective sense of holy space and holy time that pertains to its festivals. Ceremonies look to the stability of the lines of society's maps. Conversely, rituals attend precisely to those lines but focus on their crossing. Rituals are stable ways of dealing with necessary instability in the system: a boy and a girl cross lines to become husband and wife in a marriage ritual; sick people cross lines and become healthy (Lev 14; Mark 1:44); sinners become purified (Luke 18:13-14). The converse is also true: a seemingly innocent person may become guilty through a ritual trial. The status of those who cross lines is thereby changed, and so these rites are called "status transformation" rituals. If ceremonies look to the center of the map and the stable lines that make up the map, rituals look to the map's boundaries. These should be stable, but may be legitimately or fraudulently crossed.

Transformational rituals include baptism/entrance rite, birth, marriage, excommunication, and death. Ceremonies, on the other hand, are foot washing, meals, greeting with a holy kiss, collection for the poor, exercise of spiritual gifts, feasts (Passover). In chapter 2 we used these categories of transformation and ceremony to classify the types of prayers we were discussing. Because it fits into the present discourse on worship, we repeat it here.

Type of Prayer	Status Transformation or Ceremony	Distinguishing Aim
1. instrumental	status transformation	petition for what is lacking
2. interactional	status transformation	petition for revivification of relationship
3. self-focused	ceremony	contentment with current status
4. heuristic	status transformation	petition for information which is currently lacking
5. imaginative	ceremony	contentment in relationship
6. acknowledgment	ceremony	contentment in relationship
7. appreciation	ceremony	contentment in relationship

Self-focused, imaginative acknowledgment, and appreciation prayers are all ceremonies because they occur in the course of group ritual, are planned for (first day of the week; feast), recall experience in the past that is brought forward for celebration. The purpose of these types of prayers is to confirm the relationship of those praying and God. Inasmuch as most prayer was done in common and during the worship service, not only do these types of prayers confirm relationship with God but they also maintain membership in the Jesus group. Three types of prayers, however, are transformational rituals because they petition God for something that is lacking that will change current inadequate status.

This same classification of rituals and ceremonies can be applied with insight to the various elements of worship studied above.

Rituals and Other Aspects of Worship

1. prophecy	1. ceremony: confirming prophet's role as subbroker and group's role as Christian group favored by God and Christ
2. homily, sermon	2. status-transformation ritual: if it is a call to decision making (Black, Wills), repentance; ceremony: if it is an exhortation to keep on observing group's norms
3. hearing Scripture read (Luke 4:18)	3. ceremony: group confirmed as members by hearing their story
4. hearing the words of Jesus and his stories once more	4. ceremony: hearers confirmed as disciples: these are the sheep who hear the shepherd's voice
5. judgment (1 Cor 5; Matt 18:15-17)	5. status-degradation ritual: members lose honor in the group and are even expelled from it
6. agape meal and/or Eucharist	6. ceremony: membership in the group confirmed by shared sacred food and shared sacred talk
7. laying on of hands/ healing (James 5:14-16)	7. status-elevation ritual: (a) sick person moves from illness to healing and wholeness; (b) ordinary member set aside for sacred duties
8. baptism of new members	8. status-elevation ritual: a person is now "born again" and has "put on Christ"

Communication Theory and Status-Transformation Rituals and Ceremonies

The rituals of status transformation and ceremony should also be understood in terms of communication theory. Baptism, for example, expresses God's benefaction by making of the initiand a new creation, a member of the house of Abraham, and an imitator of the dying and rising of Jesus. Baptism "in the name" of the Father and of the Son and of the Holy Spirit means that God takes possession of the initiands or adopts them. Hence Paul can describe the transformation of baptism in this vein: "And because you are children, God has sent the Spirit of his Son into our hearts, crying, 'Abba! Father!' So you are no longer a slave but a child, and if a child then also an heir, through God" (Gal 4:6-7). It might be said that the initiands pray and fast so that their sins be washed away, which prayer is answered by the blessing of God and which dedicates them to the praise of God in God's family. In short, whatever is thought about the liminal process of the initiands and their status-transformation ritual, much more needs to be said about God's role in blessing the initiands and favoring them with kinship with Abraham and Jesus.

The Eucharist, too, benefits from being seen in terms of communication theory. These remarks are based on the description of the Eucharist in *Didache* 9–10 and Justin's *First Apology* 65–66, documents that will be examined later in this book. The official presiding at the Eucharist holds bread and wine that he dedicates to God, either by "blessing" or by "giving appreciation." This gesture we consider a prayer of acknowledgment and appreciation, in fact, even a "sacrifice," in that some inducement is offered to God. Here we observe two types of prayers being prayed:

acknowledgment

Didache 9.2, 3; 10.2, 4 "To you be glory forever"; 10.6 "Hosanna to the God of David"
First Apology, 65.4 ". . . praise and glory to the Father"

appreciation (forms of εὐχαριστέω)

Didache 9.2, 3; 10.2, 4 "We thank thee, our Father, for the holy vine of David. . . . We thank Thee, our Father. . . ."
First Apology 65.4 "He offers thanks at considerable length"; 65.5 "When he has concluded the prayers and thanksgivings . . ."; 65.7 "When the president has given thanks. . . ."

Thus, the group seeks to communicate with God both by its offering of bread and wine and by prayers of praise and gratitude.

God's communication in the Eucharist consists in accepting the praise and gratitude of the group and in transforming the bread and wine into a food that God returns to the group for nourishment. Justin's *First Apology* talks about this transformation: "We have been taught that the food which is blessed by the prayer of His word, and from which our blood and flesh by transmutation are nourished, is the flesh and blood of that Jesus who was made flesh" (66.2). Thus, even as God accepts our "sacrifice of praise," God returns that gift to us, but transformed into the food of eternal life. Thus both baptismal transformation and Eucharist contain communication from mortals to God (prayer), but especially communication from God as prayers are heard and benefaction is given.

What Do We Know If We Know This?

We have an adequate model of worship, primarily based on what the experts tell us goes on in the process of communication: X speaks to Y, Y speaks to X. Our model fully accounts for prayer, the communication of mortals to the Immortal One; and it itemizes ways in which the Immortal One communicates with mortals. God's speech may be heard in the Scriptures, the words and deeds of Jesus, homilies, and various kinds of oracles. Worship, moreover, expresses the communication of a group of Christian disciples with God. And so, we should note rituals that facilitate entrance to the group, ceremonies that confirm its identity, and if needed, exit rituals.

The model of worship-as-communication has many advantages to it that a descriptive approach does not have. It can distinguish more types of prayers than the common "petition and praise." And in doing so, it surfaces data that often is not seen, much less understood. Moreover, it provides the glue that holds the parts together and that provides the integration of the pieces. The other models, such as rituals of transformation and ceremonies, serve to clarify the dynamic of listening to the Scripture and breaking bread and hearing oracles of many kinds.

The proof of the pudding is in the eating. In this book we are reading documents in which we find elements of worship. Indeed, without some prior acquaintance with worship (ancient or contemporary) we would be hard pressed to itemize and systematize elements of worship. In fact, the next chapter will put this template of worship-as-communication over John 14–17, not the most obvious place to expect a full presentation of worship. Readers, therefore, are urged to return to their own worship services as performed and experienced on Sunday. This event is indubitably "worship," but how rich an experience it would be for readers to label the parts of worship as we have done here, to attend to the variety of prayers expressed from opening hymn to closing hymn. What ceremonies occur? What or whom do they confirm? Is the collection a ritual action? Is the bulletin distributed also a part of worship?

CHAPTER SIX

Worship in the Fourth Gospel:
A Cultural Interpretation of John 14–17

Introduction, State of the Question, and Hypothesis

As the title indicates, this chapter employs the model of worship developed previously as the lens through which we proposed to read and interpret worship in the Fourth Gospel, in particular John 14–17. To be sure, discussions of worship in the Fourth Gospel are rare,[1] and in most commentaries worship does not even rate a place in the topical index. Yet the author of the Gospel formally attends to matters of worship when he himself raises certain topics: (1) *where* to worship, (2) *how* to worship, (3) *of what* worship consists, (4) *when* to worship, and (5) *who* participates in worship.

Where?

At Jesus' inaugural visit to Jerusalem's temple, he upsets its sacrificial worship system (he drives the sheep and oxen out of the temple) and its revenue collection. In defense, he declares: "Destroy this temple, and in three days I will raise it up" (2:19), which his opponents misunderstand, for they think he is referring to a physical building, another fixed sacred space. The

1. Oscar Cullmann (*Early Christian Worship* [London: SCM, 1953]) describes "basic characteristics of the early Christian worship service" in a quarter of his book, and then with a sacramental focus treats the various episodes in the Fourth Gospel that have to do with water/baptism, bread/Eucharist, Sabbath, and temple. On occasion one finds a treatment of worship in the Fourth Gospel as part of a larger work, for example, David E. Aune, *The Cultic Setting of Realized Eschatology in Early Christianity* (Leiden: Brill, 1972), 45-135.

truth is, "He was speaking of the temple of his body" (2:21). The Samaritan woman asked Jesus-the-prophet to settle a dispute about *where* to worship, "on this mountain" or "in Jerusalem" (4:20). Jesus gives a sweeping answer: "neither on this mountain nor in Jerusalem" (4:21). Thus Jesus broadly negates all fixed places of worship. Finally, Jesus declares that "in my Father's house there are many dwelling places. . . . I go to prepare a place for you" (14:2). On the one hand, these locations ("house," "dwelling places," "place") suggest a "where" for worship, but they do not refer to any fixed sacred space. James McCaffrey argues that we not consider these as geographical spaces: "The text describes the redemptive work of Christ in terms which pertain to the family and its intimate personal relationships."[2] Thus *where* one worships remains throughout the Gospel a major question, for which we need a model of fixed and sacred space from cultural anthropology.

How?

True worshipers will perform actions that do not consist of sacrifice or require temple clergy, tithes, and revenues. Neither will they worship in fixed sacred space, nor in the manner of the temple. At least this seems to be the substance of Jesus' remark: "true worshipers will worship the Father in spirit and truth" (4:23).[3] This remark, however, is mute on specific forms of worship. As so much attention is given to prayer(s) in John 14–17, prayer would seem to be a most promising place to start.

When?

Although Jesus attended certain feast days in Jerusalem, scholars argue that he replaced with himself both the feasts and the benefits sought from them. Jesus is now the benefit of benefits sought at festive worship: he is the bread come down from heaven (6:33-51), the Passover lamb

---

2. James McCaffrey, *The House with Many Rooms: The Temple Theme of Jn. 14,2-3* (Rome: Pontifical Biblical Institute, 1988), 21.

3. For example, Herman Ridderbos, *The Gospel according to John* (Grand Rapids: Eerdmans, 1997), 163.

(19:33-34), the rains/water (7:37-38), and the sun/light (8:12) sought at tabernacles. But where is the evidence that Johannine disciples kept a calendar of this sort? Balancing these replacements, we learn that special significance was given to the "first day of the week" (20:1) and the "eighth day" (see 20:26 RSV).

Who?

Worship, of course, is directed to God. And God, who is spirit, seeks worshipers who worship in spirit and truth. Clearly, then, both God and a worshiping group are envisioned. But other figures function in this worship: Jesus, in whose name the disciples petition God and the Paraclete, who mediates Jesus' words to the group. But those who refuse to or are afraid to acknowledge Jesus as sent from God are not true worshipers (17:3). But is there any formal pattern to relationship of those who worship?

What, then, do we know? Oddly, we know *where not* to worship, *how not* to worship, and perhaps *when not* to worship. But the Gospel does not tell us of what worship consists, nor does it define roles and statuses of members of the worshiping group. Much more needs to be learned about worship so as to interpret the Fourth Gospel. (1) Our task begins with "worship" itself. While descriptive catalogues of early Christian "worship" are helpful, we search for a formal definition of it and a social science model that will help us interpret its forms. From this perspective, we will interpret four forms of worship: prayer, prophecy, homily, judgment. (2) Since the author puts so much emphasis on *where* the group worships, we need a model that compares and contrasts fixed and fluid sacred spaces. This will aid us in interpreting Jesus' remarks about "my Father's house" and "many dwelling places" (μοναί, 14:2). And in this light we will examine other aspects of *where* worship occurs: "being in" and "dwelling in." (3) Finally, in attempting to understand the structural relationships between God, Jesus, Spirit, and the group in worship, we turn to the model of patron-broker-client. The roles of God and group are clear, but modern scholarship often misunderstands the structural place of Jesus and the Paraclete in Johannine worship.

Worship in the Early Church

As we saw earlier, scholarly surveys[4] of early Christian worship agree that: (1) the early church borrowed heavily from synagogue worship both in form and contents, especially prayer and the study of the Scripture; (2) its activities were not tied to particular places, but could be practiced virtually anywhere; and (3) the central forms of worship were verbal.[5] Because of its comprehensiveness, David Aune's description is worth repeating: "Christian worship had a primarily verbal character, and in this respect it was similar to synagogue Judaism. . . . Yet Christians did have religious gatherings where various types of rituals were practiced. Christians gathered to eat together, to baptize new members, to read Scripture, to listen to God speaking through other Christians, to experience healing, to pray and sing hymns and thanksgivings to God. These activities were not tied to particular places, but could be practiced virtually anywhere."[6] Aune, following Delling, Cullmann, and Martin, identifies a variety of activities that fall under the genus "worship": (1) prayers, creeds and confessions, doxologies, hymns, songs, and psalms; (2) prophecy (oracles of judgment, salvation, and the like); (3) sermons and homilies; and (4) public reading of Scripture. To this Cullmann adds another, remembering specifically the words and deeds of Jesus. The archetype of worship in the New Testament was and is the remarks found in Acts 2:42 ("they devoted themselves to the apostles' teaching and fellowship, to the breaking of bread and the prayers"), the letters of Paul (i.e., 1 Cor 11:20ff.; 14:1-36), Pliny's letter to Trajan (*Epistle* 10.96), and reconstructions of early synagogue worship.[7] Aune's first element of worship is "prayer," which seems more fixated on forms of prayer than on classification of prayer according to the eight or so purposes of speech to God. More attention, we think, should be given to

---

4. The sources consulted are: Cullmann, *Early Christian Worship;* C. C. Richardson, "Worship in New Testament Times, Christian," in *IDB* 4:883-94; Gerhard Delling, *Worship in the New Testament* (London: Darton, Longman and Todd, 1962); Ralph P. Martin, *Worship in the Early Church* (London: Marshall, Morgan and Scott, 1964); Ferdinand Hahn, *The Worship of the Early Church* (Philadelphia: Fortress, 1973); David E. Aune, "Worship, Early Christian," in *ABD* 6:973-89.

5. Early Christianity differed from worship in the Greco-Roman world, in that it had no temples, no cult statues, and no regular sacrifices.

6. Aune, "Worship, Early Christian," 973.

7. See Martin, *Worship,* 18-27.

the variety of reasons for which one prays, the effect one wishes to have on God, and the relationship that should be repaired. This description, while it identifies an entrance ritual, baptism, does not include rituals of transformation or exit rituals. Ceremonial eating together is noted, but is there place for other ceremonies? The model of worship presented earlier indeed fills out the enumeration of the forms of worship, even as it provides a definition of prayer and worship and appropriate cultural lenses for viewing their parts. Thus the complete model of worship we are employing provides us the most complete index of typical verbal forms of worship as we begin our reading of John 14–17. Thus, we begin knowing several important things: (1) worship is "primarily *verbal*"; (2) members "pray and sing hymns and thanksgivings"; (3) they not only speak to God in prayer, but also *listen to God* through the Scriptures, the words of Jesus, and Spirit-inspired utterances; and (4) these activities are *not* tied to *particular places*.

Worship in John 14–17

Most readers are comfortable with understanding John 14–17 in terms of its form-critical classification as a farewell address.[8] The various prayers of Jesus and especially the so-called high priestly prayer in John 17 suggest that "worship" is not a misleading category for interpreting John 14–17. We propose to examine these chapters in terms of the two directions of worship described above: (1) speaking to God (i.e., prayers) and (2) listening to God (i.e., prophecy, homily, and oracles of salvation and judgment).

Types of Prayers in John 14–17[9]

Malina, as we have learned, provides readers with a sophisticated typology of prayers. All prayer is a communication of mortals to God, but prayers differ in the effect they seek to have with God, ranging from petition to

8. Fernando Segovia (*The Farewell of the Word* [Minneapolis: Fortress, 1991], 5) provides the most complete and exhaustive treatment of this material both in his text and in note 2.

9. Bruce Malina, "What Is Prayer?" *TBT* 18, no. 4 (1980): 214-20; and Bruce J. Malina and Richard L. Rohrbaugh, *Social-Science Commentary on the Gospel of John* (Minneapolis: Fortress, 1998), 246-47.

praise: (1) petitionary, (2) regulatory, (3) interactional, (4) self-focused, (5) heuristic, (6) imaginative, (7) acknowledgment, and (8) appreciation.

Petitionary Prayer in John 14–16

No one can read John 14–17 without noting Jesus' repetitive instructions to "ask" the Father for some benefit, which in the typology we are using means petitionary prayer. The New Testament employs a variety of verbs in the context of prayerful petitioning. In one sense they all mean "to ask for," but they differ in the urgency with which the request is made. Most frequently readers find petitionary requests expressed in δέομαι ("ask with urgency," "beg") and προσεύχομαι ("speak to," "make requests"). John's petitions, however, are expressed by different words, αἰτέω ("ask with urgency, even to the point of demanding") and ἐρωτάω ("ask," "request"), but without any change of meaning. Except for Martha's remark that Jesus could petition God for Lazarus (11:22), the other eleven instances of petitionary prayer all occur in the Farewell Address; they thus constitute a distinct body of material on this type of prayer.

14:13-14	"I will do whatever you *ask* in my name. . . . If in my name you *ask* me for anything . . ."
14:15-16	"I will *ask* the Father, and he will give you another Advocate."
15:7	"If you abide in me, and my words abide in you, *ask* for whatever you wish. . . ."
15:16b	"The Father will give you whatever you *ask* him in my name."
16:23-24	"On that day you will *ask* nothing of me. . . . If you *ask* anything of the Father . . ."
16:26	"On that day you will *ask* in my name."

In addition to the insistent instructions of Jesus, we note several things: (1) the object of the petitions is both vastly expansive ("whatever" and "anything") and specific ("Advocate"); and (2) while the patron being petitioned is always God, Jesus maintains his role as broker by indicating that the petitions will be made "in my name" and he himself will initiate the process by petitioning on pray-ers' behalf ("I will ask . . ."). Petitionary prayer, moreover, is only one type of prayer found in John 14–16. When we turn to John 17, we observe a prayer composed of many types.

Jesus' Multipurposed Prayer in John 17

Malina's taxonomy of prayer provides the means to distinguish different types of prayers occurring in John 17. In general, we consider the whole of John 17 as a *heuristic* prayer: it explores the world of God and God's workings within the Son and his disciples, individually and collectively.[10] It is not a search for meaning so much as a revelation of the state of the relationship of the pray-er and God. Thus it is heuristic in that it discovers and uncovers interpersonal perspectives implicit in all the actions culminating in Jesus' "hour." Yet this heuristic prayer is by no means the only kind of prayer in John 17. We can classify the statements of Jesus to God as petitionary, self-focused, and informative, as the chart below indicates.[11]

John 17	Prayer Text	Classification
v 1	Glorify your Son so that the Son may glorify you.	petitionary
v 3	This is eternal life, that they may (ac)know(ledge) you, the only true God, and Jesus Christ whom you have sent.	acknowledgment
v 5	Glorify me in your own presence with the glory that I had in your presence before the world existed.	petitionary
v 6	I have made your name known to those whom you gave me from the world.	self-focused

10. See Malina and Rohrbaugh, *Social-Science Commentary,* esp. 244-48.

11. It is a commonplace among commentators to divide John 17 into three sections: vv 1-8 = Jesus' prayer for himself; vv 9-19 = Jesus' prayer for his disciples; and vv 20-26 = Jesus' prayer for those his disciples will recruit. See Raymond Brown, *The Gospel according to John* (Garden City, N.Y.: Doubleday, 1966), 748-51; and with minor variations, see Charles H. Talbert, *Reading John: A Literary and Theological Commentary on the Fourth Gospel and the Johannine Epistles,* rev. ed. (Macon, Ga.: Smyth and Helwys, 2005), 224-31. As accurate as this literary division may be, it obscures the different types of prayers that occur throughout 17:1-26. Hence a different kind of model is needed that can do just this.

vv 6-8	They were yours, and you gave them to me, and they have kept your word. Now they know that everything you have given me is from you; for the words that you gave to me I have given to them, and they have received them and know in truth that I came from you; and they have believed that you sent me.	self-focused
v 9	I am asking on their behalf; I am not asking on behalf of the world, but on behalf of those whom you gave me, because they are yours.	self-focused + petitionary
v 10	All mine are yours, and yours are mine; and I have been glorified in them.	self-focused
v 11	Protect them in your name that you have given to me, so that they may be one, as we are one.	petitionary
v 12	While I was with them, I protected them in your name that you have given me. I guarded them, and not one of them was lost but the one destined to be lost.	self-focused
vv 13-14	But now I am coming to you, and I speak these things in the world so that they may have my joy made complete in themselves. I have given them your word, and the world has hated them because they do not belong to the world, just as I do not belong to the world.	self-focused
v 15	I am not asking you to take them out of the world, but I ask you to protect them from the evil one.	petitionary
v 16	They do not belong to the world, just as I do not belong to the world.	self-focused
v 17	Sanctify them in the truth.	petitionary
vv 18-19	As you have sent me into the world, so I have sent them into the world. And for their sakes I sanctify myself, that they also may be sanctified in truth.	self-focused

vv 20-21	I ask not only on behalf of these, but also on behalf of those who will believe in me through their word, that they may all be one. As you, Father, are in me and I am in you, may they also be in us, so that the world may believe that you have sent me.	self-focused + petitionary
vv 22-23	The glory that you have given me I have given them, so that they may be one, as we are one, I in them and you in me, that they may become completely one, so that the world may know that you have sent me and have loved them even as you have loved me.	self-focused
v 24	Father, I desire that those also, whom you have given me, may be with me where I am, to see my glory, which you have given me because you loved me before the foundation of the world.	petitionary
vv 25-26	Righteous Father, the world does not know you, but I know you; and these know that you have sent me. I made your name known to them, and I will make it known, so that the love with which you have loved me may be in them, and I in them.	self-focused

We observe that Jesus *petitions* God frequently (vv 2, 5, 11, 15-16, 17, 20-21, 24), the form of which is easily discerned: (1) a verb of "asking" in the imperative mood, and (2) a request for a specific benefaction from God (glory, unity, special relationship, etc.). We see, moreover, another type of prayer, which Malina calls "self-focused" (vv 6-8, 9, 10, 12, 13-14, 16, 18-19, 20, 22-23, 25-26),[12] whose form is also clearly expressed by: (1) a first-person speech: "I made manifest" . . . "I kept them in your name" . . . "I have given them your word" (versus second person in petitionary prayer), which (2) celebrates the record of Jesus' past good deeds (versus future benefactions in petitionary prayer). In John 17 Jesus tells God that he has fulfilled his apostleship and done what God sent him to do:

12. Readers are reminded of the full treatment of "self-focused" prayer in the first chapter.

- I glorified you on earth (v 4).
- I have made known your name (vv 6 and 26).
- I have given them the words you have given me (vv 8 and 14).
- I have kept them in your name (12a).
- I have guarded them (12b).
- I have sent them into the world (18).
- I have sanctified myself (19).
- I have given them the glory you have given me (22).
- I have "known" you (25).

Unlike petitionary prayer, Jesus declares to God before his disciples his perfect fulfillment of the mission he was sent to accomplish:[13] he has (1) *glorified* God on earth, (2) *manifested* to the disciples the divine *name* and kept them in it, (3) *given* the divine *words* to them, and (4) *extended* his work by sending them into the world.[14]

Labeling John 17 as "high priestly" is clearly anachronistic, although the label does convey the sense that Jesus enjoys the role of mediator or broker, a topic to be developed shortly.[15] Similarly, the prayer celebrates his effectiveness in the role of channel of God's benefaction to the disciples. Benefits came through Jesus and will continue to come through him. Jesus' self-focused prayer may also be seen as a claim to the virtue of piety or justice. Throughout the Greco-Roman world, justice was thought of as the noble fulfillment of one's basic duties. Pseudo-Aristotle states: "First among the claims of righteousness are our duties to the gods, then our duties to the spirits, then those to country and parents, then those to the departed; among these claims is piety (εὐσέβεια), which is either a part of

13. It has long been a staple of commentaries on John 17 to compare and contrast it with the Our Father found in the Synoptics. See William O. Walker, "The Lord's Prayer in Matthew and John," *NTS* 28 (1982): 237-56.

14. Although he seems to consider "prayer" only as "petitionary" speech, Ernst Käsemann (*The Testament of Jesus: A Study of John in the Light of Chapter 17* [London: SCM, 1968], 5) commented on the variety of Jesus' speech in John 17. Yet he writes: "This is not a supplication, but a proclamation directed to the Father in such manner that his disciples can hear it also. The speaker is not a needy petitioner but the divine revealer and therefore the prayer moves over into being an address, admonition, consolation and prophecy."

15. Raymond Brown (*Gospel according to John*, 747) said: "If Jesus is a high priest here, it is not primarily in the sense of one about to offer sacrifice, but more along the lines of the high priest described in Hebrews and in Rom viii 34 — one who stands before the throne of God making intercession for us."

righteousness or a concomitant of it. Righteousness is also accompanied by holiness (πίστις) and truth (ὁσιότης) and loyalty (ἀλήθεια) and hatred of wickedness" (*Virtues and Vices* 5.2-3). The distinction of the triple focus of justice is found regularly in the philosophical and rhetorical literature of antiquity,[16] and also in John 17. Here Jesus acknowledges that he has fulfilled his *duties to God* ("I glorified you . . . made your name known . . . [gave] them your word") and his *duties to "kin"* ("I have protected them . . . guarded them," etc.).[17] Thus the Just Jesus celebrates his virtuous completion of the duties he owes to God, who is Father and Patron and "kin."

Yet in 17:3 we find still a third type of prayer, namely, "acknowledgment": "This is eternal life, that they may know you, the only true God, and Jesus Christ whom you have sent." Instead of a petition, we find here an honorable acknowledgment of God in traditional words. This prayer consists of two elements: (1) we read "to know" in the sense of "to acknowledge," that is, to confess the worth, honor, sovereignty, and excellence of God.[18] The first part of 17:3 resembles the confession known as the Shema, the leading prayer in the synagogue (see Mark 12:29, 32; Deut 6:4). Thus acknowledgment of the "only true God" is an appropriate confessional honoring of God. But 17:3 also includes (2) confession of "Jesus Christ whom you have sent." So the complete honoring of God consists of the acknowledgment of both the unique God of Israel and God's unique

16. Other samples of this include *Rhetorica ad Herennium:* "(justice is shown) if we contend that alliances and friendships should scrupulously be honored; if we make it clear that the duty imposed by nature towards parents, gods, and fatherland must be religiously observed; if we maintain that ties of hospitality, clientage, kinship, and relationship by marriage must inviolably be cherished; if we show that neither reward nor favour nor peril nor animosity ought to lead us astray from the right path; if we say that in all cases a principle of dealing alike with all should be established" (3.3.4). Similarly, Menander Rhetor: "The parts of justice are piety, fair dealing and reverence: piety toward the gods, fair dealing towards men, reverence toward the departed. Piety to the gods consists of two elements: being god-loved and god-loving. The former means being loved by the gods and receiving many blessings from them, the latter consists of loving the gods and having a relationship of friendship with them" (1.361.17-25).

17. It should be noted that God is addressed as "Righteous Father" (πάτερ δίκαιε, 17:25), indicating that God too has duties toward Jesus and his disciples.

18. See Robert Picirelli, "The Meaning of 'Epignosis,'" *EvQ* 47 (1975): 85-93; see also Jerome H. Neyrey, *2 Peter, Jude* (New York: Doubleday, 1993), 149. See Titus 1:16, where "know" is juxtaposed with "deny"; Rom 1:20-21, where "knowing" does not lead to "acknowledging"; and James 2:19, where knowing that God is one does not lead the demons to honor God.

agent, Jesus.[19] While "confession" and "creed" are no strangers to New Testament scholarship, rarely do we find them discussed as "prayer."[20] John 17:3 is situated in a continuous address to God that petitions God for the disciples, who as clients should make the prayer-confession in verse 3 to their heavenly Patron while acknowledging that Jesus is the true agent sent from heaven.[21] The disciples' "knowing" of Israel's only, true God is not simply knowledge, but acknowledging and honoring God and the deity's existential plans. This prayer, moreover, is not possible in temple and synagogue (e.g., 9:22; 12:42).[22]

Listening to God: Prophecy

According to our model of communication, a *sender* sends a *message* via some *channel* to a *receiver* to have an *effect*. In prayer the senders are the Johannine members who send a message via Jesus-as-channel to God; but in prophecy the process is reversed, as God speaks to mortals, not listens to them. In prophecy (1) God, the *sender*, (2) sends a *verbal message* (3) through the *channel* of Jesus, the "Spirit of Truth," or a disciple-prophet, (4) to the *receivers*, the members of the Johannine group, (5) for the *purpose* of communicating to them special information. But in the Fourth Gospel the sender of esoteric information seems to be Jesus. While

19. In John 5:23-24, Jesus declared that God had given all judgment to the Son "so that all may honor the Son just as they honor the Father. Anyone who does not honor the Son does not honor the Father who sent him."

20. Representative of these is Cullmann (*Early Christian Worship*, 22), who asserts, "We may assume with certainty that *Confessional formulae* were recited in the early Christian service of worship. The verbs ὁμολογεῖν and ἐξομολογεῖσθαι (Rom 10,9; Phil 2,11, etc.) connect above all with the confession that Christ is the Lord, in the same way as the early liturgical prayer *Maranatha* is concerned with his second coming." See also Martin, *Worship*, 52-65; Delling, *Worship*, 77-91; Aune, "Worship, Early Christian," 981; and Otto Michel, "ὁμολογέω," in *TDNT* 5:199-213.

21. Peder Borgen, "God's Agent in the Fourth Gospel," in *Religions in Antiquity*, ed. Jacob Neusner (Leiden: Brill, 1968), 137-48; and George W. Buchanan, "Apostolic Christology," in SBLSP (1986): 172-82.

22. John 9:22 and 12:42 tell us that those who make the confession found in 17:3 will be expelled from the synagogue. Confessional prayers are sometimes (a) thanksgivings or doxologies, such as Matt 11:25//Luke 10:21; 1 Tim 1:16 and 6:12-16; (b) protestations of loyalty, such as Matt 10:32//Luke 12:8; and (c) honorific acknowledgments of Jesus' new role and status (Rom 10:9-10; 1 Cor 12:3; Phil 2:11).

in general Jesus remains mediator and broker of God's benefaction, for prophecy he functions as the source or sender. This may be because most prophetic material is concerned with remembering Jesus' words that are themselves mediated by the Spirit who will bear witness to Jesus (15:26).[23] This may be an idiosyncratic quirk from a maverick Gospel.

We need, however, a catalogue of the varieties of prophetic speech to alert us to which types of prophetic oracles are possible and their respective purposes. At the end of his study of prophecy in early Christianity and the Hellenistic world, David Aune offers the following list of "basic forms of Christian prophetic speech": (1) oracles of assurance, (2) prescriptive oracles, (3) announcements of salvation, (4) announcements of judgment, (5) legitimation oracles, and (6) eschatological theophany oracles.[24]

"Prophet" in the Fourth Gospel

The Fourth Gospel occasionally records people favorable to Jesus acclaiming him as a prophet (4:19; 6:14; 7:40 [52]; 9:17), generally because of his wisdom or powers, that is, a "prophet mighty in word and deed." But prophet/prophecy in John 14–17, while it focuses on the words of Jesus, also makes specific note of predictions of forthcoming events. Among the many remarks about "going away" and "coming back" (14:3, 18-19; 16:16), we find three statements that serve a special purpose that surpasses the mere communication of esoteric information. Some predictions by Jesus serve a prophylactic purpose of confirming loyalty in times of conflict. For example, after repeating the remark "I am going away, and I am coming to you," Jesus states the reason for telling this to his disciples: "Now I have told you this before it occurs, so that when it does occur, you may believe" (14:28-29). Similarly, after Jesus discloses the bleak future awaiting the disciples (16:1-2), he explains once again the prophylactic purpose of the prediction: "I have said these things to you so that when their hour comes you may remember that I told you about them" (16:4).[25] The Fourth Gospel would have us read these statements

---

23. M. Eugene Boring, *The Continuing Voice of Jesus* (Louisville: Westminster John Knox, 1991), 38.

24. David E. Aune, *Prophecy in Early Christianity and the Ancient Mediterranean World* (Grand Rapids: Eerdmans, 1983), 320-25.

25. Along with announcing a traitor, Jesus states the purpose of this communication: "I

as communication from Jesus in the course of his career, which, when re-membered, ameliorate a forthcoming crisis by indicating a providential knowledge of, if not control of, future, painful events. Thus, the purpose of this prophetic communication is exhortation to faithfulness, courage, and the like. Oracles of assurance? Salvation?

In a similar vein, when Jesus tells the disciples that they will be hated (15:18-25), he adds, "Remember the word that I said to you, 'Servants are not greater than their master'" (15:20). An earlier word in 13:16 reads: "Ser-vants are not greater than their master, nor are messengers greater than the one who sent them." But this remark occurs in the context of the mandate of Jesus that the disciples wash one another's feet: if Jesus (master) did so, then disciples (servants) must do likewise. While in 15:18-25 the words are the same, the context has changed. Now "hate" is the fate of both master and servants. Thus past words can be prophetic of future events, especially trials awaiting the disciples. And in both cases they communicate assur-ance and encouragement.

Statement, Misunderstanding, Clarification

Prophecy may also be understood as the communication of esoteric in-formation needed to understand Jesus' cryptic words. Throughout the Fourth Gospel the author regularly casts Jesus' discourse with friend and foe in terms of a pattern known as "statement, misunderstanding, and clarification."[26] Jesus makes a statement ("You know the way to the place where I am going," 14:4), which is misunderstood ("Lord, we do not know where you are going. How can we know the way?" 14:5), which prompts Jesus to offer a clarification ("I am the way, and the truth, and the life," 14:6).

---

tell you this now, before it occurs, so that when it does occur, you may believe that I am he" (13:19). The prediction of Peter's future death (21:18-19), which is given by the risen Jesus, likewise functions as a prophecy given to offset the shock of future suffering.

26. For a fuller exposition of the pattern along with other data on esoteric information in the Fourth Gospel, see Jerome H. Neyrey, "The Sociology of Secrecy and the Fourth Gos-pel," in *What Is John?* vol. 2, *Literary and Social Readings of the Fourth Gospel*, ed. Fernando Segovia (Atlanta: Scholars, 1998), 98-101, 107-8.

Statement	Misunderstanding	Clarification
14:1-4	14:5	14:6
14:7	14:8	14:9-11
14:18-21	14:22	14:23-24
16:16	16:17-18	16:19-24
16:25-27	16:29-30	16:31-33

Although instances of this pattern occur regularly throughout the Gospel, we observe a concentration of it in chapters 14 and 16, which are Jesus' final address to his inner circle of disciples. Previously this pattern served as catechetical enlightenment of enlightenable disciples, such as the Samaritan woman, but also as a wall shutting out unenlightenable disciples, such as Nicodemus and the Jerusalem crowds. Here, insiders and core disciples require special information about the cryptic world of Jesus, which is provided for them eventually, we suggest, by prophets speaking in the name of Jesus. Although we will take up the topic of the "Spirit of truth" enlightening or reminding the disciples, the Spirit is presumed in this discussion as a broker of Jesus. Thus this pattern functions to make and maintain boundaries; it informs, but by doing so marks and confirms certain persons as elite insiders.

The quest for esoteric information may be observed also in the pattern of questions and answers found in John 14–16. In addition to the question of Thomas noted above (14:5), Judas, not the Iscariot, asked, "How is it that you will reveal yourself to us, and not to the world?" (14:22). In several places Jesus himself asks their question to facilitate his next remarks. Although Jesus' question to Philip has much of the reproach in it (14:9), it issues in a remarkable revelation of Jesus' union with God (14:10-11), surely a singular favor. Similarly, Jesus questions the failure of the disciples to ask about a cryptic remark (16:5). At the very least, this pattern indicates that Jesus' speech is filled with esoteric information and double-meaning words, which the receivers do not fully perceive at first and which require explanation. Here at least, Jesus can lead the disciples into fuller insight by his subsequent clarifying statements. But in terms of group worship, a prophet during the group worship would presumably access the questions and provide an enlightened answer.[27] As re-

27. The classic example of later reception of the esoteric meaning of earlier speech of Jesus is found in 2:19, 21-22. Only after he was raised from the dead did his disciples remem-

gards function, the providing of special, esoteric knowledge both designates and confirms elite membership.

Furthermore, this Gospel records Jesus declaring that "I have said these things to you in figures of speech. The hour is coming when I will no longer speak to you in figures" (16:25). Does this cover only the metaphor of hard times resembling childbirth (16:20-24), or also the cryptic statements about "going away" and "coming back"? Minimally, a communication is given to the disciples that is admittedly "in figures," liable to "misunderstanding," or containing double meanings. But the veil will be lifted when in the future a prophet remembers, studies, examines, and interprets Jesus' words.

Homily

Scholars who write on early Christian sermons or homilies draw on two sources: (1) the ancient synagogue service and (2) summary remarks like Acts 2:42 (which says the early Christians were devoted to the apostles' teaching and fellowship, breaking of the bread, and prayers).[28] In the last chapter we examined types of Israelite "homilies," identifying two types: the "proem" and the *yelammedenu*. In the proem a Scripture is read, which is actually two different citations that at first glance have nothing in common. The teacher's task is to tease from each esoteric meanings so that at the conclusion, the two citations are shown to be complementary and mutually illuminating.[29] In the *yelammedenu* type, which means "Let our teacher instruct us," again an authorized person reads the Scriptures and explains them.[30] From the Hellenistic side, speeches structured in Greco-Roman rhetoric are discussed. In both Israelite and Greco-Roman con-

---

ber that he had said this; "and they believed the scripture and the word that Jesus had spoken." This insight must be mediated by someone in the group, namely, the prophet.

28. Everett Ferguson, *Early Christians Speak* (Austin, Tex.: Sweet Publishing Co., 1971), 86-87; Cullmann, *Early Christian Worship*, 12-14, 28-29; Delling, *Worship*, 92-103; Martin, *Worship*, 66-76; Richardson, "Worship," 887-89; Aune, "Worship, Early Christian," 983.

29. Joseph Heinemann, "The Proem in the Aggadic Midrashim: A Form-Critical Study," *Studia Hierosolymitana* 22 (1971): 100-22.

30. J. W. Bowker, "Speeches in Acts: A Study in Proem and Yelammedenu Form," *NTS* 14 (1967): 96-111.

texts, we know of some sort of sermon or homily, although its precise form eludes us.[31]

Although neither the Jewish nor the Greco-Roman type of homily applies to material in John 15–16, we find, nevertheless, two side-by-side exhortations. In 15:1-8 and 15:9-17 the audience is exhorted in the type of rhetoric called deliberative to choose and keep on choosing loyalty to Jesus and his Father. In terms of our communication model, "teaching" or "exhortation" or "instruction" is diagrammed as follows: (1) a *sender* (God) (2) sends a *message* (teaching, exhortation), (3) via some *channel* (Jesus → Spirit → teacher), (4) to *receivers* (Johannine group), (5) to have some *effect* on them (to confirm and to urge loyalty). We focus, then, on 15:1-8 and 15:9-17 because these exhortations most closely accord with the elements of deliberative rhetoric.

The topic of 15:1-8 is introduced in the metaphor: "I am the vine, my father is the vinedresser" (15:1).[32] In this context the entire passage exhorts the disciples to choose to "remain." This exhortation occurs seven times (vv 4, 4b, 4c, 5, 6, 7a, and 7b), sometimes in the imperative mood and sometimes in a conditional clause, surely indicative of the choice to be made. Seven occurrences! This exhortation builds on current relationships and urges the disciples to maintain them in the future, the value of which relationships provides the very argument from advantage. The relationships are: Jesus = vine, the disciples = the branches, while the Father = the vinedresser (vv 1-2, 5). The telltale signs of an argument from advantage suggest that we consider this material an example of deliberative rhetoric that "appeals for future action *on the basis of future benefits*."[33] Remaining brings sweet advantage, just as *not* remaining leads to bitterness. A branch that remains and is cleansed by the vinedresser "bears much fruit" (v 2), a phrase repeated three times (vv 4, 5, 8) to underscore the advantage that comes from "remaining." Similarly, branches that "remain" may petition God for whatever they wish and expect God's positive response (v 7) — advantage indeed! In contrast, we are told of the sanctions imposed on

31. The discussions of 15:1-8 and 15:9-17 are based on the author's translation of the passages.

32. Yet important advances have been made by Lawrence Wills, "The Form of the Sermon in Hellenistic Judaism and Early Christianity," *HTR* 77 (1984): 277-99; and C. Clifton Black, "The Rhetorical Form of the Hellenistic Jewish and Early Christian Sermon: A Response to Lawrence Wills," *HTR* 81 (1988): 1-18.

33. Black, "The Rhetorical Form," 5.

those who do *not* remain. They are taken away (v 2), and worse, "cast forth
. . . wither . . . thrown into the fire and burned" (v 6).

We find clear argumentative patterns here. "Unless the branch remains . . ." is a necessary condition frequently found in the Fourth Gospel:
"unless" one is born of the Spirit or eats the flesh of the Son of Man or is
washed by Jesus, one does not experience the benefit of God. So, too, here
the advantage of "remaining" is also cast in the form of an "unless" argument: "A branch cannot bear fruit unless (ἐὰν μή) it remains in the vine,
neither can you, unless (ἐὰν μή) you remain in me" (v 4).[34] Similarly, in
verses 6-7 conditional sentences articulate the deliberative character of
"remaining" and "*not* remaining." "Unless (ἐὰν μή) disciples remain, they
are cast forth . . . if (ἐάν) you remain in me and my words remain in you,
you may ask for whatever you wish." The speaker provides reasons for the
right choice. On the positive side, the "cleansing" of the vine (perhaps a
euphemism for testing gold in a furnace) serves the purpose (ἵνα) of caus-
ing the branches to bear more fruit, clearly an advantage. And Jesus gives
the reason why branches must "remain" in the vine: "for (ὅτι) without me
you can do nothing" (v 5). Because we observe an argument being made,
not merely information being imparted, we consider 15:1-8 a crisp example
of deliberative rhetoric, which places before the disciples the decision of
"remaining," a deliberation richly rewarded or severely sanctioned. The argument from advantage is a regular feature of exhortations, homilies, and
sermons.[35]

A second exhortation follows immediately, which begins with the
command "Remain in my love" (v 9) and concludes with "love one another" (v 17). Evidently the focus is on "love," although verses 9-17 are
linked with verses 1-8 by four more references to "remain" (vv 9-10, 16).
Thus 15:1-8 and 15:9-17 should be seen as parallel and linked exhortations,
the first one expressing a vertical series of relationships between
vinedresser, vine, and branches, and the second one horizontal relationships between "one another." As with verses 1-8, the exhortation in 9-17 is
argued by: (1) imperatively urging: "Love one another!" (2) conditional
sentences explaining this "love," such as "if (ἐάν) you keep my command-

---

34. Other "unless" demands include: 3:3, 5; 6:53; 8:24; 12:24; 13:8. See Jerome H. Neyrey,
An Ideology of Revolt: John's Christology in Social-Science Perspective (Philadelphia: Fortress,
1988), 143-44, 155-56.
35. Black, "The Rhetorical Form," 5.

ments, you will abide in my love" (v 10); and (3) analogies that clarify the topic: "as (καθώς) the Father has loved me, so have I loved you" (v 9). In language using the argument from advantage, the author first tells the disciples that "remaining" and "loving" elevate their status from that of "servants" to "friends" (φίλους). This echoes the contrasting statuses of dead versus fruitful branches in 15:1-8, with the comparison now made between "servants" and "friends." Jesus' final argument here reminds the disciples of their debt in justice to him, which he is calling in through this exhortation: "You did not choose me, but I chose you and appointed you that you should go and bear fruit and that your fruit should remain" (v 16). The verbs indicate the extent of Jesus' benefaction that creates the debt of justice: "chose," "appointed," "bear fruit," and "your fruit remain." To this he now appends one more benefaction, effective petitionary prayer: "Whatever you ask the Father in my name, he will give it to you" (v 16b), surely a significant advantage.

Therefore, this material is exhortatory, and it resumes the most important behaviors urged in the Fourth Gospel, "remaining" and "loving." Because of its exhortatory character, it stands apart from all other parts of the Farewell Address. But is "homily" or "sermon" the appropriate classification? And do such things belong in worship? The type of rhetoric in 15:1-17 is deliberative; that is, it exhorts the hearers to make a choice that will affect their future, and the argument rests primarily on pointing out the advantage to those choosing to "remain" and "love." Such rhetoric is not exclusive to homily or sermon and may occur in many types of public speaking, especially speeches to the Roman Senate or the Greek assembly. Yet it is most compatible with sermon and homily (see Heb 3:1–4:13; 6:1-12), which are admittedly parts of Christian worship.[36]

Study of the Words of Jesus

It is indisputable that the disciples in their worship told the story of Jesus again and examined his words and parables. This is, moreover, where the speeches of Acts all end: what God has done to Jesus. But John 14–17 does not contain the splendid narratives found earlier or elsewhere; on the con-

---

36. Harold W. Attridge, "Paraenesis in a Homily (λόγος παρακλήσεως): The Possible Location of, and Socialization in, the 'Epistle to the Hebrews,'" *Semeia* 50 (2004): 211-26.

trary, the chapters contain only his words, although the self-focused prayer in John 17 does summarize his mission. But as has been the case from John 2 onward, the meaning of his words is by no means clear. For example, "Destroy this temple . . ." was heard as "this [Herodian] temple." Only after his resurrection did "his disciples [remember] that he had said this; and they believed the scripture and the word that Jesus had spoken" (2:22). We have seen above the pattern of statement-misunderstanding-clarification, which demonstrates that many, even of the inner circle, failed to understand Jesus' words correctly, but required an interpreter either then or in the future. This material has been studied according to the sociology of secrecy, which argues that it was a regular feature of the Fourth Gospel to have Jesus conceal and reveal. Secrecy, we learn, is the "mandatory or voluntary, but calculated concealment of information, activities or relationships."[37] Put simply, knowledge is controlled. Not all people know everything at the same time; being "in the know" serves as an important marker of insider status.[38] Readers of John are already familiar with certain types of secrecy: riddles, irony, parables, footnotes, and asides. When was the veil lifted? When did the disciples get the correct understanding of Jesus' words? How far afield are we to suggest that Jesus' words were studied by the group at its gathering and given attention comparable to the Scriptures?

Enter the Paraclete, the Spirit of Truth. In John 14–16 this figure is described four times, every time as the broker of special knowledge about Jesus. First of all, we note that most of the time this Paraclete/Spirit of Truth reminds people of Jesus, glorifies Jesus, and takes what is Jesus' and declares it to them. The Paraclete, then, attends primarily to the Jesus story and the words of Jesus. We know, moreover, that this Paraclete spoke through someone in the group, a prophet. But the Spirit has other functions as well.

Judgment

Few scholars who list the various elements of Christian worship include "judgment" as part of it. All the more, then, are David Aune's reflections

---

37. S. K. Tefft, "Secrecy as a Social and Political Process," in *Secrecy: A Cross-Cultural Perspective*, ed. S. K. Tefft (New York: Human Sciences Press, 1980), 320.

38. Elizabeth Brandt, "On Secrecy and the Control of Knowledge: Taos Pueblo," in *Secrecy*, 125-34.

Category	14:26	15:26	16:7-10, 12
Title or Name	Paraclete Holy Spirit	Paraclete Spirit of Truth	16:7 Paraclete 16:12 Spirit of Truth
Source & Relationship to Father and Jesus	whom the Father will send in my name	whom I shall send to you from the Father . . . who proceeds from the Father	16:7 I will send him to you
Functions	1. he will teach you all things	1. ————	1. he will guide you into all the truth . . . he will declare to you the things that will come
	2. bring to your remembrance all that I have said to you	2. he will bear witness to me	2. he does not speak on his own authority . . . he will glorify me, for he will take what is mine and declare it to you

worth our attention. In *The Cultic Setting of Realized Eschatology in Early Christianity*, he argued that two elements of eschatology, declarations of salvation and judgment, have their proper place in "the worship, preaching and teaching of that community."[39] "This cultic 'coming' of the Son of man to save and to judge, to bless and to curse, was a corporate worship experience which the Johannine community conceptualized in terms of the traditional Christological expectation of the Son of man."[40] He cites with approval Käsemann's "Sentences of Holy Law" as illustrative of cultic judgment speech.[41] As we saw above, Aune listed "oracles of judgment"

39. Aune, *Cultic Setting*, 121; this is continuously argued in 45-135.

40. Aune, *Cultic Setting*, 126.

41. Ernst Käsemann, "Sentences of Holy Law in the New Testament," in his *New Testament Questions of Today* (Philadelphia: Fortress, 1979), 66-81. His location of this material in worship contexts is based on Hans Lietzmann, *Mass and the Lord's Supper: A Study in the History of the Liturgy* (Leiden: Brill, 1979), 186; and Gunther Bornkamm, "Das Anathema in der urchristlichen Abendmahlsliturgie," *TLZ* 75 (1950): 227-30.

among the types of prophecy found in the early church.[42] "Announcements of judgment and salvation," then, are not foreign to Christian worship; moreover, they were types of sanctioned speech.

For example, we recall Paul's judgment of the man in an incestuous
marriage in 1 Corinthians 5. Paul times the sentencing of the sinner to occur within a group meeting ("when you are assembled"), at which he
speaks with pneumatic authority and declares that he enjoys the "power of
the Lord," that is, authority to censure the man. Found guilty of corruption, the man is publicly expelled from the group (5:3-5).[43] Similarly, Matthew 18:15-17 records a group ritual in which an errant member should
progressively receive correction. Should the transformational ritual fail,
"the church" declares him an outsider. Both of these examples envision a
community assembly, at which an oracle of judgment takes place.

This material, we suggest, pertains to John 16:7-11, which we interpret
as a form of judgment oracle. In terms of Johannine logic, the Paraclete
will play a forensic role, similar to the presentation of Jesus in his various
trials in the Gospel.[44] Unlike 1 Corinthians 5 and Matthew 18:15-17, no one
is cast out of the group; on the contrary, the group is experiencing expulsion from the synagogue (9:22, 34; 12:42; 16:1-2). The judgment oracle,
then, serves to make and maintain boundaries with "the world" by empha-
sizing in dualistic terms how and why the Johannine group is right and
therefore does not belong in the world. The following list drawn from the
Farewell Address illustrates the studied emphasis on group boundaries
(quotations are from the RSV):

42. Aune, *Prophecy in Early Christianity*, 320-25.

43. In addition, see the curse "anathema" in 1 Cor 16:22; Gal 1:8-9; Rom 9:3.

44. Frequently in his defense Jesus, the accused, became the accuser; and his judges
were judged:

"I know that you do not have the love of God in you" (5:42; see 5:43-47).
"Do not judge by appearances, but judge with right judgment" (7:24).
"You judge by human standards" (8:15; see 8:16-18).
"You know neither me nor my Father" (8:19).
"You are from below, I am from above; you are of this world, I am not of this world"
(8:23).
"You are from your father the devil, and you choose to do your father's desires" (8:44).
"The reason you do not hear them [the words of God] is that you are not from God"
(8:47).

Jesus and His Disciples	*The World*
. . . you know him, for he dwells with you, and will be in you (14:17b)	the Spirit of truth, whom the world cannot receive, because it neither sees him nor knows him (14:17a)
. . . but you will see me (14:19b)	the world will see me no more (14:19a)
how is it that you will manifest yourself to us (14:22a)	. . . and not to the world? (14:22b)
Peace I leave with you; my peace I give to you (14:27a)	. . . not as the world gives do I give to you (14:27b)
. . . he has no power over me (14:30b)	the ruler of this world is coming (14:30a)
But because you are not of the world, but I chose you out of the world, therefore the world hates you (15:19)	If the world hates you, know that it has hated me before it hated you (15:18) If you were of the world, the world would love its own (15:19)
You will weep and lament (16:20a)	. . . but the world will rejoice (16:20b)
. . . I am leaving the world and going to the Father (16:28b)	I came from the Father and have come into the world (16:28a)
. . . but be of good cheer, I have overcome the world (16:33b)	In the world you have tribulation (16:33a)

The discourse in the Farewell Address, then, makes and maintains boundaries with "the world" to emphasize the chasm that separates the disciples from the synagogue and to make any crossing back impossible. Thus in this context we read 16:7-11 as an oracle of judgment.

The task of the Paraclete in 16:8 consists of some form of judgment, whether we translate the Greek verb used here as "convict" or "convince."[45] On the one hand, the Johannine group will surely have much to

45. See Tricia Gates Brown, *Spirit in the Johannine Writings: Johannine Pneumatology in Social-Science Perspective* (New York: T. & T. Clark, 2003), 221-27.

criticize the synagogue for, at least to confirm the synagogue's utter depravity. Thus they are equipped with ready arguments to judge the synagogue and so prove it hopelessly wrong. On the other hand, this criticism serves also to firm up the group's own beliefs of its superiority and so its necessary separation from the world. Thus the Paraclete will prove *to the disciples* that the *synagogue/world* is guilty of sin, (false) righteousness, and (false) judgment.[46] "Of sin," because the world did not believe in Jesus.[47] "Of [false] righteousness," because the synagogue judged Jesus a sinner and deceiver, yet Jesus will shortly be in the presence of the all-holy God.[48] "Of [false] judgment," because it persecutes and judges Jesus, and by doing so brings judgment upon itself.[49] Thus, we argue that part of the worship described in the Farewell Address includes an oracle of judgment, that is, a *communication* sent from *God* through the *channel* of the Paraclete to the *disciples* for the *purpose* of shoring up the disciples even as it condemns their adversaries.

Not on This Mountain nor in Jerusalem — but Where?

Jesus' declaration that his body would be the new and true temple (2:19-22) is followed by a conversation with a Samaritan woman about the right place to worship, Mount Gerizim or Mount Zion (4:20), which mountains

46. On this reading of John 16:8-11, see D. A. Carson, "The Function of the Paraclete in John 16:7-11," *JBL* 98 (1979): 547-66. See also Raymond E. Brown, *Gospel according to John*, 705.

47. As always, the premier sin is that they do not believe in Jesus (3:19; 8:21, 24; 9:41; 15:22). This means that some never had any belief and were always hostile; others were liars who faked belief to escape censure (8:30), but were exposed as "liars and murderers."

48. When Jesus qualifies "righteousness" by saying that he is going to the Father, this expresses the right relationship to God: acting as God's agent, fulfilling God's command to speak God's word and the command to lay down his life. As one who has always done his duty to God, he is welcome in God's presence. But many see their duty to God as putting Jesus to death and exterminating his disciples (16:1-2). Thus, their relationship with God is tragically wrong; their true duties are left unfulfilled; they dishonor God with wrongdoing.

49. On the principle that "as you judge, so you are judged" (see Matt 7:2), the enemies of the group share the judgment of the ruler of this world. And those who judge unjustly will be judged by the same judgment (John 7:24; 8:15; 9:16 and 24). Instead of judging Jesus justly as God's agent, they judged him according to appearances (7:24) and as having a demon (8:48; 10:20). But Jesus has already judged this ruler: "Now the ruler of this world will be driven out" (12:31).

Jesus declassifies as sacred places of worship.[50] Thus, the Johannine disciples have no *fixed sacred space,* in contrast to Samaritan and Israelite temples that are permanently fixed atop certain mountains. Nor does the local synagogue serve as the site of their worship, for public confession of Jesus as the Christ results in expulsion from that assembly (9:22; 12:42-43; 16:1-2). But if *not* Mount Gerizim *nor* Jerusalem *nor* the synagogue, then where?[51] One of the dominant themes discussed in John 14–17 is where worship will take place. We argue that parts of the answer will come from a fresh consideration of (1) "many dwelling places" (μοναί, 14:2) and (2) "being in" and "dwelling in." But first let us consider a model of "territoriality" from the anthropology of space, to appreciate the significance of Jesus' declassification of Mounts Gerizim and Zion.

Fixed versus Fluid Sacred Space (4:21-24)

"Not on this mountain nor in Jerusalem" effectively negates fixed sacred space for the Johannine group, that is, temples with the elaborate systems that surround them: priests, offerings, tithes, revenues, a temple building with its adornment and maintenance, and hosts of diverse persons to staff it, perform in it, and guard it. Needless to say, ethnic temples are clear examples of fixed sacred space, which they often express by declaring themselves as the "navel" or "center" of the world.[52] Since discussion of fixed or

---

50. See Tod D. Swanson, "To Prepare a Place: Johannine Christianity and the Collapse of Ethnic Territory," *JAAR* 62 (1994): 248-51.

51. Although the disciples remain in the world, Jesus repeatedly tells them that they do not belong to "this world" and that they are "not of this world" (17:9, 14, 15, 16).

52. Strabo attests to a long tradition that Delphi, its most sacred shrine, was the "center" and the "navel of the earth": "For it (temple at Delphi) is almost in the center of Greece taken as a whole . . . it was also believed to be in the center of the inhabited world, and people called it the *navel of the earth*" (Strabo, *Geography* 9.3.6); see also Plato, *Republic* 427b-c; Pausanias, *Descriptions of Greece* 16.2.3; see also Bruce J. Malina and Jerome H. Neyrey, *Portraits of Paul: An Archaeology of Ancient Personality* (Louisville: Westminster John Knox, 1996), 120-22. Judean authors applied the "navel of the world" label to Jerusalem: "Just as the navel is found at the center of a human being, so the land of Israel is found at the center of the world . . . and it is the foundation of the world. Jerusalem is at the center of the land of Israel, the Temple is at the center of Jerusalem, the Holy of Holies is at the center of the Temple, the Ark is at the center of the Holy of Holies and the Foundation Stone is in front of the Ark, which spot is the foundation of the world" (*Tanchuma, Kedoshim* 10).

fluid space depends on some social theory of space, let us briefly examine a model commonly used in the anthropology of space, namely, "territoriality." Robert Sack, a representative of modern research, defines territoriality as "the attempt by an individual or group to affect, influence, or control people, phenomena, and relationships, by delimiting and asserting control over a geographic area. . . . Territories require constant effort to establish and maintain."[53] This means that groups typically engage in a three-step process: (1) *classification* of the space (mine/yours, sacred/profane, etc.), (2) *communication* of the classification (fences, gates, walls), and (3) *control* of the space. Within this model, let us examine "fluid" versus "fixed" sacred space. On this point we turn to Mary Douglas and one of her best interpreters, Bruce J. Malina. Of *fixed* sacred space, Malina writes: "Just as persons have their statuses by ascription and perdure in that status indefinitely, the same holds true for places. The topography of the main places where people in this script live out their lives is rather permanent. A palace location, a temple location, and a homestead stay in the same place and with the same lineage through generations."[54] Thus *fixed* sacred space correlates with *fixed* roles and statuses. All of this is characterized by redundant aspects of stability, permanence, and continuity. The temple-city of Jerusalem exemplifies this well.[55] Of *fluid* sacred space, Malina writes:

> This situation of porous boundaries and competing groups stands in great contrast to the solid, hierarchical, pyramidal shape of strong group/ high grid [fixed space]. . . . as groups form and re-form anew, permanence is no longer to be found outside the group; and where the group is, there is stability. Sacred space is located in the group, not in some imper-

53. Robert D. Sack, *Human Territoriality: Its Theory and History* (Cambridge: Cambridge University Press, 1986), 19. Other important definitions have been given by Godelier, in Michael J. Casimir, *Mobility and Territoriality: Social and Spatial Boundaries among Foragers, Fishers, Pastoralists, and Peripatetics* (Oxford: Oxford University Press, 1992), 19; and Ralph B. Taylor, *Human Territorial Functioning: An Empirical Evolutionary Perspective on Individual and Small Group Territorial Cognitions, Behaviors, and Consequences* (Cambridge: Cambridge University Press, 1988), 6.

54. Bruce Malina, *Christian Origins and Cultural Anthropology: Practical Models for Biblical Interpretation* (Atlanta: John Knox, 1986), 31.

55. Malina's description of a leading city such as Jerusalem is similar to Jonathan Z. Smith's (*Map Is Not Territory* [Leiden: Brill, 1978], 132-33, 160-61, and 293) attention to "archaic urban cultures." As noted, the latter constantly appeals to the Pan-Babylonian School at the end of the nineteenth century, whose focus was the archaic, agricultural city-empire.

sonal space like a temple. The group is the central location of importance. . . . Discourse within these groups, whether the words of a portable Torah, the story of Jesus, or the exhortations of the philosopher-teacher, becomes the mobile, portable, exportable focus of sacred place, in fact more important than the fixed and eternal sacred places.[56]

Malina bases his classification on considerations of space and time, at which we must look more closely. The following chart should make explicit the contrasts on every level between fixed and fluid sacred space.

Fixed: Temple	Fluid: Group
1. topological, actual space	1. place where the group meets
2. place perduring over time	2. space of opportunistic, occasional group meetings
3. major mode of worship: sacrifice	3. major mode of worship: verbal forms
4. focus on altar	4. focus on sacred writings
5. hierarchical arrangement of persons by birth	5. significant individuals whose competency is based on spirit giftedness or closeness to the group's hero

This model of fluid (versus fixed) sacred space alerts us to certain aspects of worship as they may appear in John 14–17. First, significant attention is given to the group, not to any place; second, the medium of the communication that is worship is certainly not sacrifice, performed by a priest whose competency rests on birth into the appropriate clan or family, but verbal worship as articulated by competent figures in the group.[57] In short, where the group is, there is the place of worship.

In My Father's House Are Many Rooms (14:2)

Beginnings are generally significant rhetorical places to establish a topic, and we read John 14:2 in this manner, as a topic statement. This verse con-

56. Malina, *Christian Origins*, 38.

57. Because birth by blood or water avails nothing and because the flesh is of no avail, the Fourth Gospel sees no value in any form of hereditary roles or statuses.

tains two phrases: (1) "in my Father's house are many rooms (μοναὶ πολλαί)" and (2) "I go to prepare a place (τόπον) for you."[58] A recent dissertation on these verses offers a critical, inventive interpretation of them. McCaffrey notes that "my Father's house" has been variously explained as heaven, the heavenly temple, the messianic kingdom, and even the universe.[59] Since the author of the Fourth Gospel declassifies any mountain or earthly temple as sacred space for God's dwelling, we look to God's "realm" as the place for worshiping God — wherever that may be. McCaffrey, moreover, gives special attention to the term "in my Father's *house*" (οἰκίᾳ), which suggests intimate kinship relationships,[60] such as Father and Son, God and disciples, and perhaps other Christians yet to be brought in — "many rooms."[61] And when Jesus states that "I go to prepare a place for you," he goes not as an architect but as a broker of relationships that will secure access to God through himself. Thus we are inclined to read 14:2 in terms of personal relationships and not in terms of buildings or space.

Jesus next states that he goes away and comes back — he goes "to prepare a place for you" and then says he "will come again and will take you to myself." He states as his purpose that "where I am you may be also." After brokering his relationship with the Father, he returns to solidify his relationship with God's clients. He does not say that he will take the disciples to the "Father's house," but rather that he will facilitate his brokerage by maintaining a favored relationship with the disciples. Thus, I would extend the sense of "relationship" to the "place" Jesus prepares. As we will shortly argue, Jesus functions as broker in a patron-client relationship that is first linked with his Father-Patron and then with his disciples-clients. As tortured as it may sound, Jesus is in two "places" at once: in heaven (in relationship with God, wherever God is) and on earth (in relationship with disciples, wherever they gather). Balancing his remark that he has access to God's presence, he also takes the disciples "to myself." Thus they too have access to God's house, but only in relation to Jesus. Poor Thomas, who does not know the way to the Father's house! Jesus tells him, "I am the way . . ." (14:6), that is, the exclusive relationship with God and the unique

---

58. The discussion in this section uses the RSV.

59. McCaffrey, *House with Many Rooms*, 49-64.

60. McCaffrey, *House with Many Rooms*, 29-32. See also Sjef van Tilborg, *Imaginative Love in John* (Leiden: Brill, 1993).

61. See John 17:20-22; also Swanson, "To Prepare a Place," 244-45, 248-51, 257-60.

broker of God: "No one comes to the Father, but by me." Jesus, then, is both relationship and access, but he is not "place."

Later Jesus amplifies the meanings we argue for "Father's house" and "place": "If a man loves me, he will keep my word, and my Father will love him, and we will come to him and *make our home* with him" (14:23). Once more, the key to this "geography" is relationship: (1) a disciple *loving* Jesus and *keeping* his word, (2) the Father *loving* this disciple, and (3) the Father and Son *coming to him* and making a *"home"* with him. Again Jesus functions as the key link, the broker or mediator between God and the clients. The disciple-client, moreover, must maintain faithfulness with this mediator, which relationship will be honored by the Father-Patron. Thus a link between disciple and Father is forged in and through Jesus. The purpose or utility of this relationship comes from the benefaction the Patron then shows the client, namely, "we will make *our home* with him." Any disciple may fit this description, and any earthly place is suitable for this relationship to occur. The only exclusive thing that makes this place "sacred" is the fact that Father and clients are located only in relationship with Jesus.

Later Jesus petitions God for a benefaction that relates to the Johannine statement studied above, namely, that "place" = relationship: "Father, I desire that they also, whom you have given me, may be with me *where I am,* to behold my glory which you have given me in your love for me before the foundation of the world" (17:24, slightly altered). The related figures include "Father," "I," those the Father has "given me," that is, the same persons described in terms of patron-broker-client relationships above. The Patron has already established the broker with his clients, but he is now petitioned by Jesus to bestow on the clients a unique blessing, "to behold my glory which you have given me in your love for me before the foundation of the world." What can "be with me where I am" mean? Several times in John 17 Jesus recognizes the *non*relatedness of the disciples to "the world": while "they are in the world" (17:11), "they are not of the world" (17:14). Nevertheless, Jesus does not ask that they be removed *from the world:* "I do not pray that you should take them out of the world, but that you should keep them from the evil one" (17:15, slightly altered). Thus that they "be with me where I am" is no heavenly ascent nor a spatial relocation. Rather, the directional and spatial patterns we observe suggest that such language is best understood in terms of relationships. The relationship of Jesus with the Father contains elements of obedience, love, and generosity. In John 17 we are told thirteen times that the Father "gave" Jesus

195

something, such as "power over all flesh" (17:2), "those you gave him" (17:6, 9, 24), "everything" (17:7), "the words" (17:8, 14), "the name" (17:11-12), and "glory" (17:22, 24). And Jesus' numerous petitions suggest that God will continue giving, but giving in Jesus' name. Similarly, the relationship of Jesus-broker and disciples-clients itself contains strains of loyalty, generosity, and faithfulness. For example, Jesus, gifted with the "name" of God, reveals it to his disciples (17:6, 11, 12, 26); he has given them God's "word" (17:14, 17) and "glory" (17:22, 24). It is not enough that God play patron to his disciples via a broker; the fullest benefaction will occur when the broker "takes" the disciples close to the Patron — a relationship, not a geographical or fixed sacred place. Brokerage given in the past will continue in the future because the relationships of Patron, Broker, and clients are faithfully maintained.

Thus we return to the phrase "to behold my glory which you have given me in your love for me before the foundation of the world." The "place" of Jesus' precreation glory must be in the presence of God, even the bosom of God (1:18; 17:5). To repeat, Jesus' petition in 17:24 does not require that the disciples be taken to a new place or be transported heavenward. His prayer may be accomplished by some sort of Christophany in which the disciples "behold my glory." That is, they who are still in the world will see into heaven, just as Nathanael and others were promised a vision (in 1:50-51), if not of heaven itself, then certainly of heavenly persons.[62] In summary, Jesus' declaration in 14:2 that there are "many rooms" in the Father's house and its repetition in 14:23 are best understood as descriptions of relationships, not places such as were declassified in 4:21. No specific earthly place in the world is envisioned, but rather a relationship between Father, Jesus, and the disciples, which we describe as a Patron-Broker-client relationship.

"Being In" and "Dwelling In"

We find in chapters 14 and 15 a number of remarks by Jesus describing his relationships with both the Father and disciples, which are seemingly ex-

---

62. One thinks of Stephen's vision of the heavens opened and his sight of Jesus at the throne of God (Acts 7:55-56). Moreover, Jesus' remark to Philip should not be forgotten: "Whoever has seen me has seen the Father" (14:9).

pressed in spatial terms. He expresses his relationship with the Father in two ways: (1) "I am *in* the Father and the Father *in* me" (14:10, 11, 20), and (2) "the Father . . . *dwells* in me" (14:10b).[63] Similarly, Jesus' relationship with the disciples parallels that between him and God: "I am *in* my Father, and you *in* me, and I *in* you" (14:20). Although one might initially think that "in" is a spatial term ("in my Father's house are many rooms"), as we have noted, the disciples do not travel to another place and "being in" does not necessarily imply spatial location.

Similarly with "dwell in." In terms of Jesus' relationship with God, we are told that the Father "*dwells* in me" (14:10b). The same verb is used ten times in 15:4-10 to express the relationship of Jesus with the disciples. On the one hand, the disciple must "dwell" in or remain in or sustain loyalty to Jesus: "the branch cannot bear fruit . . . unless it [dwells] in the vine" (15:4). Conversely, if a branch "dwells" in the vine, the vine curiously will "dwell" in the branch: "dwell in me and I in you" (15:4, 5b, author's translation). An alternate way of expressing this in 15:7 indicates the basis for this type of dwelling: "If you dwell in me and my words dwell in you . . ." (author's translation). The words of Jesus "dwelling" point to a relationship of loyalty and faithfulness. Finally, the Spirit will "dwell" in you and "be" in you (14:17). When we ask what types of relationships are envisioned, several types seem suitable here: (1) kinship relationships (father, son, household) and (2) patron-broker-client relationships.

Juxtaposed to the exhortation to "dwell" in Jesus and to "love," we are told about "hate." Those outside the relationships described above hate the disciples (15:18-25), which results in physical expulsion from the synagogue (16:1-2). There will be no "dwelling" there, for it would mean acceptance of their criticism of Jesus. Moreover, Jesus explains why he tells them this prediction — "to keep you from falling away." This prophecy, then, is intended to cement their relationship with Jesus, that is, to "dwell" in him even as he is "in" them. In the discourse on "hate," "scandal," and "scattering," the exhortation to "dwell," while metaphorically on the level of physical separation and distancing, expresses a close relationship of the highest sort. Thus "being in" and "dwelling in" correspond to "love" and "faithfulness," but "scandal" and "scattering" and "hate" are the converse. Loyal and faithful relationships, we argue, best explain these erstwhile spatial terms.

63. The discussion in this section uses the RSV.

Patron-Broker-Client Relations

Patrons and Clients

Worship inevitably brings together persons of varying roles and statuses. What people? What roles? Let us look through the lenses of patron-client relationships. Patron-client relations have long enjoyed the attention of classicists.[64] Frederick Danker's book *Benefactor* brought to the attention of New Testament scholars the tradition of honoring benefactors, a form of patron-client relation characteristic of the eastern Mediterranean.[65] And Bruce Malina pioneered the formal use of the anthropology of patron-client relations to interpret early Christian literature.[66] Malina's model[67] of patron-client relations describes those that arise between people of unequal status and resources: landlord/vassal, aristocrat/peasant, king/subject, father/son, and God/Israel.[68] Thus patron-client relationships describe the vertical dimension of exchange between higher-status and lower-status persons.

64. For example, Richard P. Saller, *Personal Patronage under the Early Empire* (Cambridge: Cambridge University Press, 1982); and Andrew Wallace-Hadrill, ed., *Patronage in Ancient Society* (London: Routledge, 1989).

65. Frederick W. Danker, *Benefactor: Epigraphic Study of a Graeco-Roman and New Testament Semantic Field* (St. Louis: Clayton Publishing House, 1982).

66. The initial study is Bruce J. Malina, "Patron and Client: The Analogy behind Synoptic Theology," *Forum* 4, no. 1 (1988): 2-32; this article was made more widely available in Malina's *The Social World of Jesus and the Gospels* (London: Routledge, 1996), 143-75. See also Halvor Moxnes, "Patron-Client Relations and the New Community in Luke-Acts," in *The Social World of Luke-Acts: Models for Interpretation*, ed. Jerome H. Neyrey (Peabody, Mass.: Hendrickson, 1991), 241-68.

67. The important anthropological literature includes Steffen Schmidt, James Scott, Carl Landé, and Laura Guasti, *Friends, Followers, and Factions: A Reader in Political Clientalism* (Berkeley: University of California Press, 1977); Jeremy Boissevain, *Friends of Friends: Networks, Manipulators, and Coalitions* (New York: St. Martin's Press, 1974); and Shlomo Eisenstadt and Louis Roniger, *Patrons, Clients, and Friends: Interpersonal Relations and the Structure of Trust in Society* (Cambridge: Cambridge University Press, 1984).

68. The description of patron-client relationships by A. Blok is particularly helpful: "Patronage is a model or analytic construct which the social scientist applies in order to understand and explain a range of apparent different social relationships: father-son, God-man, saint-devotee, godfather-godchild, lord-vassal, landlord-tenant, politician-voter, professor-assistant, and so forth" ("Variations in Patronage," *Sociologische Gids* 16 [1969]: 366).

EXCURSUS: BASIC FEATURES OF PATRON-CLIENT RELATIONS

The basic features include: (1) Patron-client relations are particularistic, thus characterized by favoritism. (2) They involve the exchange of a whole range of goods and services, power, influence, inducement, and commitment. (3) The exchange entails a package deal, so that the elements of patronage cannot be given separately (i.e., concretely useful goods must go along with loyalty). (4) Solidarity here entails a strong element of unconditionality and long-range social credit. (5) Hence, patron-client relations involve a strong element of personal obligation. (6) These relations are not fully legal or contractual, but still are very strongly binding. (7) In principle, patron-client relations entered into voluntarily can be abandoned voluntarily, although always proclaimed to be lifelong, long-range, forever, etc. (8) Patron-client relations are vertical and dyadic (between individuals or networks of individuals), and thus they undermine the horizontal group organization and solidarity of clients and other patrons. (9) They are based on strong inequality and differences between patrons and clients. Patrons monopolize certain positions of crucial importance to clients, especially access to means of production, major markets, and centers of society.[69]

As noted above, the topic of patron-client relations is now part of New Testament scholarship,[70] and so does not need to be rehearsed here. We should, however, widen the model to accommodate another person in the patron-client relationship, namely, the broker.[71] In social or commercial terms, a broker places people in touch with each other, such as a real estate broker, a stockbroker, or a marriage broker.[72] A broker must be suitably

69. See Malina, "Patron and Client," 3-4.

70. See Stephen Charles Mott, "The Power of Giving and Receiving: Reciprocity in Hellenistic Benevolence," in *Current Issues in Biblical and Patristic Interpretation*, ed. Gerald Hawthorne (Grand Rapids: Eerdmans, 1975), 60-72; Bruce J. Malina, "The Social World Implied in the Letters of the Christian Bishop-Martyr (Named Ignatius of Antioch)," in SBLSP (1978): 2:71-119; Holland Hendrix, "Benefactor/Patron Networks in the Urban Environment Evidence from Thessalonika," *Semeia* 56 (1992): 39-58; and Seth Schwartz, "Josephus in Galilee: Rural Patronage and Social Breakdown," in *Josephus and the History of the Greco-Roman Period*, ed. F. Parente and J. Sievers (Leiden: Brill, 1994), 290-306.

71. To my knowledge, Bruce J. Malina and Richard L. Rohrbaugh were the first to introduce the role of "broker" to the study of Fourth Gospel (*Social-Science Commentary*, 117-19).

72. This discussion of broker borrows heavily from Malina, "Patron and Client," 11-18.

placed to be accessible both to clients seeking aid and patrons who might provide assistance. Thus a broker is a bridge (i.e., *pontifex*) or link or mediator between patrons and clients.

Broker in Patron-Client Relations

Writing on the term "mediator," Albert Oepke identified the following social roles in the ancient world that exemplify the role of broker or mediator. A mediator is a person who (1) is "neutral" to two parties and negotiates peace or guarantees agreements, (2) arranges business deals, (3) receives as king divine laws and offers sacrifice for the people, (4) offers as priest prayers and sacrifice to God on behalf of individuals and the people, (5) brings as prophet a teaching or mighty work from God, (6) founds a new cult or religion, and (7) delivers an angelic communication from God.[73]

Oepke notes that when the New Testament calls Jesus a broker, it shades the term into many meanings: he is the unique mediator (μεσίτης) between the one God and humankind (1 Tim 2:5), the mediator of the new covenant (Heb 8:6; 9:15; 12:24), and a "priest . . . according to the order of Melchizedek" (Heb 5:6; 6:20; 7:17). In contrast to Levitical priesthood, Jesus' priesthood/brokerage is vastly superior because Jesus "is able for all time to save those who approach God through him, since he always lives to make intercession for them" (Heb 7:25).

We are hardly the first to read John 17 in terms of mediation. Already in patristic times the prayer that constitutes John 17 was labeled "the high priestly" prayer, a tag still affixed to it. Our interpretation accepts the perception of Jesus' role as a mediator figure, not simply in chapter 17, but in the whole of the Farewell Address. Building on past studies of John 14–17, we wish to use the social science model of patron, broker, and client to interpret the role of Jesus as broker as an essential part of understanding worship in the Fourth Gospel.[74]

How does a broker or mediator function in a system of patron-client

73. A. Oepke, "μεσίτης," in *TDNT* 4:598-624.

74. Jesus' brokerage in the Fourth Gospel is best understood in terms of his being "sent" by God; see Malina and Rohrbaugh, *Social-Science Commentary*, 118; Borgen, "God's Agent in the Fourth Gospel"; Buchanan, "Apostolic Christology."

relations? One anthropologist identifies four elements of a broker's functioning: (1) *capital,* what the broker brokers; (2) *tariff,* remuneration for
his services; (3) *debt,* the promises he makes; and (4) *interest,* his calculation of when and how his tariff will be paid.[75] Inasmuch as he brokers
goods and services, what is exchanged in a patron-broker-client relationship? Clients typically seek protection and access to scarce resources,
which are called first-order resources.[76] A broker most frequently has
second-order goods, namely, access to patrons and skill in connecting the
right client with the right patron. In the rough-and-tumble of village or
urban life in antiquity, there might be many clients working through many
brokers to gain access to many patrons.[77] But in the Fourth Gospel there is
only one patron (God) and one clientage (Israel), but competing brokers
(Jesus versus Moses, Abraham, temple, synagogue).[78]

Jesus as Broker in John 14–17

Let us situate Jesus first in relationship to the Patron-Father and then in
relationship to the clients-disciples. It is generally agreed that a successful
broker must be part of the two worlds he joins. The author expresses Jesus' relation to the heavenly world in many ways. For example, Jesus was
sent by God (17:3, 21), which social-science interpreters call his ascribed
authority or honor. Moreover, in 17:5 and 24 Jesus speaks of glory he had
from his Patron before the world was made, which clearly describes Jesus
as belonging to the heavenly world or totally dedicated to the affairs of the

75. Boissevain, *Friends of Friends,* 158-62.

76. The petition in the Our Father, "deliver us from the Evil One," seeks protection or
God's power; requests to Jesus for healing are similar, especially if spirit aggression is the
dominant cause of sickness. Nicolas of Myra is reputed to have provided dowries for a man's
three daughters, in this scheme, wealth. Job might be said to beg of God knowledge, a different resource. Thus, using the model of exchange found in Turner and then in Malina, a patron has "first order" goods: power, commitment, inducement, and influence.

77. As all know, non-Israelite persons in antiquity might become clients of many deities; there was no sense of monotheism to preclude a multiplicity of patron-client relations.

78. Oepke, "μεσίτης," 618-20; Ronald A. Piper, "Glory, Honor and Patronage in the
Fourth Gospel: Understanding the *Doxa* Given to the Disciples in John 17," in *Social Scientific Models for Interpreting the Bible: Essays by the Context Group in Honor of Bruce J. Malina,*
ed. John J. Pilch (Leiden: Brill, 2001), 295-97. In this regard, one thinks of rival rabbinic
teachers, such as Shammai and Hillel.

Father.[79] Thus Jesus' relationship to the Patron is ancient, intimate, and enduring. In John 17, moreover, Jesus repeatedly tells us how loyally he has served the interests of his Patron:

17:4   I glorified you on earth by finishing the work that you gave me to do.

17:6   I have made your name known to those whom you gave me.

17:8   The words that you gave me I have given to them.

17:12   While I was with them, I protected them in your name that you have given me.

17:14   I have given them your word.

He accomplished what God gave him to do, which specifically means manifesting the Patron's name (also in 17:11, 12) and delivering the Patron's words. In addition, Jesus brokered the following for his earthly clients: (1) power (17:2), (2) protection (17:12), and (3) glory (17:22). Thus Jesus belongs to the Patron's world, shares in the riches of that world, and loyally serves the interests of his Patron.

Jesus the broker also belongs to the clients' world and serves their interests as well. For example, Jesus confesses to the Patron the many ways in which he has brokered the safety of the clients:

17:12   I protected them in your name. . . . Not one of them was lost except . . .

17:13   I speak these things in the world so that they may have my joy made complete in themselves.

17:15   I am not asking you to take them out of the world, but I ask you to protect them from the evil one.

17:19   For their sakes I sanctify myself, so that they also may be sanctified in truth.

He not only protects them, but seeks their continued safety. Moreover, he envisions a future brokerage that includes: (1) keeping them from the Evil One (17:15) and (2) being with Jesus where he is in glory (17:24). In an ex-

---

79. In this vein, one might include claims such as 1:18. Expressions such as "no one . . . but the Son" serve to articulate Jesus' relationship to God and the heavenly world: see 3:2, 13; 6:44; and 14:6.

pression of limitless brokering, Jesus repeatedly declares that his clients are assured of his brokerage when they "ask in my name":

14:13   I will do whatever you ask in my name.
14:14   If in my name you ask me for anything, I will do it.
15:16   The Father will give you whatever you ask him in my name.
16:24   Until now you have not asked for anything in my name. Ask and you will receive.
16:26   On that day you will ask in my name. I do not say to you that I will ask the Father on your behalf; for the Father himself loves you.

Jesus is the unique broker, for "no one comes to the Father except through me" (14:6).

Summary, Conclusions, Further Questions

Summary and Conclusions

This study began by providing a current descriptive inventory of worship. In addition, we developed a social science model of worship based on communication theory that adequately explains how both prayer and other types of worship (prophecy, homily, etc.) all belong together as diverse aspects of worship. The communications model identifies and interprets the two directions of communication: (1) worshipers sending a message to the deity for a specific purpose and (2) the deity sending a message to the worshipers for various purposes via various persons in the group. The model identifies both the medium of the communication and the channel along which it is sent, as well as a wide variety of purposes for the communication.

In regard to prayer, the communication model provides a rich typology of prayer, which advances our understanding of the various effects prayer seeks to have on the deity. While we are all familiar with the purpose of petitionary prayer, we found the typology of prayer particularly helpful in identifying petitionary and self-reflective prayers in John 14–17. Moreover, the communication model allowed for a nuanced reading and understanding of other forms of worship, which in the model describe the communication of the deity with worshipers. We identified the following such types of communication in John 14–17: prophecy (oracles of assurance and of judgment), homily, and study of the words of Jesus.

In examining the issue of "where" the Johannine group worshiped, we were greatly aided by the use of a model of fixed versus fluid sacred space. Fluid sacred space, unlike fixed spaces as found in temples, does not embody the system of temple personnel such as we find in Jerusalem's temple.[80] But we can go further than the standard rejections of Mounts Gerizim and Zion and their facile replacements of "spirit and truth." The model of fluid sacred space urges us to examine how both the person of Jesus and the persons of the group become the sacred space. Jesus does not take his disciples out of the world, even though he has prepared a place (i.e., "relationship") for them. The key element in understanding the "where" of worship for the Johannine group lies in appreciating how the risen Jesus continues to offer Christophanies to the group, especially in the revealing of the sacred name "I AM" to them. In short, God draws near to the group through Jesus and the disciples are drawn near to God through Jesus, especially as the figure who bridges the heavenly and earthly worlds. Thus we look to relationships as the "where" of worship.

We addressed the issue of the roles that constitute the relationship just described. The model of patron/broker/client, known both from ancient authors and from modern anthropologists, seems particularly applicable to worship as we find it described in John 14–17. Broker — both the choice of New Testament writers and our best understanding of Jesus' role vis-à-vis God and his disciples — provides an adequate interpretation of the communication in John 14–17: the client's petitions to the heavenly Patron are all made "in my name," just as the Patron's "words" and "commands" all come through Jesus to the disciples. Whether we label him "broker," "mediator," or "priest," we have both a social and a functional understanding of Jesus' role in the verbal worship of the Johannine group.

Finally, scholars agree on the prayer aspect of the section of the Fourth Gospel labeled as a "Farewell Address." But it also contains materials that have never been considered as elements of worship that have remained in the shadows for want of an adequate model to identify them. When one

80. See Joachim Jeremias, *Jerusalem in the Time of Jesus* (Philadelphia: Fortress, 1969), 21-27, 127-221; and K. C. Hanson and Douglas E. Oakman, *Palestine in the Time of Jesus* (Minneapolis: Fortress, 1998), 131-60.

adds to discussions of worship both a communications model and notions of fluid versus sacred space, one finds that a surprising amount of material in John 14–17 can then be seen to be part of a large discourse on worship in the Fourth Gospel. A familiar text is thus freshly interpreted precisely because new models of reading and interpretation suggest new data.

Further Questions

Because we have focused on John 14–17, our investigation of worship is not complete in two ways. First, how are we to interpret pilgrimage feasts to Jerusalem? How do we understand baptism (3:22-26) and eating the bread of life (6:32-56)? As Aune earlier stated, worship consists of "various types of rituals . . . Christians gathered to eat together, to baptize new members, to experience healing."[81] The very presence of the foot washing in 13:12-17 suggests a ceremonial welcome of group members by its officials. Is this the raw material of a study of group worship? The details of a purificatory ritual described in 20:23 are absent, although Jesus authorizes those on whom he breathes to "forgive" and "retain" sins. What, then, still needs to be identified and interpreted? The inquiry is just beginning. Second, the more forms of worship that are identified, the more we need to consider roles and statuses within the group. How might the patron-broker-client model assist us in interpreting the roles of elite members of the group, if this is possible? Third, we have focused only on John 14–17; are there other data in the Gospel about various forms of worship and various aspects of it (time, place, ritual)? We claimed to find most of the elements of worship described by those who make surveys of what constitutes early Christian worship. What, however, have we *not* found in John 14–17? Finally, the worship models exposed here can only benefit from their application to other worship materials in the New Testament.

---

81. See Aune, "Worship, Early Christian," 973.

The *Didache* and Justin's *First Apology:*
Descriptions of Christian Worship

I n this final chapter we turn to other documents, the *Didache* and Justin's *First Apology,* to examine them with our model of worship. The *Didache* as we have it was edited in the early second century, while Justin's *First Apology* is dated mid–second century. Although neither document is an order of worship, each nevertheless talks consciously about worship in the assembly, which in the second century was finding a regular shape. Certain elements appear regularly. And this is our focus: What parts of worship are in view? A model of worship can take us well beyond the translator's chapter headings, for it can surface more data than are generally noticed and provide a more in-depth interpretation. Thus we are using our model of worship both to X-ray and to assess the contents of these two documents, and allowing the "fit" between document and model to confirm its accuracy and utility in reading. These two documents, moreover, are the most self-conscious in the early church concerning worship; it is not that they define and explain it, but they have the largest canvas on which to display the elements of worship as practiced then. They contain the pieces of the mosaic, to which the model of worship ascribes pattern or design.

The briefest repetition of the model of worship will help us keep a sharp focus while reading. According to the model, worship is communication both by mortals to God and by God to mortals. The earlier part of this book was devoted to "prayer," the premier communication of mortals to God. The communication from God to the group is generally realized in the following verbal forms: (1) hearing the Scripture; (2) hearing the words and deeds of Jesus; (3) homilies to the group members; (4) prophetic oracles that assure, judge, prescribe, and announce; and (5) the blessings that accompany baptism and Eucharist. Although we accept the remark that early Christian worship was "verbal," we must include rites of entrance into and exit from the worshiping group, as well as ceremonies regularly performed in the assembly that confirm group identity and unity.

The *Didache*

In considering John 14–17 as worship, we needed a model of worship to be able to identify elements of worship scattered through the Farewell Address and to gather them in a unity as parts of worship: prayers communicating with God and God communicating with the disciples. The *Didache*, on the other hand, presents a scenario of events that typically took place when the group assembled; the author understands them to be parts of a worship service, although he ever uses such terms. The *Didache*, then, would seem to be an easy document to interpret because we know that it is self-consciously parading basic parts of a worship service, even presenting them in a fixed chronological sequence.

Reading the *Didache* in terms of a specific model, much less one from the social sciences, is foreign to current studies of the *Didache*. In general we tend to find studies of (1) specific sections or passages or terms, (2) the work's relationship to earlier works (Matthew, *Barnabas*), (3) liturgical rituals such as "prayer" and "Eucharist," and (4) the Semitic background of various parts, such as the "two ways." We expect, however, from reading the *Didache* in terms of our model, to identify many more elements of worship, both familiar and less so. Surfacing data is one of the model's benefits; interpreting them is another. Even a casual skimming of the document identifies the following elements.

1. Exhortation: The Two Ways (1–6)
2. Baptism, Entrance Ritual (7)
3. Prayer (8)
4. Eucharist (9–10)
5. Ceremonial Personnel (11–13; 15)
6. Purity Ritual (14)
7. Final Exhortation (16)

This is but a preliminary catalogue of worship, a list that will grow much longer as we read and interpret.

Exhortation

Chapter 1. The Two Ways

1There are two ways, one of life and one of death, but a great difference between the two ways. 2The way of life, then, is this: First, you shall love God who made you; second, love your neighbor as yourself, and do not do to another what you would not want done to you. 3And of these sayings the teaching is this: Bless those who curse you, and pray for your enemies, and fast for those who persecute you. For what reward is there for loving those who love you? Do not the Gentiles do the same? But love those who hate you, and you shall not have an enemy. 4Abstain from fleshly and worldly lusts. If someone strikes your right cheek, turn to him the other also, and you shall be perfect. If someone impresses you for one mile, go with him two. If someone takes your cloak, give him also your coat. If someone takes from you what is yours, ask it not back, for indeed you are not able. 5Give to every one who asks you, and ask it not back; for the Father wills that to all should be given of our own blessings (free gifts). Happy is he who gives according to the commandment, for he is guiltless. Woe to him who receives; for if one receives who has need, he is guiltless; but he who receives not having need shall pay the penalty, why he received and for what. And coming into confinement, he shall be examined concerning the things which he has done, and he shall not escape from there until he pays back the last penny. 6And also concerning this, it has been said, Let your alms sweat in your hands, until you know to whom you should give.

Scholars generally agree that *Didache* 1–6 forms a rhetorical unit under the topic "instruction for baptismal candidates." The key piece of evidence that this exhortation was intended for those preparing for baptism is found in the beginning of the section that describes baptism: "Having first said all these things, baptize into the name of . . ." (7.1). There is nothing specific about baptism or rebirth in this exhortation; moreover, many of the items presented are found in the parenetic sections of Paul's letters. Whether it is a "baptismal" exhortation or more neutrally a group exhortation, it communicates Scripture and the words of Jesus; it is a communication from God to the church, and so we consider it a homily or exhortation. And we will be considering it in terms of deliberative rhetoric, that is, rhetoric that urges right choice.

EXCURSUS ON DELIBERATIVE RHETORIC

When rhetoricians define deliberative rhetoric, they understand it as either ex-hortation (protreptic) or dissuasion (apotreptic). Its time orientation is the future, that is, what should be done. And it argues from advantage; some things are advantageous *(sympheron)* and others harmful *(blaberon)* (Aristotle, *Rhetoric* 1.3.5-6).

The exhortation begins with a topic statement: "There are two ways, one of life and one of death, but a great difference between the two ways" (1.1). In terms of rhetorical structure, this is the statement of the thing to be argued (πρόθεσις, Aristotle, *Rhetoric* 3.13.2; or *propositio*, Quintilian, *Institutio oratoria* 3.9.5; 4.2.7). In deliberative rhetoric the speaker states quite clearly what is to be chosen or avoided. This element is essential to a discourse, for as Aristotle states, "It is necessary to state the subject and then prove it" (3.13.1), for how can one argue something that has not been clearly set forth? It is, he states, one of the essential parts of a discourse: "At most, the parts [of a speech] are four in number — exordium, *statement* (πρόθεσις), argument, epilogue" (3.13.4; see Quintilian 3.3.1). The length of the statement varies, and the rhetoricians indicate that it can be succinct ("The statement of facts will be brief," Quintilian 4.2.40 and 4.4.8), which is the case in *Didache* 1.1.

According to rhetorical theory, the proof (πίστις, *argumentatio*) follows the topic statement, which proof is often achieved through comparison ("comparison is an amplification of one's own case, and therefore also part of the proof," Aristotle 3.13.3). Since the topic of this deliberative exhortation is the contrast between the way of life and the way of death, it is hardly surprising that comparison or juxtaposition becomes the chief mode of argumentation. And since deliberative rhetoric argues from "advantage," clearly "life" is to be chosen because it is advantageous, while "death" should be avoided because it is utterly disadvantageous. Let us now consider *Didache* 1–6 as deliberative rhetoric, indeed, as a homily.

The author first develops the "way of life" in considerable detail. Even here we find a topic statement that basically informs us of what that way is. The author sets before the hearers their basic duties: (1) *duties to God* ("You shall love the God who made you") and (2) *duties to one's neighbor* ("Do not do to another what you would not want done to you"). The duty to God is rooted in the Scripture (Lev 19:18) and was stated by Jesus as well (Matt 22:37-39). Nothing more, however, is said about one's duties to God, as the focus turns exclusively to duties to one's neighbor, namely, the "golden rule." This "rule," also, is a word of Jesus, found in his premier exhortation, the Sermon on the Mount (Matt 7:12). Thus, as one might expect, the exhortation on the "way of life" begins with citations from the Scripture and the Jesus tradition, from which the rest of the material will be drawn. In many ways, then, this resembles a "proem" type of homily that develops for the "golden rule" of Jesus.

Excursus: The Virtue of Justice

In claiming that the author of the *Didache* is exhorting the group to virtue, especially to fulfill one's duties, we should examine what "justice" meant in popular discourse. First, we find in Pseudo-Aristotle a commonplace description of justice and duties: "To righteousness it belongs to be ready to distribute according to desert, and to preserve ancestral customs and institutions and the established laws, and to tell the truth when interest is at stake, and to keep agreements. First among the claims of righteousness are our duties to the gods, then our duties to the spirits, then those to country and parents, then those to the departed; among these claims is piety, which is either a part of righteousness or a concomitant of it. Righteousness is also accompanied by holiness and truth and loyalty and hatred of wickedness" (*Virtues and Vices* 5.2-3).

After stating the "golden rule," the author immediately develops it: "And of these sayings the teaching is this . . ." (1.3). He makes a selection of Jesus' sayings from the Antitheses of the Sermon in Matthew 5. This has the feel of a study of Jesus and the Gospels. This consideration of Jesus' teaching is communication from God and the heavenly world to the assembly. Various duties are spelled out, namely, the duties of the disciples to all others, even enemies. In essence, these duties explain how according to the "golden rule" a disciple does not return evil for evil. Subsequently, we find a "woe" balancing a "blessing." The statement is made that we ought to give and not refuse, which is supported by a commandment from God, "For the Father wills that to all should be given of our own blessings (free gifts)" (1.5). "Happy is he who gives according to the commandment," but "woe to him who [only] receives." The argument from advantage obviously sees benefit (blessings) in giving but disadvantage (woe) in failure to give.

Chapter 2. Duties to Others

1And the second commandment of the Teaching; 2You shall not commit murder, you shall not commit adultery, you shall not commit pederasty, you shall not commit fornication, you shall not steal, you shall not practice magic, you shall not practice witchcraft, you shall not murder a child by abortion nor kill that which is born. You shall not covet the things of your neighbor, 3you shall not swear, you shall not bear false witness, you shall not speak evil, you shall bear no grudge. 4You shall not be double-minded nor double-tongued, for to be double-tongued is a snare of death. 5Your speech shall not be false, nor empty, but fulfilled by deed. You shall not be covetous, nor rapacious, nor a hypocrite, nor evil disposed, nor haughty. 6You shall not take evil counsel against your neighbor. 7You shall not hate any man; but some you shall reprove, and concerning some you shall pray, and some you shall love more than your own life.

Next appears the Decalogue, another part of Scripture, which the author labels "the second commandment of the Teaching" (2.1). If love of God is the first tablet of the Ten Commandments, then love of neighbor would be the second tablet. These commandments appear to be a list of the core duties that individuals have toward others. In addition to the commandments, we find an exhortation to avoid certain vices that harm social intercourse: double-mindedness and double-tongued, vain speech (one promises to do something but does not act), hypocrisy, etc. (2.4-7). This exhortation, moreover, even if a mere recitation of the "second commandment," is nevertheless a communication from God to the group from the Scriptures.

Chapter 3. Paternal Exhortation of Other Duties

1My child, flee from every evil thing, and from every likeness of it. 2Be not prone to anger, for anger leads to murder. Be neither jealous, nor quarrelsome, nor of hot temper, for out of all these murders are engendered. 3My child, be not a lustful one, for lust leads to fornication. Be neither a filthy talker, nor of lofty eye, for out of all these adulteries are engendered. 4My child, be not an observer of omens, since it leads to idolatry. Be neither an enchanter, nor an astrologer, nor a purifier, nor be willing to look at these things, for out of all these idolatry is engendered. 5My child, be not a liar, since a lie leads to theft. Be neither money-loving, nor vainglorious, for out of all these thefts are engendered. 6My child, be not a murmurer, since it leads the way to blasphemy. Be neither self-willed nor evil-minded, for out of all these blasphemies are engendered. 7Rather, be meek, since the meek shall inherit the earth. 8Be long-suffering and pitiful and guileless and gentle and good and always trembling at the words which you have heard. 9You shall not exalt yourself, nor give over-confidence to your soul. Your soul shall not be joined with lofty ones, but with just and lowly ones shall it have its intercourse. 10Accept whatever happens to you as good, knowing that apart from God nothing comes to pass.

The audience is addressed as "my child," which accepts the fiction that it is the duty of a true parent to instruct and discipline his children. The author later exhorts the parent to "teach [children] the fear of God from their youth" (4.9). More duties are stated, many of which appeared earlier. But in this part the hearers are instructed to control their bodies, because according to the Judean purity system the critical bodily orifices must be regulated. For example, disciples must control their genitals: "lust leads to fornication . . . out of all these adulteries are engendered" (3.3). "Lust," of course, begins in the eyes, which must also be controlled: be not "of lofty eye" (3.3). "An observer of omens" uses the eyes for esoteric information (3.4). The mouth, too, gets attention: "be not a liar . . . a murmurer . . . self-willed" (3.5-6). Many of these statements sport a reason for them ("for"), which indicates how something minor, if left unattended, will lead to great ruin: be not a murmurer, *for* this leads to blasphemy, nor a thinker of evil, "*for* out of all these blasphemies are engendered" (3.6). Concern, then, is expressed over a lesser problem before it turns into a severe one. There is great advantage, then, in being concerned about minor things, lest they sicken into major ones.

Chapter 4. Duties to Others

1My child, remember night and day him who speaks the word of God to you, and honor him as you do the Lord. For wherever the lordly rule is uttered, there is the Lord. 2And seek out day by day the faces of the saints, in order that you may rest upon their words. 3Do not long for division, but rather bring those who contend to peace. Judge righteously, and do not respect persons in reproving for transgressions. 4You shall not be undecided whether or not it shall be. 5Be not a stretcher forth of the hands to receive and a drawer of them back to give. 6If you have anything, through your hands you shall give ransom for your sins. 7Do not hesitate to give, nor complain when you give; for you shall know who is the good repayer of the hire. 8Do not turn away from him who is in want; rather, share all things with your brother, and do not say that they are your own. For if you are partakers in that which is immortal, how much more in things which are mortal? 9Do not remove your hand from your son or daughter; rather, teach them the fear of God from their youth. 10Do not enjoin anything in your bitterness upon your bondman or maidservant, who hope in the same God, lest ever they shall fear not God who is over both; for he comes not to call according to the outward appearance, but to them whom the Spirit has prepared. 11And you bondmen shall be subject to your masters as to a type of God, in modesty and fear. 12You shall hate all hypocrisy and everything which is not pleasing to the Lord. 13Do not in any way forsake the commandments of the Lord; but keep what you have received, neither adding thereto nor taking away therefrom. 14In the church you shall acknowledge your transgressions, and you shall not come near for your prayer with an evil conscience. This is the way of life.

Still more duties are articulated here. First, the hearer has a duty to the leader of the group, "who speaks the word of God to you." Because he is God's agent, hearers are asked to "honor him as you do the Lord" (4.1). Hence in honoring this person, one fulfills one's duty to God, who authorized him. Secondly, the hearers are enjoined to "seek out day by day the faces of the saints," which we consider a duty one has to the Jesus group. The following material about almsgiving and generosity can be understood as one's duty to the poor members of the group (4.5-8). This parallels the earlier material on giving from what one has received (1.5-6), which at the time we considered as a duty to one's neighbor in general. Following this is an exhortation for right relationships in a family, a topic known to New Testament scholars as a "code of household duties." In view are "son or daughter," "bondman or maidservant" (4.9-11). This part ends with instructions that pertain to the congregation, and so we consider them as duties to the group. "Do not in any way forsake the commandments of the Lord; but keep what you have received" (4.13), an injunction similar to Deuteronomy 4:2, 12:32, and Revelation 22:18-19. The purity of the group is again the author's concern, for he urges the hearer to "acknowledge your transgressions" when necessary (4.14). Duties, then, are quite in evidence here: to the leader, to the saints, to the poor within the group, to one's household, and finally to the congregation once more. Within the group we observe many rituals. First, frequent contact with group members is urged, which confirms identity and membership. Almsgiving is an act of patronage, all the more so when the donation is made to a group member, thus confirming identity in the same group and duties to one another. Finally, in the assembly one should confess his transgressions, which appears to be a form of petitionary prayer for purification.

Chapter 5. The Way of Death

1And the way of death is this: First of all it is evil and accursed: murders, adultery, lust, fornication, thefts, idolatries, magic arts, witchcraft, rape, false witness, hypocrisy, double-heartedness, deceit, haughtiness, depravity, self-will, greediness, filthy talking, jealousy, over-confidence, loftiness, boastfulness; 2persecutors of the good, hating truth, loving a lie, not knowing a reward for righteousness, not cleaving to good nor to righteous judgment, watching not for that which is good, but for that which is evil; from whom meekness and endurance are far, loving vanities, pursuing revenge, not pitying a poor man, not laboring for the afflicted, not knowing Him Who made them, murderers of children, destroyers of the handiwork of God, turning away from him who is in want, afflicting him who is distressed, advocates of the rich, lawless judges of the poor, utter sinners. Be delivered, children, from all these.

Finally the author takes up the second topic, the "way of death," although not as thoroughly as the "way of life." The deliberative character of the "way of life" was communicated by imperatives: don't do x; be not y, which had much of exhortation in them. But the "way of death" is simply a cascade of evils and vices (5.1-2), indeed similar to the "vice lists" common in gospels and letters. The "way of death" concludes with an exhortation that is part prayer: "Be delivered, children, from all these" (5.2). The "way of death," then, is all disadvantage that should be avoided.

Chapter 6. Perfection and Possibility

1See that no one causes you to err from this way of the Teaching, since apart from God it teaches you. 2For if you are able to bear the entire yoke of the Lord, you will be perfect; but if you are not able to do this, do what you are able. 3And concerning food, bear what you are able; but against that which is sacrificed to idols be exceedingly careful; for it is the service of dead gods.

The exhortation formally ends not so much with a summary highlighting previous material, but with an exhortation to use discretion in following the "way of life." First, the hearers are cautioned about teachers; not all are orthodox and some will be threatening: "See that no one causes you to err from this way of the Teaching" (6.1). In terms of communication, not all speakers speak for God. Exhortation: avoid them. Although perfection comes from bearing the "entire yoke of the Lord," those who cannot are asked to do what they can (6.2). The same exhortation is given about foods: "Bear what you are able" (6.3).

Excursus on Wholeness

Wholeness, an essential element in the purity system of Israel, assesses what is "too much" or "too little." People who have two faces, have too much: "But do not, my children, wear two faces like unto them, of goodness and of wickedness; but cleave unto goodness only, for God has his habitation therein, and men desire it. But flee away from wickedness, destroying the inclination by your good works; for they that are double-faced serve not God but their own desires so that they may please Beliar and men like themselves" (*Testament of Asher* 3.1-2). And people without some body part have too little: "With regard to the priests there are the following laws. It is ordained that the priest should be perfectly sound throughout, without any bodily deformity. No part, that is, must be lacking or have been mutilated, nor on the other hand redundant, whether the excrescence be congenital or an after growth due to disease. Nor must the skin have been changed into a leprous state or into malignant tatters or warts or any other eruptive growth" (Philo, *On the Special Laws* 1.80).

In summary, we consider *Didache* 1–6 to be a homily and exhortation for the following reasons. (1) It is deliberative rhetoric, which exhorts the audience to choose good and avoid evil. (2) The argument is based on appeal to advantage and disadvantage, i.e., "blessing" versus "woe." (3) After the topic of the homily is announced, the "way of life" begins with Scripture ("Love God who made you") and with a word of the Lord ("Do not do to another what you would not want done to you"; see Matt 7:12), a feature of ancient homilies. (4) This statement of Jesus, moreover, becomes the "text" for the "way of life," in that it organizes the subsequent material and brings into consideration more words of Jesus from the Sermon on the Mount for illustration and proof. (5) We suggest as a subtext for the homily, exhortation to "justice," which means that one acquits oneself of one's duties to God, polis (or group), and family. The hearers were exhorted to honor God (1.2), their neighbors, the leader of the group, the poor of the group, their households, and the congregation. Hence, the homily urges the hearers to do good (fulfill their duties) and avoid evil. It seems not to matter in this analysis whether the homily was intended as catechetical exhortation to those preparing for baptism or as instruction to a post-baptismal group. It stands on its own as a homily, an exhortation.

Entrance Ritual

Chapter 7. Concerning Baptism

1And concerning baptism, baptize this way: Having first said all these things, baptize into the name of the Father, and of the Son, and of the Holy Spirit, in living water. 2But if you have no living water, baptize into other water; and if you cannot do so in cold water, do so in warm. 3But if you have neither, pour out water three times upon the head into the name of Father and Son and Holy Spirit. 4But before the baptism let the baptizer fast, and the baptized, and whoever else can; but you shall order the baptized to fast one or two days before.

We are informed of many details of this transformation ritual. Presumably there is some liminal process in view, a common feature of transformation rituals. After leaving familiar surroundings, family, and previous roles, initiands begin to learn what is needed for the new life, namely, discipline, special knowledge, obedience, endurance. At the completion of the liminal period, initiands undergo a transformative ritual by which they assume new statuses and/or new roles. Most importantly, this transformation must then be acknowledged by others, in this case the group who welcomes them. The liminal period is alluded to in the instruction "Having first said all these things. . . ." This presumably refers to the earlier exhortation on the "two ways," which both informs and forms the initiands to leave the "way of death" and walk in the "way of life." The initiands climax the liminal process by fasting one or two days. They do not fast alone, but are accompanied by the persons who officiate at the baptism and by others in the group, thus dramatizing how the group is already praying for them and acknowledging their new status. Evidently the entrance ritual consists of word and action. The action of baptismal washing employs water for washing, with preference for running and cold water. The words used are a strict formula of blessing in the "name" of Father, Son, and Spirit. Along with a status-transformation ritual, we find also prayer, namely, petitionary prayer expressed in fasting.

Prayer (and Fasting)

Chapter 8. Fasting and Prayer (the Lord's Prayer)

1But let not your fasts be with the hypocrites, for they fast on the second and fifth day of the week. Rather, fast on the fourth day and the Preparation (Friday). 2Do not pray like the hypocrites, but rather as the Lord commanded in His Gospel, like this: "Our Father who art in heaven, hallowed be Thy name. Thy kingdom come. Thy will be done on earth, as it is in heaven. Give us today our daily (needful) bread, and forgive us our debt as we also forgive our debtors. And bring us not into temptation, but deliver us from the evil one; for Thine is the power and the glory for ever." 3Pray this three times each day.

Inasmuch as prayer, fasting, and almsgiving were regularly linked in Judaism and Christianity (Matt 6:1-18), the sequencing of fasting and prayer here seems quite logical. The instruction on prayer closely resembles that of the Sermon on the Mount. First we are told how *not* to pray ("Do not pray like the hypocrites," 8.2), and then positively how to pray, "as the Lord commanded in His Gospel." As blame and praise are awarded to types of prayers, the author seeks to persuade his audience to avoid blameworthy and disadvantageous prayer but to choose praiseworthy and advantageous prayer. An expanded version of the Our Father appears, complete with a concluding doxology. Finally, the speaker requests that the group pray this prayer three times a day, perhaps mimicking the synagogue's praying of the Shema or echoing Matthew's report that Jesus prayed this prayer three times in the garden (26:39, 42, 44). (See chapter 3 for a full exegesis of the prayer.) But it should be noted that both fasting and prayers are a communication of senders to God. As regards prayer, praying the Our Father thrice daily is a ceremony — a regular and fixed time for prayer and an official text prayed only by the Jesus group. Obedience to this injunction confirms membership as well as right understanding of God. As regards types of prayers, we observe petitionary (fasting; the last four petitions of the Our Father) and acknowledgment ("Thou petitions"; doxology).

Eucharist

Chapter 9. Concerning Giving Thanks

1Now concerning the Eucharist, give thanks this way. 2First, concerning the cup: We thank Thee, our Father, for the holy vine of David Thy servant, which You madest known to us through Jesus Thy Servant; to Thee be the glory for ever. 3And concerning the broken bread: We thank Thee, our Father, for the life and knowledge which You madest known to us through Jesus Thy Servant; to Thee be the glory for ever. 4Even as this broken bread was scattered over the hills, and was gathered together and became one, so let Thy Church be gathered together from the ends of the earth into Thy kingdom; for Thine is the glory and the power through Jesus Christ for ever. 5But let no one eat or drink of your Eucharist, unless they have been baptized into the name of the Lord; for concerning this also the Lord has said, "Give not that which is holy to the dogs."

The author states the common topic of this chapter and the next, "concerning the Eucharist," by which he means both prayers and ceremonies. We will argue that *Didache* 9–10 is mostly prayers and mostly prayers of appreciation, the meaning of εὐχαριστέω, which we argued earlier. Two blessing prayers are spoken, first over wine and then over bread:

We give thanks (εὐχαριστήσατε) to thee, our Father,
   for the holy vine of David your child

which you have made known to us through Jesus your child.
To you be glory forever.

We give thanks (εὐχαριστήσατε) to thee, our Father,
    for the life and knowledge
    which you made known to us through Jesus your child.
To you be glory forever.

God is addressed as a generous patron, "our Father," who provides us with
(1) *inducement* (wine and bread), (2) *influence* ("made known to us through
Jesus . . . the life and knowledge which you made known"), and (3) *commitment* ("our Father . . . Jesus your child"). Favoritism in this patronage is made
clear by the injunction to withhold these foods from those not baptized, a
command given by Jesus himself: "Give not that which is holy to the dogs."
For such benefaction the disciples pray prayers of gratitude and appreciation. Each prayer ends with a doxology ("To you be glory forever"), a prayer
of acknowledgment. Immediately following these prayers, the author petitions God to gather those who worship, using terms similar to the petition
expressed by Jesus in John 17:11. The prayer petitions God for shepherding of
the disciples, instead of scattering. The petition endures until all are gathered
into God's kingdom, a future time utterly unknowable by us. Although the
ceremony of the Eucharist is referred to, most of the worship here is prayer
of three types: petitionary, acknowledgment, and appreciation.

Chapter 10. Prayer after Communion

1But after you are filled, give thanks this way: 2We thank Thee, holy Father, for Thy holy name which You caused to tabernacle in our hearts,
and for the knowledge and faith and immortality, which You made
known to us through Jesus Thy Servant; to Thee be the glory for ever.
3Thou, Master almighty, did create all things for Thy name's sake; You
gave food and drink to men for enjoyment, that they might give thanks
to Thee; but to us You freely give spiritual food and drink and life eternal through Thy Servant. 4Before all things we thank Thee that You are
mighty; to Thee be the glory for ever. 5Remember, Lord, Thy Church, to
deliver it from all evil and to make it perfect in Thy love, and gather it
from the four winds, sanctified for Thy kingdom which You have prepared for it; for Yours is the power and the glory for ever. 6Let grace
come, and let this world pass away. Hosanna to the God (Son) of David!

If any one is holy, let him come; if any one is not so, let him repent. Maranatha. Amen. 7But permit the prophets to make Thanksgiving as much as they desire.

This chapter continues the same topic as the previous one, "concerning the Eucharist," but with instructions on prayers of gratitude: "Give thanks (εὐχαριστήσατε) this way," the identifying mark for this kind of prayer that is used four times in this section (10.1, 2, 3, 4).

> We give thanks (εὐχαριστοῦμεν) to you, O Holy Father,
>> for your Holy Name which you made to tabernacle in our hearts,
>> for the knowledge, faith, and immortality which you made known to us
>>> through Jesus your child.
>>> *To you be glory forever.*
>
> Above all we give thanks (εὐχαριστοῦμεν) to you
>> for you are mighty.
>> *To you be glory forever.*

Again we observe two kinds of prayers: (1) *appreciation/gratitude* ("we give thanks") and (2) *acknowledgment* ("To you be glory forever"). Considering *Didache* 10 as a whole, the benefactions for which the group shows gratitude are: (1) *commitment* (Holy Name tabernacles in our hearts; Holy Father; communication through a family member, through your holy child); (2) *power* (almighty Lord . . . you are mighty); (3) *influence* (knowledge and faith made known through Jesus); and (4) *inducement* (God creates all things, especially food and drink for all humans; spiritual food and drink and eternal light). And in a gesture of favoritism, God has given to the disciples of Jesus "spiritual food and drink and life eternal." Eventually we are presented with petitionary prayer:

> Remember, Lord, your church:
>> to deliver it from all evil.
>> to make it perfect in your love,
>> to gather it together in its holiness. . . .
> For Yours is the power and the glory forever.

The petition here resembles that found after the prayers of gratitude in 9.4, a prayer for God's extended providential care of God's favorites. The nuance here looks to the holiness of the church, its separation from evil and its perfection in love. The communication to God in the petitionary prayer is supported by the command "If any one is holy, let him come; if any one is not so, let him repent." A final prayer of acknowledgment concludes the chapter: "Hosanna to the God of David!" Prayer, then, is the dominant motif of *Didache* 9–10.

Who Has Voice? Who May Speak?

Chapter 11. Concerning Teachers, Apostles, and Prophets

1Whoever, therefore, comes and teaches you all these things that have been said before, receive him. 2If the teacher himself turns and teaches another doctrine to the destruction of this, hear him not. But if he teaches so as to increase righteousness and the knowledge of the Lord, receive him as the Lord. 3Concerning the apostles and prophets, act according to the decree of the Gospel. 4Let every apostle who comes to you be received as the Lord. 5But he shall not remain more than one day; or two days, if there's a need. But if he remains three days, he is a false prophet. 6And when the apostle goes away, let him take nothing but bread until he lodges. If he asks for money, he is a false prophet. 7And every prophet who speaks in the Spirit you shall neither try nor judge; for every sin shall be forgiven, but this sin shall not be forgiven. 8But not every one who speaks in the Spirit is a prophet; but only if he holds the ways of the Lord. Therefore from their ways shall the false prophet and the prophet be known. 9And every prophet who orders a meal in the Spirit does not eat it, unless he is indeed a false prophet. 10And every prophet who teaches the truth, but does not do what he teaches, is a false prophet. 11And every prophet, proved true, working unto the mystery of the Church in the world, yet not teaching others to do what he himself does, shall not be judged among you, for with God he has his judgment; for so did also the ancient prophets. 12But whoever says in the Spirit, Give me money, or something else, you shall not listen to him. But if he tells you to give for others' sake who are in need, let no one judge him.

Because worship is also a communication from God, who speaks to the group is an important concern. Clearly issues such as "who has voice?" and "who may speak?" impinge upon the conduct of the assembled group, although the process of settling this is not necessarily itself worship. Thus, the material in chapters 11–13 instructs the worshiping group about those who speak to it: Who is authorized to speak? Who has voice? Who is communicating God's word to the group? There seems to be a presumption here that the group has specified local members in it who are acknowledged as worthy teachers. And so, the issues raised in these chapters concern persons who "come" into the group, presumably itinerant apostles, teachers, and prophets.

This body of materials begins with a topic statement about whom to receive and whom not to listen to. Receive the teacher who teaches according to "all these things that have been said before" (11.1). But speakers who teach "another doctrine to the destruction of this" should not be listened to. In short, only teachers who teach so as to "increase righteousness and the knowledge of the Lord" should be received.

The body of instruction begins with a typical topic heading: "*concerning* the apostles and prophets" (11.3), which the author has used repeatedly as a topic indicator: "concerning food" (6.3), "concerning baptism" (7.1), and "concerning the Eucharist" (9.1). The instruction about apostles and prophets is quite general: "act according to the decree of the Gospel" (11.3), presumably a reference to a Gospel discourse by Jesus himself (Matt 10:5-15). On the one hand, "receive" the apostle, but if he overstays his welcome, he is a false prophet. Send him on his way with his daily bread; but if he asks for money, he is a false prophet. Hospitality is to be presumed, until abuse appears; hospitality in this case is a ceremony, for by providing sustenance for the traveling prophets the group acknowledges its role. Continuing with discourse on prophets, the author speaks antithetically about speaking in a spirit. On the one hand, the group should not test or examine this person; but on the other, since not all speakers in a spirit are genuine, they may be evaluated on whether they have the behavior of the Lord (11.7-8). But what behavior is not that of the Lord? First, if a prophet in the spirit orders a meal (more abuse of hospitality), he is false; second, if he does not teach the truth, he is false; third, if he says in the Spirit, "Give me money, or something else" (still more abuse), he is false. As we see, the request for money or goods and the taxing of the resources of the group are just indicators that the speakers' claims to be communicators of God are proved false. Who, then, communicates God's word to the group? Until abuse appears, any of the aforementioned apostles and prophets have voice in the assembly.

Chapter 12. Reception of Christians

1But receive everyone who comes in the name of the Lord, and prove and know him afterward; for you shall have understanding right and left. 2If he who comes is a wayfarer, assist him as far as you are able; but he shall not remain with you more than two or three days, if need be. 3But if he wants to stay with you, and is an artisan, let him work and eat. 4But if he has no trade, according to your understanding, see to it that, as a Christian, he shall not live with you idle. 5But if he wills not to do, he is a Christ-monger. Watch that you keep away from such.

Although this section is not labeled "concerning travelers," like the previous material, it speaks consistently to that topic. Once more, the basic principle is that the group must show hospitality in general to those who come "in the name of the Lord" (12.1). The author specifies this principle through four conditional statements, all begun by the word "if." First, *if* the person is a traveler, help him, but not more than two or three days (12.2). Second, *if* he wishes to remain with you, he must earn his bread. Third, *if* he has no craft to earn his bread, the group must provide for him, but he shall not live in idleness. Fourth, *if* the traveler will not earn his keep, "he is a Christ-monger," that is, "making traffic of Christ" (12.5). Presumed, then, is that those who come "in the name of the Lord" speak for God; but those who tax the group's resources are shown to be false.

Chapter 13. Support of Prophets

1But every true prophet who wants to live among you is worthy of his support. 2So also a true teacher is himself worthy, as the workman, of his support. 3Every first-fruit, therefore, of the products of wine-press and threshing-floor, of oxen and of sheep, you shall take and give to the prophets, for they are your high priests. 4But if you have no prophet, give it to the poor. 5If you make a batch of dough, take the first-fruit and give according to the commandment. 6So also when you open a jar of wine or of oil, take the first-fruit and give it to the prophets; 7and of money (silver) and clothing and every possession, take the first-fruit, as it may seem good to you, and give according to the commandment.

The final part of this section speaks to the "worthiness" of a prophet. The topic sentence states that true prophets who settle among the group are "worthy of [their] support." The argument rests on the parallel drawn between a workman and the prophet, both of whom are worthy of support because of their labors, just as Jesus said in Matthew 10:10 (see 1 Cor 9:3-12). The status and role of the prophets are increased when the author claims for them that "they are your high priests" (13.3). Just as tithes were brought to the priests for temple support, so too firstfruits are to be assigned to the prophet. What follows is a catalogue of goods that the prophet should receive: wine, grain, oxen, sheep, money, and clothing. And if bread is baked, he gets the firstfruits; if vessels of wine and oil are opened, he receives the firstfruits.

Teaching should be interpreted as a ceremony. At a precise time and place (the assembly), someone speaks in the name of the Lord in accord with tradition. He may also pray the Eucharist in a unique manner (see 10.7). Every time the teacher or prophet speaks, his role is confirmed. Despite his elevation as "high priest," he does not experience any status transformation; on the contrary, his teaching confirms the identity of the group as disciples of Jesus who hear once more the teaching of Jesus. We suggest, moreover, that the persistent concern with money, hospitality, and goods is also part of the ceremonial confirmation of the teacher or prophet. When hospitality is shown, it is because the person claims the role of teacher or prophet; the ceremonial acknowledgment of this is expressed by the support of the group. If the teacher misuses the group's resources, they withdraw their confirmation of him. Finally, the prophet who is labeled a high priest rightfully receives tithes or firstfruits. Every time members of the group bring them to the prophet, his role and status are confirmed. Indirectly, then, we find the teacher and prophet functioning in a ceremonial context in which their voice or authorization is confirmed.

Transformation Rituals

Chapter 14. Rituals of the Lord's Day

1But every Lord's day gather yourselves together, and break bread, and give thanksgiving after having confessed your transgressions, that your sacrifice may be pure. 2But let no one who is at odds with his fellow come together with you, until they be reconciled, that your sacrifice may not be profaned. 3For this is that which was spoken by the Lord: "In every place and time offer to me a pure sacrifice; for I am a great King, says the Lord, and my name is wonderful among the nations."

Although it is doubtful that this group worships in a fixed sacred space, it does have a fixed, calendrical time for worshiping on the "Lord's day" (and fasting on Wednesdays and Fridays; 8.1). On the Lord's Day two rituals occur: (1) breaking bread and holding Eucharist and (2) confessing transgressions. This, of course, is the kind of topic statement we have seen frequently in this document. The first part, the Eucharist, is skipped, presumably because it was treated earlier. Which "transgressions"? Presumably the intragroup quarrels mentioned next. These quarrels are considered so weighty that they threaten to "profane" the worship; yet the Lord demands a "pure" sacrifice. This echoes the command of Jesus for a disciple who has offended another to "make friends" before offering a sacrifice (Matt 5:23-24). The Eucharist, we have seen, is a ceremonial meal confirming membership in the body of Christ. The individual participants as well as the group must be holy. But "confessing one's transgressions" means participating in a status-transformation ritual, changing from unclean to clean. Although confession is mentioned after the Eucharist here, it precedes it temporally because the Eucharist is held "after" confession of transgressions. In view are ceremonial meals and transformation penance rites.

Judgment Oracles

Chapter 15. A Potpourri

1Appoint, therefore, for yourselves, bishops and deacons worthy of the Lord, men meek, and not lovers of money, and truthful and proved; for they also render to you the service of prophets and teachers. 2Therefore do not despise them, for they are your honored ones, together with the prophets and teachers. 3And reprove one another, not in anger, but in peace, as you have it in the Gospel. But to anyone that acts amiss against another, let no one speak, nor let him hear anything from you until he repents. 4But your prayers and alms and all your deeds so do, as you have it in the Gospel of our Lord.

Similar to the judgment ritual described in Matthew 18:12-18, we find two different status-transformation rituals. First, a member of the group may "reprove" another, presumably changing him from sinner back to saint. Second, a shunning process allows the group to stop all communication with a member of the group who has injured his neighbor (15.3). Should we consider the treatment of an erring member an oracle of judgment? This material seems related to what we read in 14.1-3. We are not told that these judgments are part of a worship service, but it is hard to imagine that they did not begin in the group assembly and find their resolution there.

Final Exhortation

Chapter 16. Final Exhortation

1Watch for your life's sake. Let not your lamps be quenched, nor your loins unloosed; but be ready, for you know not the hour in which our Lord will come. 2But come together often, seeking the things which are befitting to your souls: for the whole time of your faith will not profit you, if you are not made perfect in the last time. 3For in the last days false prophets and corrupters shall be multiplied, and the sheep shall be turned into wolves, and love shall be turned into hate; 4for when lawlessness increases, they shall hate and persecute and betray one another, and then shall appear the world-deceiver as Son of God, and shall do signs and wonders, and the earth shall be delivered into his hands, and he shall do iniquitous things which have never yet come to pass since the beginning. 5Then shall the creation of men come into the fire of trial, and many shall be made to stumble and shall perish; but those who endure in their faith shall be saved from under the curse itself. 6And then shall appear the signs of the truth: first, the sign of an outspreading in heaven, then the sign of the sound of the trumpet. And third, the resurrection of the dead — yet not of all, but as it is said: "The Lord shall come and all His saints with Him." 8Then shall the world see the Lord coming upon the clouds of heaven.

The document ends with an appropriate concluding exhortation. The topic, as we have come to see, is stated immediately: "Watch for your life's sake. Let not your lamps be quenched, nor your loins unloosed . . ." (16.1). The "text" for this exhortation seems to come from Jesus' farewell instruction while seated on the Mount of Olives (Matt 24:36-44). The author addresses the whole group, for he commands them to "come together often, seeking the things which are befitting to your souls" (16.2). Thus, we understand these remarks as confirmation of the group's identity; the point is to avoid any status transformation, which will mean a loss of holiness and identity. With the end in view, the author catalogues the wickedness that the loyal disciples will face (16.3-4), a list of remarks taken from Jesus' words.

When we consider this final exhortation in terms of deliberative rhetoric, many things fall in place. First, the addressees are urged to choose, not between good and evil, but to choose to hold firm to what they now have. Reasons are provided that argue the advantage of the choice to "watch . . . be ready." First, do not throw away your investment: "The whole time of your faith will not profit you, if you are not made perfect in the last time" (16.2). Second, terrible times are coming, which you now know of and against which you are now strengthened — advantage. Third, those who endure will be saved — maximum advantage. The Lord is indeed coming on the clouds of heaven to gather his saints. Choices must be made, but only advantageous ones.

What Do We Know If We Know This?

The flow of communication is clear: (1) the group communicates with God in its prayers, and (2) God communicates with the group by means of Scripture, the words of Jesus, and the president's homily. As regards prayer, the *Didache* is particularly rich in kinds of prayers that should be prayed. Fasting, we maintain, is a petitionary prayer. In addition, we find petitionary prayers (9.4; 10.5), prayers of acknowledgment (9.2, 3, 4; 10.2, 4, 6), and prayers of appreciation (9.2, 3; 10.2, 3, 4). The following summary brings together the various references to prayer that are found throughout the *Didache*.

Fasting

Let not your fasts be with the hypocrites (8.1).

Petitionary

Our Father (8.2).
Remember, Lord, Thy Church, to deliver it . . . to make it perfect . . .
    and gather it from the four winds (10.5).

Acknowledgment (doxologies)

To Thee be the glory for ever (9.3).
For Thine is the glory and the power . . . for ever (9.4).
To Thee be the glory for ever (10.2).
For Thine is the glory . . . for ever (10.4).

Appreciation

We thank (εὐχαριστοῦμεν) Thee, our Father, for the holy vine of David (9.2).
We thank (εὐχαριστοῦμεν) Thee . . . for the life and knowledge which You madest known to us through Jesus Thy Servant (9.3).
We thank (εὐχαριστοῦμεν) Thee . . . for Thy holy name which You caused to tabernacle in our hearts, and for the knowledge and faith and immortality, which You made known to us through Jesus Thy Servant (10.2).
You gave food and drink to men for enjoyment, that they might give thanks (εὐχαριστήσωσιν) to Thee (10.3).
We thank (εὐχαριστοῦμεν) Thee that You are mighty (10.4).

The group, moreover, possesses a prayer unique to itself, the Our Father, which should be prayed three times a day. The repetition of a fixed text thrice daily is a ceremony that brings a piece of the past to present relevance and confirms the identity of the group who prays it as disciples of Jesus.

In regards to God's communication to the group, we found references to the Scriptures, but especially to the words of Jesus.

EXCURSUS: DIDACHE, THE GOSPEL (MOSTLY MATTHEW), AND THE SCRIPTURES

Here is a sample of the Gospel materials that appear in the *Didache:*

1.2 = Matt 22:37-39 (love God . . . love neighbor)
1.2b = Matt 7:12 (the Golden Rule)
1.3-4 = Matt 5:38-39, 40-41, 48 (bless those who curse you . . . be perfect)

1.4   = Matt 5:42 (give to him who begs . . .)
1.5   = Matt 5:26 (. . . until he pays the last penny)
2.3   = Matt 5:33 (you shall not commit perjury)
5.1-2 = Matt 15:19 (out of the heart come murder, adultery, fornica-
        tion . . .)
6.1   = Matt 24:4 (take heed that no one leads you astray)
7.1   = Matt 28:19 (baptize in the name of the Father, the Son, and the
        Holy Spirit)
8.1-3 = Matt 6:1-16 (instructions on prayer and the Our Father)
9.5   = Matt 7:6 (do not give what is holy to the dogs)
10.5 = Matt 24:31 (angels gathering the elect from the four winds)
11.7 = Matt 12:31 (the unforgivable sin)
12.1 = Matt 21:9 (who comes in the name of the Lord)
13.1 = Matt 10:10 (the laborer is worthy of his hire)
14.2 = Matt 5:23 (leave your gift on the altar . . . be reconciled)
16.1-8 = Matt 24

Materials from the Scriptures are relatively rare: (1) the Ten Commandments (love God = first commandment; love neighbor = second commandment: Exod 20:13-17); (2) the warning not to add to or take away from the commandments (4.13 = Deut 4:2 and 12:32); (3) the prophecy of Malachi about Christian worship (14.1 = Mal 1:11 and 14).

With so many references to Matthew in view, it seems safe to say that this group had some version of that Gospel. The person who exhorts in the early chapters of the *Didache* apparently draws from this same Gospel many items suitable to his argument. But was there a ceremonial reading from the Gospel as a regular part of worship? It would seem probable. This is confirmed by the attention paid to the one "who *speaks the word of God to you*." He is due the same honor as the Lord because when he proclaims the lordship of Jesus, "there is the Lord" (4.1). Problems arise with the advent of "teachers, apostles, and prophets." Only those who do not abuse the group's hospitality are worthy of speaking.

Within this broad framework of worship-as-communication, we find many other aspects of group life, both status transformations and ceremonies. (1) *Transformation rituals* include entrance into (baptism) and exit from (shunning) the group, while others look to the restoration to holiness of members who have committed transgressions (confession of trans-gressions). If the homily is indeed a part of the liminal process leading up to baptism, then it functions to lead the initiands from ignorance to light and from death to life. (2) *Ceremony* best explains the Eucharist, for all eat-ing events in antiquity were ceremonies confirming identity and status: "Likes eat with likes." The foods, moreover, are group-specific, namely, "spiritual food and drink." Since only members of the group may eat this food, partaking of the blessed foods identifies them as holy members of the group, the body of Christ. Many other ceremonies are in view, such as the predictable and regular day of meeting, the Sunday. Although we just stated that the exhortation is a status-transformation ritual, this is so for initiands; for all others who hear an exhortation and who are in no need of a first conversion, the homily confirms identity as worthy disciples who ac-cept the teaching of Jesus. Group hospitality to traveling prophets, apos-tles, and teachers is also a ceremony. It is a regular feature of the group to welcome others. And if that monetary welcome is balanced by a word of instruction or exhortation from the traveler, both speaker and hearers are confirmed as disciples who live from the Gospel. Roles and statuses, more-over, are confirmed on both parts.

The *First Apology* of Justin

We turn now to another document from the second century that contains extensive materials pertaining to worship. We are examining only chap-ters 61 and 65–67 of Justin's *First Apology,* a section at the end of the work. By the time Justin's material on worship is discussed, this apology to the emperor has discoursed on many topics, from Roman justice for the Christians, to Christian understanding of God, and later to the Jesus story. Even here, events in the Lord's life were prophesied in the Scrip-tures, giving heavenly weight to their communication as the word of God. Finally, Justin discourses on the worship of the Christians, beginning with baptism.

Chapter 61

1I will also relate the manner in which we dedicated ourselves to God when we had been made new through Christ. 2As many as are per-suaded and believe that what we teach and say is true, and undertake to be able to live accordingly, are instructed to pray and to entreat God with fasting, for the remission of their sins that are past, we praying and fasting with them. 3Then they are brought by us where there is water, and are regenerated in the same manner in which we were ourselves regenerated. For, in the name of God, the Father and Lord of the universe, and of our Savior Jesus Christ, and of the Holy Spirit, they then receive the washing with water. 4For Christ also said, "Except ye be born again, ye shall not enter into the kingdom of heaven." Now, that it is impossible for those who have once been born to enter into their mothers' wombs, is manifest to all. 5And how those who have sinned and repent shall escape their sins, is declared by Isaiah the prophet, as I wrote above; he thus speaks: "Wash you, make you clean; put away the evil of your doings from your souls; learn to do well; judge the fatherless, and plead for the widow: and come and let us reason together, saith the Lord. 6And though your sins be as scarlet, I will make them white like wool; and though they be as crimson, I will make them white as snow."

7And for this [rite] we have learned from the apostles this reason. 8Since at our birth we were born without our own knowledge or choice, by our parents coming together, and were brought up in bad habits and wicked training; 9in order that we may not remain the children of necessity and of ignorance, but may become the children of choice and knowledge, and may obtain in the water the remission of sins formerly committed, there is pronounced over him who chooses to be born again, and has repented of his sins, the name of God the Father and Lord of the universe; 10he who leads to the laver the person that is to be washed calling him by this name alone. 11For no one can utter the name of the ineffable God; and if any one dare to say that there is a name, he raves with a hopeless madness. 12And this washing is called illumination, because they who learn these things are illuminated in their understandings. 13And in the name of Jesus Christ . . . and in the name of the Holy Ghost, who through the prophets foretold all things about Jesus, he who is illuminated is washed.

When Justin describes the ritual that allows entrance into the worshiping group, he understands it as a typical rite of passage. As all know, transformation rituals when performed most fully have four stages: (1) separation, (2) liminal experience, (3) ritual of change, and (4) acknowledgment of the change. Almost the whole of this process is in view here. While an actual separation from former status and role is not formally described, the liminal process is. Initiands must learn discipline and self-abasement through the instruction on how "to pray and to entreat God with fasting, for the remission of their sins that are past" (61.2). More-over, they learn not only the folly of their past lives, but of the wisdom of the new one. In the past they "were brought up in bad habits and wicked training . . . the children of necessity and of ignorance" (61.8-9). Now they are instructed in the virtuous life characteristic of disciples: "Wash you, make you clean; put away the evil of your doings from your souls; learn to do well; judge the fatherless, and plead for the widow" (61.5). The author calls attention to this instruction when he says, "This wash-ing is called illumination, because they who learn these things are illumi-nated in their understandings" (61.12). Thus in their liminal process, initiands seek to "live accordingly" as they are taught (61.2), to pray and learn self-abasement, and to be instructed or illuminated about the new life.

The key element of the baptism is the status transformation of wash-ing and of prayer in the name of Father, Son, and Spirit. The initiands are led by someone in the group, most likely the mentor who schooled them through the liminal period, to a place of water for washing. "Washing" is more than water poured over the head. Baptismal washing means rebirth that was mandated by Jesus as an absolute necessity (61.4 = John 3:3) for entering the kingdom of God. But washing also has to do with purifica-tion, as Isaiah makes clear: "And though your sins be as scarlet, I will make them white like wool; and though they be as crimson, I will make them white as snow" (61.6 = Isa 1:18). The washing, then, facilitates a new status for the initiands: rebirth/regeneration or purification from scarlet sins. The "change" effected by baptism has long been described as movement *from* X *to* Y, or transition from "past" to "present."

Before		After
darkness	v.	light
ignorance	v.	knowledge
passion/flesh	v.	spirit
deceit	v.	truth
death	v.	life
drunkenness/asleep	v.	soberness/awake
lust	v.	holiness
blindness	v.	sight

The initiands receive the washing "in the name of God, the Father and Lord of the universe, and of our Savior Jesus Christ, and of the Holy Spirit" (61.3), a formula later repeated in 61.10 and 13. What is the purpose of baptizing "in the name of . . ."? Is it a prayer that petitions God for purification? Might it be communication from God to the initiands? It is most assuredly the latter, for the document makes this explicit: "There is pronounced over him . . . the name of God the Father and Lord of the universe" (61.9). The communication flows from God to the person being baptized; in the baptismal situation, the blessing of God comes upon the person. Moreover, the washing is also an illumination; that is, a heavenly benefaction is given. This is mediated "in the name of Jesus Christ . . . [and] of the Holy Ghost, who through the prophets foretold all things about Jesus" (61.13). All three figures are honored for their deeds, which are in fact benefactions: creator, savior, giver of prophecies. Thus we observe an extensive transitional ritual that includes considerable petitionary prayer. This communication with God is balanced by God's communication with the initiands in Scripture and the words of Jesus and in the blessing in the name that makes them a possession of God.

Chapter 65

1But we, after we have thus washed him who has been convinced and has assented to our teaching, bring him to the place where those who are called brethren are assembled, 2in order that we may offer hearty prayers in common for ourselves and for the baptized [illuminated] person, and for all others in every place, that we may be counted worthy, now that we have learned the truth, by our works also to be found good citizens and keepers of the commandments, so that we may be saved with an everlasting salvation. 3Having ended the prayers, we salute one another with a kiss. 4There is then brought to the president of the brethren bread and a cup of wine mixed with water; and he taking them, gives praise and glory to the Father of the universe, through the name of the Son and of the Holy Ghost, and offers thanks at considerable length for our being counted worthy to receive these things at His hands. 5And when he has concluded the prayers and thanksgivings, all the people present express their assent by saying Amen. 6This word Amen answers in the Hebrew language to γένοιτο [so be it]. 7And when the president has given thanks, and all the people have expressed their assent, those who are called by us deacons give to each of those present to partake of the bread and wine mixed with water over which the thanksgiving was pronounced, and to those who are absent they carry away a portion.

This chapter describes the final stage of status-transformation rituals, namely, the acceptance and acknowledgment of the change by a significant audience. The persons who have passed through the liminal passage of baptism are formally brought into "the place where those who are called brethren are assembled" (65.1). This clearly acknowledges that the baptized have experienced a change of identity and so are no longer outsiders. They are acknowledged as genuine insiders, as reborn or regenerated. Proof of this occurs when the reborn immediately share ritual actions with them. In particular, we are told, the parent group prays earnestly for the newly reborn: "We . . . offer hearty prayers in common for ourselves and for the baptized [illuminated] person" (65.2). These petitionary prayers beg God "that we may be counted worthy . . . be found good citizens and keepers of the commandments" (65.2), which are then climaxed with a petition "that we may be saved with an everlasting salvation" (65.2). This ritual of common prayer is concluded with the holy kiss. Inasmuch as kissing generally indicates close relationship, either kinship or fictive kinship, the kiss completes the acknowledgment part of the transformational ritual of baptism. The group not only prays with and for the reborn, but embraces them as kin. Thus a complete transformation ritual and common petitionary prayer characterize this first part of the worship.

Nothing is said here about a service of the Word, that is, the hearing of the Word of God. But in chapter 67 we find a succinct instruction about it: "the memoirs of the apostles or the writings of the prophets are read, as long as time permits; then, when the reader has ceased, the president verbally instructs, and exhorts to the imitation of these good things" (67.2-3). We saw in 61.4-6 above that a word of Jesus was stated concerning the meaning and necessity of baptism, which was followed by Isaiah's prophecy about the transformation of sinners. Whereas those remarks were brief and topical, it would seem that "the memoirs of the apostles or the writings of the prophets" imply larger selections, even continuous reading "as long as time permits." Then follows the homily, which Justin says includes both "instruction" and "exhortation." Prayers communicate the needs and praise of mortals to God; but God communicates with the group by the written Scriptures and the interpretative word of the president. The reading and hearing of the Word, moreover, is a ceremonial action that is part of a larger ceremony. Here, at a regular place in the worship on a regular day, predictable reading from predictable Scriptures is done. Even if the hearers become enlightened or changed in some way, the group confirms its identity by reading and hearing. God speaks to them, not to others; they have the words of everlasting life.

Justin states that after the prayers a different event occurs, which we consider the ceremony of the Eucharist. A ceremonial person, "the president," receives bread and wine and prays a prayer of praise and acknowledgment: "gives praise and glory" (αἶνον καὶ δόξαν) to God and "offers thanks (εὐχαριστίαν) at considerable length" for benefits received (65.4). Aspects of a ceremony include: (1) a regular offering and eating at a specific time in the service, namely, after the prayers and the kiss; (2) actions and words that do not change and should not change because they currently recall what Jesus did in the past; (3) the bringing of the past and its significant actions into the present to be celebrated; and (4) the confirmation, through the actions, of identity, role, and status in the group. In 66.1 we will learn that these foods are to be consumed only by group members; so their identity as members is confirmed. Moreover, only a "president" receives the bread and wine; only he "prays the prayers and thanksgiving," thus confirming his role as president. Only the deacons distribute the bread and wine to those present or to those absent; these particular actions thereby confirm their role. After the president prays the prayers and thanksgiving, "the people present express their assent by saying Amen" (65.5). Their "Amen" confirms what the president prays on their behalf; "Amen" is, in this case, a prayer of praise and appreciation. "Amen" was commonly spoken by people to affirm what an official person had just stated (1 Chron 16:36; Neh 5:13). Thus we observe status transformations (baptism) and ceremonies (kiss and Eucharist); in addition, we find in chapter 65 these types of prayers: (1) petitionary prayers (εὐχάς, 65.2-3), prayed without a leader and prayed for one another; (2) prayers of praise and glory (αἶνον καὶ δόξαν, 65.4); (3) appreciation or "Eucharist" (εὐχαριστίαν, 65.4-5, 7), prayed only by the leader; and (4) "Amen," assent to the prayers of praise and thanksgiving (65.5).

Chapter 66

1And this food is called among us Εὐχαριστία [the Eucharist], of which no one is allowed to partake but the man who believes that the things which we teach are true, and who has been washed with the washing that is for the remission of sins, and unto regeneration, and who is so living as Christ has enjoined. 2For not as common bread and common drink do we receive these; 3but in like manner as Jesus Christ our Savior, having been made flesh by the Word of God, had both flesh and blood for our salvation, so likewise have we been taught that the food which is blessed by the prayer of His word, and from which our blood and flesh by transmutation are nourished, is the flesh and blood of that Jesus who was made flesh. 4For the apostles, in the memoirs composed by them, which are called Gospels, have thus delivered unto us what was enjoined upon them; 5that Jesus took bread, and when He had given thanks, said, "This do in remembrance of Me, this is My body;" and that, after the same manner, having taken the cup and given thanks, He said, "This is My blood;" and gave it to them alone. 6And we afterwards continually remind each other of these things.

This chapter continues the discussion of the premier ceremony of the group, the Eucharist. Its ceremonial character is emphasized by the note that the foods are restricted to believers who have been washed. "Likes eat with likes" and "You are what you eat": only Christians eat the eucharistic foods, and consuming the flesh and blood of the Lord, they are confirmed as parts of his body. Lest we think this restriction odd, let us read comparable instruction from a later period.

Excursus: Restricted Table Fellowship

"We do not partake of food from the table of Gentiles, nor indeed are we able to share their hospitality, because they live uncleanly. But when we have persuaded them to mind the truth and do it, and have baptized them with the thrice-blessed invocation, then we have table-fellowship with them. Otherwise, even if it be a father or mother or wife or child or brother, or any other who by nature has our affection, we cannot dare to eat with them. For by our religion we make this distinction. So do not take it as an insult that your son does not eat with you until you adopt this belief and practice" (Clementine Homilies 13.4).

Whereas in the discussion of Eucharist in the previous chapter the emphasis was put on prayers of praise and gratitude to God, here the author stresses the etiology and significance of the Eucharist in relation to Jesus. A significant past event is being commemorated and brought into the present. What is being consumed? Not common bread and drink, but "flesh and blood." Justin argues that Jesus "[was] made flesh," and so "had both flesh and blood for our salvation," so that the food blessed by his word is itself "the flesh and blood of that Jesus who was made flesh" (66.3). No ordinary food, this Eucharist. Then follows the Gospel story of the inaugural Eucharist: "Jesus took bread, and when He had given thanks, said, 'This do in remembrance of Me, this is My body;' and that, after the same manner, having taken the cup and given thanks, He said, 'This is My blood'" (66.5). Justin, moreover, introduces this story with the tag "[I] deliver what [I] was enjoined" (66.4), the same formula used by Paul to introduce significant traditions related to Jesus. "I hand on what I received" introduces his accounting of Jesus' last meal (1 Cor 11:23) and his proclamation of the resurrection and appearances of Jesus (1 Cor 15:3-7). The ceremonial meal is eaten during a regularly scheduled meeting. And since it is eaten only by group insiders, it functions to confirm them as disciples of Jesus and members of his group.

Chapter 67

1And the wealthy among us help the needy; and we always keep together; and for all things wherewith we are supplied, we bless the Maker of all through His Son Jesus Christ, and through the Holy Ghost. 2And on the day called Sunday, all who live in cities or in the country gather together to one place, and the memoirs of the apostles or the writings of the prophets are read, as long as time permits; 3then, when the reader has ceased, the president verbally instructs, and exhorts to the imitation of these good things. 4Then we all rise together and pray, and, as we before said, when our prayer is ended, bread and wine and water are brought, and the president in like manner offers prayers and thanksgivings, according to his ability, and the people assent, saying Amen; 5and there is a distribution to each, and a participation of that over which thanks have been given, and to those who are absent a portion is sent by the deacons. 6And they who are well to do, and willing, give what each thinks fit; and what is collected is deposited with the president, who succors the orphans and widows and those who, through sickness or any other cause, are in want, and those who are in bonds and the strangers sojourning among us, and in a word takes care of all who are in need. 7But Sunday is the day on which we all hold our common assembly, because it is the first day on which God, having wrought a change in the darkness and matter, made the world; and Jesus Christ our Savior on the same day rose from the dead. 8For He was crucified on the day before that of Saturn (Saturday); and on the day after that of Saturn, which is the day of the Sun, having appeared to His apostles and disciples, He taught them these things, which we have submitted to you also for your consideration.

Justin finally concludes his description of Christian worship, in many ways repeating previous topics in the discourse, but making some notable additions. If saying something twice is a mark of emphasis, then special attention is due the beginning and ending of the chapter. Similar topics are treated: almsgiving (67.1 and 6) and Sunday as the designated day of worship (67.2 and 7). From Matthew 6:1-18, moreover, we learned to join together almsgiving, prayer, and fasting as regular aspects of Christian worship. *Fasting*, which was mentioned earlier, is part of an initiand's rite of passage. *Prayer* has been prayed throughout the discourse, both petitionary prayer and prayer of praise/acknowledgment. The remarks on *almsgiving* warrant close attention.

> The wealthy among us help the needy; and we always keep together; and for all things wherewith we are supplied, we bless the Maker of all through His Son Jesus Christ, and through the Holy Ghost. . . . And they who are well to do, and willing, give what each thinks fit; and what is collected is deposited with the president, who succors the orphans and widows and those who, through sickness or any other cause, are in want, and those who are in bonds and the strangers sojourning among us, and in a word takes care of all who are in need. (67.1, 6)

In the first reference the wealthy, not the members in general, show patronage to the needy. In the context of almsgiving, an important strategy emerges that provides a rationale for it: "For all things wherewith we are supplied, we bless the Maker of all" (67.1). This might simply be a general thanksgiving to the Maker of all for all that the group is supplied with, but it can also remind the wealthy of the source of their blessing, which prompts them to share with needy group members what God has given them. Those who have ample benefaction from the Patron-Benefactor must themselves be benefactors in turn. In the second remark about almsgiving, the wealthy are again addressed: "They who are well to do, and willing, give what each thinks fit" (67.6). But as was the case in Acts 4:34-35, what is collected is deposited with the president. This aspect of almsgiving, we argue, functions as a ceremony in the group, for when distribution is made the status of the well-to-do as God-blessed is confirmed. The direction of all donations to the president deepens the ceremonial character of the action because it confirms his particular role in the group, not only as its leader in preaching and praising, but as a patron in his own right, although with patronage not originally his own.

It is a mark of a ceremony to occur at predictable times. Its significance increases when it looks to the past to recognize some event and thus bring it into the present to celebrate it. They hold their common assembly on the day named Sunday. Why Sunday? "Because it is the first day on which God . . . made the world; and Jesus Christ our Savior on the same day rose from the dead" (67.2 and 7). Thus, believers who give "praise and glory to the Father of the Universe" (65.4) and praise "the name of God, the Father and Lord of the universe" (61.3) gather to commemorate this day of special significance to the God of Genesis. But the day draws meaning from the Jesus tradition because it is the day he was raised from the dead. We have been told about this Jesus blessing the bread and wine (66.3-5), about his crucifixion (61.13), and now about his resurrection. The day of assembly, then, reaches into the past (God = creation; Jesus = resurrection) and brings these events into the present.

The group gathers to worship, although that term is not used. What we see are prayers (petitionary and praise) and rites (baptism, Eucharist). But here we find a clear reference to what has come to be known as "the service of the Word." At this point worship as God's communication with the group is most plainly seen. First, the Gospels and the Scriptures are read at the assembly, surely every assembly. The writings of the prophets take precedence over the books of Torah. And so we can say that the words spoken to the assembly are group-specific in that Christians scoured the Scriptures for prophecies about Jesus (chaps. 31–53). The words of and the story about Jesus also were regularly heard. Following this, the president, whom we have observed performing ceremonial actions before, undertakes another, namely, to instruct and exhort. As spokesman for God in this communication, he delivers the homily and exhortation. Inasmuch as he seems to be the only person with this role, when he exercises it he confirms his position in the group. Those who listen and understand are likewise confirmed as disciples of Jesus who feed on his word. This entire communication from God in Scripture and Gospel is worship in and of itself, and a ceremony confirming the identity of those who hear the words of their Master. Following this, we are told of another ceremony of common prayer. Even if the group petitions God to change things in their lives, the fact that they pray together at this point in the service confirms their fictive kinship.

Next, the author mentions the ceremony of the Eucharist, albeit in an abbreviated form. He earlier provided an extended treatment. We are told that the president receives "bread and wine and water" and "offers prayers and thanksgivings," to which the people assent, saying Amen. As the author said earlier, specific persons give to the members some of what has been blessed, and to those absent they bring a portion.

What, Then, Do We Know If We Know This?

We observe the communication of the group with God most notably in its prayers, as well as God's communication with them in the Scriptures, in the Gospel of Jesus, in the homily, and in baptism and Eucharist. Justin was certainly not transcribing the text of a worship service, but simply describing what Christians did and why. Reading by means of a model of worship has highlighted familiar matters and surfaced new data for consideration.

Prayers

Justin has nothing to say about the Our Father, not just here but in all his writings. But he has much to say about other prayers prayed in the group.

Fasting

". . . to pray and to entreat God with fasting, for the remission of their sins that are past, we praying and fasting with them" (61.2)

Petitionary

"As many . . . are instructed to pray and to entreat God" (εὔχεσθαί τε καὶ αἰτεῖν, 61.2); "we may offer hearty prayers (καινὰς εὐχάς) in common . . . that we may be counted worthy . . . to be found good citizens" (65.2)

Praise or Acknowledgment

"[The president] gives praise and glory (αἶνον καὶ δόξαν) to the Father of the universe" (65.4); "and when he has concluded the prayers" (τὰς εὐχάς, 65.5); "we bless (εὐλογοῦμεν) the Maker of all through His Son Jesus" (67.1)

Appreciation

"[The president] offers thanks (εὐχαριστίαν) at considerable length for our being counted worthy to receive these things" (65.4); "and when he has concluded the . . . thanksgivings" (εὐχαριστίαν, 65.5); "when the president has given thanks (εὐχαριστήσοντος), and all the people have expressed their assent" (65.7)

Justin is very clear about each type of prayer, for he uses specific terms for each one: (1) petitionary prayer is to "pray and entreat" and to "pray for" something; (2) prayer of praise and acknowledgment uses terms such as "praise and glory," "sing in praise of," and "bless"; and (3) prayers of appreciation all use some form of "Eucharist," which this translator has rendered as "thanksgiving" or "giving thanks." In comparison with the *Didache*, we do not find the prayers prayed to be unusual in any way.

Status-Transformation Ritual

The premier transformation ritual, baptism, is shown to contain the typical four stages of an initiation rite: (1) separation, (2) liminal state, (3) the rite of transformation, which is then (4) acknowledged by the group. The liminal phase includes fasting and prayer, but also significant instruction from Jesus and Isaiah about the need for and results of the rite. The rite itself contains both washing with water and prayer invoking "the name of God, the Father and Lord of the universe, and of our savior Jesus Christ, and of the Holy Spirit" (61.3). The final stage of the transformation ritual occurs when the baptized is brought "to the place where those who are called brethren are assembled" (65.1). A second transformation ritual is found in the prayers prayed "in common for ourselves and for the baptized [illuminated] person, and for all others in every place" (65.2). The prayers admit that the group is not yet "worthy," and so the group petitions God to change them and make them more and more holy.

Ceremonies

Among the many items concerning ritual behavior, Justin gives considerable attention to the Eucharist. (1) An official person (the president) takes the bread and wine and praises the giver of these gifts; i.e., he "gives praise and glory to the Father of the universe" (65.4). Here the emphasis is put on prayer, both praise for the bread and wine and gratitude "at considerable length for our being counted worthy to receive these things" (65.4). (2) The past is brought forward into the present. When next the Eucharist is considered, its rootedness in Jesus is stressed: the food is Jesus' "flesh and blood" (66.3) and the current practice goes back to Jesus' own action (66.4-5). (3) Specific people perform specific acts. If the president gives praise and thanks to God over the bread and wine, deacons give the eucharistic foods to those present and take a portion to those absent. (4) We know, moreover, that the Eucharist takes place on a calendar-specific, regular day of the week. (5) The function of the Eucharist is to confirm membership in the group, for "likes eat with likes." Outsiders do not eat this food. And inasmuch as "you are what you eat," consuming the flesh and blood of Jesus confirms that the disciples are members of the body of Christ.

We find many other ceremonies mentioned in Justin. The *kiss* is one. The group's prayers are concluded by a kiss (65.3), a mark of affection and identification between group members.

Another ceremony, the *"Amen"* concludes the prayers and thanksgivings of the Eucharist (65.5) and expresses the assent of those who say it. As such, the prayer of the president and the "Amen" of the people are part of the same ceremony, praying antiphonally. Both have a specific, formal speaking role in which they speak words specific to their role; thus, when each speaks, the role of each is confirmed. The "Amen," moreover, always occurs at a regular and fixed time in the service.

Almsgiving, when practiced by the group, has features of a ceremony.

The assistance given by the wealthy in the group to the needy is a regularly scheduled part of the pattern of worship, the portion of the service that has as its aim the solidarity of the group: "The wealthy among us help the needy; and we always keep together; and for all things wherewith we are supplied, we bless the Maker of all through His Son Jesus" (67.1). As chronology goes, it occurs after the "prayers and thanksgivings." The contributors play the role of patrons, thus their giving confirms that role. Moreover, according to 67.6, what is collected is deposited with the president, who distributes it in terms of specific needs. He too is confirmed in his role of president by this. Thus almsgiving so described confirms many roles. It is, moreover, a regularly scheduled feature of the worship service.

Meeting on Sunday is its own ceremonial contribution. Besides being a regular and predictable day, Sunday was chosen because of two events in the past of great importance. When ritually remembered, the past becomes present. "Sunday" reaches back, first, to God's creation ("it is the first day on which God, having wrought a change in the darkness and matter, made the world," 67.7), and second, to Jesus' new creation ("Jesus Christ our Savior on the same day rose from the dead," 67.7). It is, moreover, the day that "all who live in cities or in the country gather together to one place" (67.2).

During the Sunday worship, readings are taken from the Gospels and the Prophets. The reading and the exhortation that follows become ceremonial actions in their own right. First of all, the readings are exclusively from Gospels and Prophets; only these are read. They are read for a variety of reasons, such as confirmation in the status of disciples who hear once more the master's voice. The Gospels, when assented to, are themselves confirmed as the official text of the group. Prophets are included, but not the Pentateuch or Torah, because they are thought by Justin to be prophetic of Jesus. Jesus' role and status are confirmed when the prophecies are explained, and those books of Scripture are singled out as forming a unity with the Gospels. Presumably, the reading is done by a specific person; in time this role will be elevated to the role of lector.

Following the readings, the president "instructs" and "exhorts" those who have heard the readings. His homily should be considered a ceremony. He speaks at a specific time in the sequence of worship, which is itself performed on a fixed day. Although his "text" will vary, he nevertheless "instructs" them about the readings. The president alone does this task, just as the president alone gives praise and thanks over the bread and wine:

this is his role, which he confirms by performing it. His "exhortation" is probably aimed at constancy and faithfulness; if so, it is a prayer that things not change.

CONCLUSION

W hat do we know if we know this? We have learned to understand prayer "in other words," that is, to use appropriate models from the social sciences to interpret a wide variety of materials that are generally lumped together as "petition" and "worship." We now have a typology of eight varieties of prayer, based on the purpose of the communication to God. In particular we have come to appreciate self-focused prayer, such as Jesus prayed in John 17, as well as to make a needed distinction between prayer of acknowledgment (i.e., "praise") and prayer of appreciation (i.e., "thanksgiving").

In addition to viewing prayer in terms of communication, we applied a checklist of various social science models for an in-depth interpretation of prayers. It matters whether we bring an appropriate set of cultural values to the task. The prayers we have studied originated in a world in which mortals were subject to drought, flood, storm, etc.; hence they are not active as modern folk are in regard to their lives, but passive recipients of what God or the gods bring them. They live in present time ("today . . ."), occasionally recalling the past for signs of what God intends and to commemorate former benefactions. Their children are born in a selfish mode and must be beaten straight, lest they embarrass their parents. In such a world, then, one would expect strong emphasis on prayers of petition and acknowledgment. Other important elements of our checklist for social science interpretation include appreciation of the pivotal value of honor, the patron-client relationship, the four media of exchange, types of reciprocity that might be employed, and finally models of status transformation and ceremony. Individually and in combination, these models truly provide an

X-ray into the skeleton of prayer, enlightening us about structure and energy. Thus, we understand prayer "in other words."

Worship, we learned, is foremost communication: from mortals to God (prayer) and from God to mortals. Communication from God, we saw, might take many forms, such as reading the Scriptures, hearing the Jesus story, hearing a homily on these and other materials, and oracles of many sorts. Since the communication with God comes in the relationship of the Jesus group with the Deity, entrance and exit rituals are also part of worship, with God either blessing new members at baptism or censuring a flagrant sinner in the group. Within the worshiping group, moreover, we find ceremonies that confirm identity and membership, as well as role and status.

What is not here? This study of prayer and worship "in other words" did not treat of sacrifice, whether animal sacrifice, rational sacrifice, or sacrifice of praise. Nor was the role of priest/president considered, particularly the "priest according to the type of Melchizedek." We would do well to bring to this study the materials on patron-*broker*-client seen early in this book. Nor did we give sufficient time to the many transformational rituals (laying on of hands, either as commissioning or as healing; death and burial) and ceremonies (foot washing; collection for the poor of the mother church; Passover). Much is left to be done, but we are confident that the social science models learned here will continue to be beneficial when used to read other materials related to worship.

Can we trust these social science models when we read ancient documents? The models themselves are developed out of cross-cultural comparison. They aim to avoid the quicksand of ethnocentricity and the cliffs of anachronism. They were developed for this particular study the way we buy our shoes: we keep trying on shoes until we get the best fit possible. Part of that fit comes from a detailed reading of Greco-Roman literature to understand how the proposed model explains the document under study. This has never been clearer than in the use of the values of honor and shame, patron-client relations, anti-individualistic personality, reciprocity, and exchange. The fit we find with the biblical materials only confirms that the model is appropriate, sensitive, and productive. Models are ultimately judged on their suitability to surface data and interpret them with profit.

What might a reader do now? Keep on reading the Bible and materials from the early church, now with this new set of glasses! And should readers wonder what importance these models might have in their own communities of worship, they need only attend to the hymns they sing, most of which are petitionary prayer or acknowledgment of God's honor. It would greatly benefit readers to study the order of worship their denomination follows on Sundays. Surely there are entrance rituals as well as purificatory ones, and perhaps also an exit ritual. The reverence shown the book of the Scriptures (kissing, incensing, attended by candles) expresses belief that when the Scriptures are read, it is Jesus or God who speaks "today." The chief ceremony of Christian churches is the Lord's Supper, whether celebrated each Sunday or less frequently. Most Christian churches restrict eating of the Eucharist to the confessed members of the group. Indeed, the processes of worship described in the *Didache* and Justin's *First Apology* themselves model the parts of worship and prayer we see in contemporary worship.

We include one final passage in the hope that readers will have learned to read "in other words" and so interpret with profit. The passage is from the document *Joseph and Aseneth,* which was possibly written in the second century, as were the *Didache* and Justin's *First Apology.* There are two points that concern us. First, the protagonist, Joseph, refuses to kiss Aseneth because of purity concerns. In telling Aseneth why he refuses to kiss her, he sketches a wonderful scene of the elements of worship he regularly practices: "It is not fitting for a man who worships God, who will bless with his mouth the living God and eat blessed bread of life and drink a blessed cup of immortality and anoint himself with blessed ointment of incorruptibility to kiss a strange woman who will bless with her mouth dead and dumb idols and eat from their table bread of strangulation and drink from their libation a cup of insidiousness and anoint herself with ointment of destruction" (8.5). While we do not have a complete worship scene here (reading of the Scriptures is absent), we have other elements of communication, blessing and eating, that are communication with God and from God. These actions, moreover, would clearly be confirming ceremonies, not status-transformation rituals. After Aseneth departs, Joseph prays this prayer: "Lord God of my father Israel, Highest, powerful, The one who gives all things life, and called them from darkness to light, and from error to truth, and from death to life, you, Lord, bring (this one) to life and bless this virgin. And renew her by your spirit, and form her with your hidden hand, and make her alive again by your life, and let her eat your bread of life, and drink your blessed cup, which you chose before it was brought into being, and let her enter into your rest, which you have made ready for your chosen ones" (8.10-11). Joseph petitions for a status transformation of Aseneth, that she may be blessed and so enter into Joseph's covenant with God. Once within, she may partake of his ceremonies, one of which includes partaking of bread and blessed cup.

Alcock, Susan E., and Robin Osborne, eds. *Placing the Gods: Sanctuaries and Sacred Space in Ancient Greece.* Oxford: Oxford University Press, 1994.

Alderink, Larry, and Luther Martin. "Prayer in Greco-Roman Religions." In *Prayer from Alexander to Constantine: A Critical Anthology,* edited by Mark Kiley, 123-27. London: Routledge, 1997.

Altmann, A. "*Homo Imago Dei* in Jewish and Christian Theology." *JR* 48 (1968): 235-39.

Anderson, B. W. *Out of the Depths: The Psalms Speak for Us Today.* Philadelphia: Westminster, 1983.

Anderson, Gary A. "The Praise of God as a Cultic Event." In *Priesthood and Cult in Ancient Israel,* edited by Gary A. Anderson and Saul M. Olyan, 15-33. Sheffield: Sheffield Academic Press, 1991.

Athanassakis, Apostolos N. *The Orphic Hymns: Text, Translation, and Notes.* Missoula: Scholars, 1977.

Athanassiadi, Polymnia, and Michael Frede. *Pagan Monotheism in Late Antiquity.* Oxford: Clarendon, 1999.

Attridge, Harold. "The Philosophical Critique of Religion under the Early Empire." *ANRW* II.16.1 (1978): 46-78.

———. "Paraenesis in a Homily (λόγος παρακλήσεως): The Possible Location of, and Socialization in, the 'Epistle to the Hebrews.'" *Semeia* 50 (2004): 211-26.

Aune, David E. *The Cultic Setting of Realized Eschatology in Early Christianity.* Leiden: Brill, 1972.

———. *Prophecy in Early Christianity and the Ancient Mediterranean World.* Grand Rapids: Eerdmans, 1983.

———. "Worship, Early Christian." In *ABD* 6:973-89.

———. *Revelation 1–5.* Dallas: Word, 1997.

———. "Prayer in the Greco-Roman World." In *Into God's Presence: Prayer in the*

New Testament, edited by Richard N. Longenecker, 23-42. Grand Rapids: Eerdmans, 2001.

Ayo, Nicholas. *The Lord's Prayer.* New York: Rowman and Littlefield, 1992.

Bahr, Gordon J. "The Use of the Lord's Prayer in the Primitive Church." *JBL* 84 (1965): 153-59.

Barr, James. "Abba Isn't Daddy." *JTS* 37 (1988): 28-47.

Beckwith, Roger T. "The Daily and Weekly Worship of the Primitive Church in Relation to Its Jewish Antecedents. Pt 1." *EvQ* 56 (1984): 65-80.

Bemile, Paul. *The Magnificat within the Context and Framework of Lukan Theology: An Exegetical Theological Study of Lk 1:46-55.* Frankfurt: Peter Lang, 1986.

Bergant, Diane. "An Anthropological Approach to Biblical Interpretation: The Passover Supper in Exodus 12:1-20 as a Case Study." *Semeia* 67 (1994): 43-62.

Berlo, David K. *The Process of Communication.* New York: Holt, Rinehart and Winston, 1960.

Betz, Hans Dieter. *The Sermon on the Mount.* Minneapolis: Fortress, 1995.

Betz, Otto. "'To Worship God in Spirit and in Truth': Reflections on John 4,20-26." In *Standing before God: Studies on Prayer in Scriptures and in Tradition with Essays,* edited by Asher Finkel and Lawrence Frizzell, 53-72. New York: Ktav, 1981.

Beyer, Hermann W. "εὐλογέω." In *TDNT* 2:754-65.

Bickerman, Elias J. "The Civic Prayer for Jerusalem." In *Essays in Greco-Roman and Related Talmudic Literature,* edited by Henry Fischel, 266-88. New York: Ktav, 1977.

Black, C. Clifton. "The Rhetorical Form of the Hellenistic Jewish and Early Christian Sermon: A Response to Lawrence Wills." *HTR* 81 (1988): 1-18.

Black, Matthew. "The Doxology to the *Pater Noster* with a Note on Matthew 6:13b." In *A Tribute to Geza Vermes,* edited by Philip R. Davies and Richard T. White, 327-28. Sheffield: JSOT Press, 1990.

Boissevain, Jeremy. *Friends of Friends: Networks, Manipulators, and Coalitions.* New York: St. Martin's Press, 1974.

Borgen, Peder. "God's Agent in the Fourth Gospel." In *Religions in Antiquity,* edited by Jacob Neusner, 137-48. Leiden: Brill, 1968.

Boring, M. Eugene. *The Continuing Voice of Jesus.* Louisville: Westminster John Knox, 1991.

Bornkamm, Gunther. "Das Anathema in der urchristlichen Abendmahlsliturgie." *TLZ* 75 (1950): 227-30.

Bossmann, David. "Images of God in the Letters of Paul." *BTB* 18 (1988): 67-76.

Bowker, J. W. "Speeches in Acts: A Study in Proem and Yelammedenu Form." *NTS* 14 (1967): 96-111.

Bremer, Jan-Maarten. "Greek Hymns." In *Faith, Hope, and Worship: Aspects of Reli-*

gious Mentality in the Ancient World, edited by H. S. Versnel, 193-215. Leiden: Brill, 1981.

―――. "The Reciprocity of Giving and Thanksgiving in Greek Worship." In *Reciprocity in Ancient Greece,* edited by Christopher Gill, Norman Postlethwaite, and Richard Seaford, 127-38. Oxford: Oxford University Press, 1998.

Brown, Raymond E. "The Pater Noster as an Eschatological Prayer." *TS* 22 (1961): 175-208. Reprinted in his *New Testament Essays* (Garden City, N.Y.: Doubleday, 1968), 275-320.

Brown, Tricia Gates. *Spirit in the Johannine Writings: Johannine Pneumatology in Social-Science Perspective.* New York: T. & T. Clark, 2003.

Buchanan, George W. "Worship, Feasts and Ceremonies in the Early Jewish-Christian Church." *NTS* 26 (1980): 279-97.

―――. "Apostolic Christology." In SBLSP (1986): 172-82.

Butts, James R. "The 'Progymnasmata' of Theon: A New Text with Translation and Commentary." Ph.D. diss., Claremont Graduate School, 1987.

Carman, John B., and Frederick J. Streng. *Spoken and Unspoken Thanks: Some Comparative Soundings.* Cambridge: Center for the Study of World Religions, Harvard University, 1989.

Casimir, Michael J. *Mobility and Territoriality: Social and Spatial Boundaries among Foragers, Fishers, Pastoralists, and Peripatetics.* Oxford: Oxford University Press, 1992.

Catechism of the Catholic Church, The. Rome: Libreria Editrice Vaticana, 1994.

Charlesworth, James H. "A Prolegomenon to the Study of the Jewish Background of the Hymns and Prayers in the New Testament." *JJS* 33 (1982): 264-85.

―――. "Jewish Hymns, Odes, and Prayers (ca. 167 B.C.E.–135 C.E.)." In *Early Judaism and Its Modern Interpreters,* edited by Robert A. Kraft and George W. E. Nicklesburg, 411-36. Atlanta: Scholars, 1986.

―――. "Prayer in the New Testament in Light of Contemporary Jewish Prayers." In SBLSP (1993): 773-86.

―――, ed. *Old Testament Pseudepigrapha.* 2 vols. Garden City, N.Y.: Doubleday, 1983.

Charlesworth, James H., Mark Harding, and Mark Kiley. *The Lord's Prayer and Other Prayer Texts from the Greco-Roman Era.* Valley Forge, Pa.: Trinity, 1994.

Chilton, Bruce. "Two Recent Ethnographic Theories of Sacrifice." In his *The Temple of Jesus: His Sacrificial Program within a Cultural History of Sacrifice,* 173-80. University Park: Pennsylvania State University Press, 1992.

Conzelmann, Hans. "εὐχαριστέω." In *TDNT* 9:407-15.

Couratin, A. H. "The Thanksgiving: An Essay." In *The Sacrifice of Praise: Studies on the Themes of Thanksgiving and Redemption in the Central Prayers of the Eucharistic and Baptismal Liturgies,* edited by B. D. Spinks, 20-61. Rome: Edizione Liturgiche, 1981.

Cullmann, Oscar. *Early Christian Worship.* London: SCM, 1953.

Cunningham, Lawrence S. *Catholic Prayer.* New York: Crossroad, 1992.

Dahms, J. V. "The Johannine Use of *Monogenes* Reconsidered." *NTS* 29 (1983): 222-32.

Danker, Frederick W. *Benefactor: Epigraphic Study of a Graeco-Roman and New Testament Semantic Field.* St. Louis: Clayton Publishing House, 1982.

Daube, David. "A Prayer Pattern in Judaism." In *Studia Evangelica: Papers Presented to the International Congress on "The Four Gospels in 1957,"* edited by Kurt Aland, 549-55. Berlin: Akademie-Verlag, 1959.

Davies, W. D., and D. C. Allison. *Matthew 1-7.* London: T. & T. Clark, 1988.

Deichgräber, Reinhard. *Gotteshymnus und Christushymnus in der frühen Christenheit.* Göttingen: Vandenhoeck & Ruprecht, 1967.

Delling, Gerhard. *Worship in the New Testament.* London: Darton, Longman and Todd, 1962.

Des Places, Edouard. "La prière cultuelle dans la Grèce ancienne." *RSR* 33 (1959): 343-59.

———. "La prière des philosophes grecs." *Greg* 41 (1960): 253-72.

Detienne, Marcel, and Jean-Pierre Vernant, eds. *The Cuisine of Sacrifice among the Greeks.* Chicago: University of Chicago Press, 1989.

Downing, F. Gerald. "Ethical Pagan Theism and the Speeches of Acts." *NTS* 27 (1981): 544-63.

———. "The Ambiguity of 'The Pharisee and the Tax Collector' (Luke 18:9-14) in the Greco-Roman World of Late Antiquity." *CBQ* 54 (1992): 80-99.

Dupont, Jacques. "Μόνῳ Σοφῷ Θεῷ." *ETL* 22 (1964): 362-75.

Eisenstadt, Shlomo, and Louis Roniger. *Patrons, Clients, and Friends: Interpersonal Relations and the Structure of Trust in Society.* Cambridge: Cambridge University Press, 1984.

Elliott, J. K. "The Language and Style of the Concluding Doxology to the Epistle to the Romans." *ZNW* 72 (1981): 124-30.

Farris, Stephen C. *The Hymns of Luke's Infancy Narratives: Their Origin, Meaning, and Significance.* Sheffield: JSOT Press, 1985.

Ferguson, Everett. *Early Christians Speak.* Austin, Tex.: Sweet Publishing Co., 1971.

———. "Spiritual Sacrifice in Early Christianity and Its Environment." *ANRW* II.23.2 (1980): 1151-89.

Fiensy, David A. *Prayers Alleged to Be Jewish: An Examination of the "Constitutiones Apostolorum."* Chico, Calif.: Scholars, 1985.

Finkel, Asher. "The Prayer of Jesus in Matthew." In *Standing before God: Studies on Prayer in Scriptures and in Tradition with Essays,* edited by Asher Finkel and Lawrence Frizzell, 131-70. New York: Ktav, 1981.

Fitzmyer, Joseph A. "Abba and Jesus' Relation to God." In *A cause de l'évangile:*

études sur les Synoptiques et les Actes offertes au P. Jacques Dupont, O.S.B. à loc-casion de son 70e anniversaire, edited by F. Refoulé, 15-38. Paris: Cerf, 1985.

Fortes, Meyer. "Pietas in Ancestor Worship." In his *Time and Social Structure and Other Essays,* 164-200. London: Athlone, 1970.

Fraser, John W. "Paul's Knowledge of Jesus: II Corinthians V.16 Once More." *NTS* 17 (1971): 293-313.

Froelich, K. "The Lord's Prayer in Patristic Literature." *PSB* Supp. 2 (1992): 71-87.

Garnsey, Peter. *Famine and Food Supply in the Graeco-Roman World.* Cambridge: Cambridge University Press, 1988.

Gaventa, Beverly. "The Prayer in Acts 4:24-31." In *Spiritual Life in the Early Church,* edited by Bonnie Thurston, 55-65. Minneapolis: Fortress, 1993.

Geertz, Clifford. "Religion as a Cultural System." In his *Anthropological Approaches to the Study of Religion,* 1-43. New York: Praeger, 1966.

Gill, Christopher, Norman Postlethwaite, and Richard Seaford, eds. *Reciprocity in Ancient Greece.* Oxford: Clarendon, 1998.

Goldsmith, Dale. "'Ask, and It Will Be Given . . .': Toward Writing the History of a Logion." *NTS* 35 (1989): 254-65.

Grant, Robert M. *Gods and the One God.* Philadelphia: Westminster, 1986.

Greeven, Heinrich. "προσκυνέω." In *TDNT* 6:758-66.

Gunkel, Hermann. *The Psalms: A Form-Critical Introduction.* Philadelphia: Fortress, 1967.

Hahn, Ferdinand. *The Worship of the Early Church.* Philadelphia: Fortress, 1973.

Hall, Edward T. *Beyond Culture.* New York: Doubleday, 1976.

———. *The Dance of Death: The Other Dimension of Time.* New York: Doubleday, 1983.

Hands, A. R. *Charities and Social Aid in Greece and Rome.* Ithaca, N.Y.: Cornell University Press, 1968.

Hanson, K. C. "Transformed on the Mountain: Ritual Analysis and the Gospel of Matthew." *Semeia* 67 (1994): 147-77.

———. "Was Bigger Better? Political Religion in Roman Palestine." In *Palestine in the Time of Jesus,* edited by Douglas E. Oakman and K. C. Hanson, 131-59. Minneapolis: Fortress, 1998.

Hanson, R. P. C. "The Christian Attitude to Pagan Religions up to the Time of Constantine the Great." *ANRW* II.23.2 (1980): 910-73.

Harding, Mark. "A Hebrew Congregational Prayer from Egypt." *NDIEC* 8 (1998): 145-47.

Harner, Philip B. *Understanding the Lord's Prayer.* Philadelphia: Fortress, 1975.

Heinemann, Joseph. "The Proem in the Aggadic Midrashim: A Form-Critical Study." *Studia Hierosolymitana* 22 (1971): 100-200.

———. *Prayer in the Talmud: Forms and Patterns.* Berlin: De Gruyter, 1977.

———. "The Background of Jesus' Prayer in the Jewish Liturgical Tradition." In

The Lord's Prayer and Jewish Liturgy, edited by J. J. Petuchowski and M. Brocke, 81-91. New York: Seabury Press, 1978.

Hendrix, Holland. "Benefactor/Patron Networks in the Urban Environment Evidence from Thessalonika." *Semeia* 56 (1992): 39-58.

Hewitt, J. W. "On the Development of the Thank-offering among the Greeks." *TAPA* 43 (1912): 95-111.

Hill, D. "'Our Daily Bread' (Matt 6:11) in the History of Exegesis." *IBS* 5 (1983): 2-11.

Hock, Ronald F., and Edward N. O'Neil. *The Chreia in Ancient Rhetoric.* Volume I. *The Progymnasmata.* Atlanta: Scholars, 1986.

Jameson, Michael H. "Sacrifice and Ritual: Greece." In *Civilization of the Ancient Mediterranean*, edited by Michael Grant, 2:959-79. New York: Scribner, 1988.

Jay, Eric George. *Origen's Treatise on Prayer.* London: SPCK, 1954.

Jay, Nancy. "Sacrifice and Descent." In her *Throughout Your Generations Forever*, 30-60. Chicago: University of Chicago Press, 1992.

Jeremias, Joachim. "The Lord's Prayer in Modern Research." *ExpT* 71 (1960): 141-46.

————. *The Parables of Jesus.* Rev. ed. New York: Scribner, 1963.

————. *The Lord's Prayer.* Philadelphia: Fortress, 1964.

————. *Abba.* Göttingen: Vandenhoeck & Ruprecht, 1966.

————. *Jerusalem in the Time of Jesus.* Philadelphia: Fortress, 1969.

————. *The Prayers of Jesus.* Philadelphia: Fortress, 1978.

Jungmann, Joseph A. *The Mass of the Roman Rite: Its Origins and Development.* New York: Benziger Brothers, 1951.

Käsemann, Ernst. *New Testament Questions of Today.* Philadelphia: Fortress, 1979.

Kiley, Mark, et al., eds. *Prayer from Alexander to Constantine: A Critical Anthology.* New York: Routledge, 1997.

Killinger, J. *The God Named Hallowed: The Lord's Prayer for Today.* Nashville: Abingdon, 1988.

Kilmartin, Edward J. "Sacrificium Laudis: Content and Function of Early Eucharistic Prayers." *TS* 35 (1974): 268-87.

Kistemaker, S. J. "The Lord's Prayer in the First Century." *JETS* 21 (1978): 323-28.

Knoppers, Gary N. "'There Was None Like Him': Incomparability in the Books of Kings." *CBQ* 54 (1992): 411-31.

Kraus, Hans-Joachim. *Psalms 1–59: A Commentary.* Minneapolis: Augsburg, 1988.

Labuschagne, C. J. *The Incomparability of Yahweh in the Old Testament.* Leiden: Brill, 1966.

Lachs, S. T. *A Rabbinic Commentary on the New Testament.* Hoboken, N.J.: Ktav, 1987.

Lampe, Geoffrey. "'Our Father' in the Fathers." In *Christian Spirituality: Essays in Honour of Gordon Rupp*, edited by Peter Brooks, 11-31. London: SCM, 1975.

Leach, Edmund. "The Logic of Sacrifice." In *Anthropological Approaches to the Old Testament*, edited by Bernhard Lang, 136-50. Philadelphia: Fortress, 1985.

Liefeld, Walter L. "Parables on Prayer (Luke 11:5-8; 18:1-14)." In *The Challenge of Jesus' Parables*, edited by Richard N. Longenecker, 240-62. Grand Rapids: Eerdmans, 2000.

Lietzmann, Hans. *Mass and the Lord's Supper: A Study in the History of the Liturgy.* Leiden: Brill, 1979.

Llewellyn, S. R. "The Development of Systems of Liturgies." *NDIEC* 7 (1994): 93-111.

Lohmeyer, Ernst. *The Lord's Prayer.* London: Collins, 1965.

Longenecker, Richard. "Prayer in the Pauline Letters." In *Into God's Presence: Prayer in the New Testament*, edited by Richard N. Longenecker, 203-27. Grand Rapids: Eerdmans, 2001.

Malina, Bruce J. "The Social World Implied in the Letters of the Christian Bishop-Martyr (Named Ignatius of Antioch)." In SBLSP (1978): 2:71-119.

———. "What Is Prayer?" *TBT* 18, no. 4 (1980): 214-20.

———. *Christian Origins and Cultural Anthropology: Practical Models for Biblical Interpretation.* Atlanta: John Knox, 1986.

———. "Religion in the World of Paul: A Preliminary Sketch." *BTB* 16 (1986): 92-101.

———. "Patron and Client: The Analogy behind Synoptic Theology." *Forum* 4, no. 1 (1988): 2-32.

———. "Christ and Time: Swiss or Mediterranean?" *CBQ* 51 (1989): 1-31.

———. *The New Testament World: Insights from Cultural Anthropology.* Rev. ed. Louisville: Westminster John Knox, 1993.

———. *Windows on the World of Jesus: Time Travels to Ancient Judea.* Louisville: Westminster John Knox, 1993.

———. "Religion in the Imagined New Testament World: More Social Science Lenses." *Scriptura* 51 (1994): 1-26.

———. "Mediterranean Sacrifice: Dimensions of Domestic and Political Religion." *BTB* 26 (1996): 26-44.

———. *The Social World of Jesus and the Gospels.* London: Routledge, 1996.

Malina, Bruce J., and Jerome Neyrey. *Portraits of Paul: An Archaeology of Ancient Personality.* Louisville: Westminster John Knox, 1996.

Manson, T. W. "The Lord's Prayer." *BJRL* 38 (1956): 436-48.

Marshall, I. Howard. "Jesus — Example and Teacher of Prayer." In *Into God's Presence: Prayer in the New Testament*, edited by Richard N. Longenecker, 113-31. Grand Rapids: Eerdmans, 2001.

Martin, Ralph P. *Worship in the Early Church.* London: Marshall, Morgan and Scott, 1964.

McCaffrey, James. *The House with Many Rooms: The Temple Theme of Jn. 14,2-3.* Rome: Pontifical Biblical Institute, 1988.

McKenna, John. "From 'Berakah' to 'Eucharistia' to Thomas Talley and Beyond." *Proceedings of the North American Academy of Liturgy* (1995): 87-100.

Michaels, J. Ramsey. "Finding Yourself an Intercessor: New Testament Prayer from Hebrews to Jude." In *Into God's Presence: Prayer in the New Testament*, edited by Richard N. Longenecker, 228-51. Grand Rapids: Eerdmans, 2001.

Miller, Patrick. *They Cried to the Lord: The Form and Theology of Biblical Prayer.* Minneapolis: Fortress, 1994.

Mott, Stephen C. "The Power of Giving and Receiving: Reciprocity in Hellenistic Benevolence." In *Current Issues in Biblical and Patristic Interpretation*, edited by Gerald Hawthorne, 60-72. Grand Rapids: Eerdmans, 1975.

Moule, C. F. D. "An Unsolved Problem in the Temptation Clause in the Lord's Prayer." *RTR* 33 (1974): 65-76.

Moxnes, Halvor. "Patron-Client Relations and the New Community in Luke-Acts." In *The Social World of Luke-Acts: Models for Interpretation*, edited by Jerome H. Neyrey, 241-68. Peabody, Mass.: Hendrickson, 1991.

Neyrey, Jerome H. "'Without Beginning of Days or End of Life' (Hebrews 7:3): Topos for a True Deity." *CBQ* 53 (1991): 439-55.

———. "The Footwashing in John 13:6-11: Transformation Ritual or Ceremony?" In *The Social World of the First Christians: Essays in Honor of Wayne A. Meeks*, edited by L. Michael White and O. Larry Yarbrough, 198-213. Minneapolis: Fortress, 1995.

———. *Honor and Shame in the Gospel of Matthew.* Louisville: Westminster John Knox, 1998.

———. "The Sociology of Secrecy and the Fourth Gospel." In *What Is John?* vol. 2, *Literary and Social Readings of the Fourth Gospel*, edited by Fernando Segovia, 79-109. Atlanta: Scholars, 1998.

———. "Spaces and Places, Whence and Whither, Homes and Rooms: 'Territoriality' in the Fourth Gospel." *BTB* 32 (2002): 60-74.

———. "God, Benefactor and Patron: The Major Cultural Model for Interpreting the Deity in Greco-Roman Antiquity." *JSNT* 27 (2005): 465-92.

———. "Worship in the Fourth Gospel: A Cultural Interpretation of John 14–17." *BTB* 36 (2006): 107-17.

———. "'I Am the Door' (John 10:7, 9): Jesus the Broker in the Fourth Gospel." *CBQ* 69 (2007): 271-91.

Neyrey, Jerome H., and Anselm Hagedorn, "'It Was Out of Envy That They Handed Jesus Over' (Mark 15:10): The Anatomy of Envy and the Gospel of Mark." *JSNT* 69 (1998): 15-56.

Nilsson, Martin P. *Greek Popular Religion.* New York: Columbia University Press, 1940.

———. *Greek Piety.* Oxford: Clarendon, 1948.

Nock, Arthur Darby. *Essays on Religion and the Ancient World.* Cambridge: Harvard University Press, 1972.

Norden, Eduard. *Agnostos Theos.* Darmstadt: Wissenschaftliche Buchgesellschaft, 1956.

Oakman, Douglas E. "Jesus and Agrarian Palestine: The Factor of Debt." In SBLSP (1985): 57-73.

———. *Jesus and the Economic Questions of His Day.* Lewiston, N.Y.: Edwin Mellen Press, 1986.

———. "The Lord's Prayer in Social Perspective." In *Authenticating the Words of Jesus,* edited by Bruce Chilton and Craig Evans, 137-86. Leiden: Brill, 1999.

O'Brien, Peter T. "Prayer in Luke-Acts." *TynB* 24 (1973): 111-27.

———. "Thanksgiving and the Gospel of Paul." *NTS* 21 (1974): 144-55.

———. *Introductory Thanksgivings in the Letters of Paul.* Leiden: Brill, 1977.

O'Brien, Peter T., and David G. Peterson. *God Who Is Rich in Mercy.* Grand Rapids: Baker, 1986.

Orchard, Bernard. "The Meaning of *ton epiousion* (Mt 6:11/Lk 11:3)." *BTB* 13 (1973): 274-82.

Orr, David G. "Roman Domestic Religion: The Evidence of the Household Shrines." *ANRW* II.16.2 (1978): 1557-91.

O'Toole, Robert. "Paul at Athens and Luke's Notion of Worship." *RB* 89 (1982): 185-97.

Pao, David W. *Thanksgiving: An Investigation of a Pauline Theme.* Downers Grove, Ill.: InterVarsity, 2002.

Parker, Robert. "Pleasing Thighs: Reciprocity in Greek Religion." In *Reciprocity in Ancient Greece,* edited by Christopher Gill et al., 105-26. Oxford: Oxford University Press, 1998.

Parsons, Talcott. *Politics and Social Structure.* New York: Free Press, 1969.

Pearson, A. C. *The Fragments of Zeno and Cleanthes.* New York: Arno Press, 1973.

Pendrick, Gerard. "Μονογενής." *NTS* 41 (1995): 587-600.

Peterson, David G. "Prayer in the General Epistles." In *Teach Us to Pray: Prayer in the Bible and the World,* edited by D. A. Carson, 328-32. Grand Rapids: Baker, 1990.

———. *Possessed by God: A New Testament Theology of Sanctification and Holiness.* Downers Grove, Ill.: InterVarsity, 1995.

———. "The Worship of the New Community." In *Witness to the Gospel: The Theology of Acts,* edited by I. H. Marshall and D. Peterson, 373-95. Grand Rapids: Eerdmans, 1998.

Petuchowski, Jakob J., and Michael Brocke. *The Lord's Prayer and Jewish Liturgy.* New York: Seabury Press, 1978.

Pilch, John J. "Prayer in Luke." *TBT* 18 (1980): 221-25.

————. "'Beat His Ribs While He Is Young' (Sir 30:12): A Window on the Mediterranean World." *BTB* 23 (1993): 101-13.

————. "Insights and Models for Understanding the Healing Activity of the Historical Jesus." In SBLSP (1993): 154-77.

————. "Altered States of Consciousness in the Synoptics." In *The Social Setting of Jesus and the Gospels,* edited by Wolfgang Stegemann, Bruce J. Malina, and Gerd Theissen, 103-16. Minneapolis: Fortress, 2002.

————. "No Thank You!" *TBT* 40 (2002): 49-53.

————. "Holy Men and Their Sky Journeys." *BTB* 35 (2005): 106-11.

Pilch, John J., and Bruce J. Malina. *Biblical Social Values and Their Meanings.* Peabody, Mass.: Hendrickson, 1993.

Piper, Ronald A. "Glory, Honor and Patronage in the Fourth Gospel: Understanding the *Doxa* Given to the Disciples in John 17." In *Social Scientific Models for Interpreting the Bible: Essays by the Context Group in Honor of Bruce J. Malina,* edited by John J. Pilch, 295-97. Leiden: Brill, 2001.

Pitt-Rivers, Julian. "Honour and Social Status." In *Honour and Shame: The Values of Mediterranean Society,* edited by J. G. Peristiany, 19-78. London: Weidenfeld and Nicolson, 1965.

————. *The Fate of Shechem or the Politics of Sex: Essays in the Anthropology of the Mediterranean.* Cambridge Studies in Social Anthropology 19. Cambridge: Cambridge University Press, 1977.

Pleket, H. W. "Religious History as the History of Mentality: The Believer as Servant of the Deity in the Greek World." In *Faith, Hope, and Worship: Aspects of Religious Mentality in the Ancient World,* edited by H. S. Versnel, 171-73. Leiden: Brill, 1981.

Plymale, Steven F. *The Prayer Texts of Luke-Acts.* New York: Peter Lang, 1991.

Price, Simon R. F. "From Noble Funeral to Divine Cult: The Consecration of Roman Emperors." In *Rituals of Royalty: Power and Ceremonial in Traditional Societies,* edited by David Cannadine and Simon Price, 56-105. Cambridge: Cambridge University Press, 1987.

Pulleyn, Simon. *Prayer in Greek Religion.* Oxford: Clarendon, 1997.

Quere, R. "'Naming' God 'Father.'" *CurTM* 12 (1985): 5-14.

Quincey, J. H. "Greek Expressions of Thanks." *JHS* 86 (1966): 133-58.

Robinson, J. A. "The 'Apostolic Anaphora' and the Prayer of St. Polycarp." *JTS* 21 (1920): 97-105.

————. "The Doxology in the Prayer of St. Polycarp." *JTS* 24 (1923): 141-44.

Rogers, Everett M., and F. Floyd Shoemaker. *Communication of Innovations: A Cross-Cultural Approach.* New York: Free Press, 1971.

Runia, David T. "Naming and Knowing: Themes in Philonic Theology with Special Reference to *De Mutatione Nominum.*" In *Knowledge of God in the Greco-*

Roman World, edited by R. van den Broek, T. Baarda, and J. Mansfeld, 69-91. Leiden: Brill, 1988.

―――. "God of the Philosophers, God of the Patriarchs: Exegetical Backgrounds in Philo of Alexandria." In his *Philo and the Church Fathers,* 2-17. Leiden: Brill, 1995.

Rüpke, Jörg. "Controllers and Professionals: Analyzing Religious Specialists." *Numen* 43 (1996): 241-62.

Russell, D. A., and Nigel Wilson. *Menander Rhetor.* Edited with Translation and Commentary. Oxford: Clarendon, 1981.

Sack, Robert D. *Human Territoriality: Its Theory and History.* Cambridge: Cambridge University Press, 1986.

Saffrey, Henri D. "The Piety and Prayers of Ordinary Men and Women in Late Antiquity." In *Classical Mediterranean Spirituality: Egyptian, Greek, and Roman,* edited by A. H. Armstrong, 195-213. New York: Crossroad, 1986.

Safrai, Shlomo. "Religion in Everyday Life." In CRINT 2 (1976): 793-833.

―――. "The Temple." In CRINT 2 (1976): 865-933.

Sahlin, Marshall. *Stone Age Economics.* Chicago: Aldine-Atherton, 1972.

Saller, Richard P. *Personal Patronage under the Early Empire.* Cambridge: Cambridge University Press, 1982.

Schmidt, Steffen, James Scott, Carl Landé, and Laura Guasti. *Friends, Followers, and Factions: A Reader in Political Clientalism.* Berkeley: University of California Press, 1977.

Schwartz, Seth. "Josephus in Galilee: Rural Patronage and Social Breakdown." In *Josephus and the History of the Greco-Roman Period,* edited by F. Parente and J. Sievers, 290-306. Leiden: Brill, 1994.

Seaford, Richard. "The Law of Gratitude: Reciprocity in Anthropological Theory." In *Reciprocity in Ancient Greece,* edited by Christopher Gill et al., 1-12. Oxford: Oxford University Press, 1998.

Smith, Jonathan Z. *Map Is Not Territory.* Leiden: Brill, 1978.

Smith, Morton. "The Common Theology of the Ancient Near East." *JBL* 71 (1952): 135-47.

Sponheim, Paul R. *A Primer on Prayer.* Philadelphia: Fortress, 1988.

Stegner, William R. "The Ancient Jewish Synagogue Homily." In *Greco-Roman Literature and the New Testament,* edited by David E. Aune, 51-70. Atlanta: Scholars, 1988.

Sterling, Greg. "'Pray Always': Prayer in Luke/Acts." In *Preaching from Luke/Acts,* edited by David Fleer and Dave Bland, 67-103. Abilene, Tex.: ACU Press, 2000.

Swanson, Tod D. "To Prepare a Place: Johannine Christianity and the Collapse of Ethnic Territory." *JAAR* 62 (1994): 241-63.

Talbert, Charles H. *What Is a Gospel? The Genre of the Canonical Gospels.* Philadelphia: Fortress, 1977.

Taylor, Ralph B. *Human Territorial Functioning: An Empirical Evolutionary Perspective on Individual and Small Group Territorial Cognitions, Behaviors, and Consequences.* Cambridge: Cambridge University Press, 1988.

Tefft, S. K., ed. *Secrecy: A Cross-Cultural Perspective.* New York: Human Sciences Press, 1980.

Tilborg, Sjef van. *Imaginative Love in John.* Leiden: Brill, 1993.

Trites, Allison A. "The Prayer Motif in Luke-Acts." In *Perspectives on Luke-Acts,* edited by Charles H. Talbert, 168-86. Edinburgh: T. & T. Clark, 1978.

Turner, Max M. V. "Prayer in the Gospels and Acts." In *Teach Us to Pray: Prayer in the Bible and the World,* edited by D. A. Carson, 58-83. Grand Rapids: Baker, 1990.

Turner, Victor. *The Forest of Symbols: Aspects of Ndembu Ritual.* Ithaca, N.Y.: Cornell University Press, 1967.

Van der Horst, Pieter W. "Hellenistic Parallels to Acts (Chapters 3-4)." *JSNT* 35 (1989): 37-46.

Van der Toorn, Karel. "Theology, Priests, and Worship in Canaan and Ancient Israel." In *Civilizations of the Ancient Near East,* edited by Jack Sasson, 3:2043-58. New York: Scribner, 1995.

Van Straten, F. T. "Gifts for the Gods." In *Faith, Hope, and Worship: Aspects of Religious Mentality in the Ancient World,* edited by H. S. Versnel, 65-151. Leiden: Brill, 1981.

Van Unnik, W. C. "*Dominus Vobiscum:* The Background of a Liturgical Phrase." In *New Testament Essays: Studies in Memory of T. W. Manson,* edited by Angus John Brockhurst Higgins, 270-305. Manchester: University of Manchester Press, 1959.

Versnel, H. S., ed. *Faith, Hope, and Worship: Aspects of Religious Mentality in the Ancient World.* Leiden: Brill, 1981.

Veyne, Paul. *Bread and Circuses: Historical Sociology and Political Pluralism.* London: Penguin Press, 1990.

Vokes, F. E. "The Lord's Prayer in the First Three Centuries." *StPat* 10 (= TU 107) (Berlin: Akademie-Verlag, 1970), 253-60.

Volz, Carl A. "Prayer in the Early Church." In *A Primer on Prayer,* edited by Paul R. Sponheim, 36-50. Philadelphia: Fortress, 1988.

Wahlde, Urban C. von. "Acts 4:24-31: The Prayer of the Apostles in Response to the Persecution of Peter and John — and the Consequences." *Biblica* 77 (1996): 237-44.

Walker, William O. "The Lord's Prayer in Matthew and John." *NTS* 28 (1982): 237-56.

Wallace-Hadrill, Andrew, ed. *Patronage in Ancient Society.* London: Routledge, 1989.

Watt, J. G. van der. *Family of the King: Dynamics of Metaphor in the Gospel according to John.* Leiden: Brill, 2000.

Werline, Rodney Alan. *Penitential Prayer in Second Temple Judaism: The Development of a Religious Institution.* Atlanta: Scholars, 1998.

Werner, Eric. "The Doxology in Synagogue and Church: A Liturgico-Musical Study." *HUCA* 19 (1945-46): 275-351.

West, M. L. *The Orphic Poems.* Oxford: Clarendon, 1983.

Westermann, Claus. *The Praise of God in the Psalms.* Richmond, Va.: John Knox, 1965.

———. *The Psalms, Structure, Content, and Message.* Minneapolis: Augsburg, 1980.

———. *Praise and Lament in the Psalms.* Atlanta: John Knox, 1981.

Whittaker, John. "Neopythagoreanism and Negative Theology." *Symbolae Osloensis* 44 (1969): 109-125.

Wiles, Gordon P. *Paul's Intercessory Prayers: The Significance of the Intercessory Prayer Passages in Paul's Letters.* Cambridge: Cambridge University Press, 1974.

Wills, Lawrence. "The Form of the Sermon in Hellenistic Judaism and Early Christianity." *HTR* 77 (1984): 277-99.

Winter, Paul. "Μονογενὴς Παρὰ Πατρός." *ZRGG* 5 (1953): 335-65.

———. "Magnificat and Benedictus — Maccabean Psalms?" *BJRL* 37 (1955): 328-47.

Wire, Antoinette C. *The Corinthian Women Prophets: A Reconstruction through Paul's Rhetoric.* Minneapolis: Fortress, 1990.

Wolfson, Harry A. *Philo: Foundations of Religion Philosophy in Judaism, Christianity, and Islam.* Cambridge: Harvard University Press, 1947.

———. "Albinus and Plotinus on Divine Attributes." *HTR* 45 (1952): 115-30.

———. "Negative Attributes in the Church Fathers and the Gnostic Basilides." *HTR* 50 (1957): 145-56.

Wright, N. T. *The Lord and His Prayer.* Grand Rapids: Eerdmans, 1996.

Wyschogrod, Michael. "The 'Shema Israel' in Judaism and the New Testament (Deut 6:4-9; 11:13-21; Num 15:37-41)." In *The Roots of Our Common Faith*, edited by H. G. Link, 23-32. Geneva: World Council of Churches, 1984.

Young, B. *The Jewish Background to the Lord's Prayer.* Austin, Tex.: Center for Judaic-Christian Studies, 1984.

Young, Frances M. "The Idea of Sacrifice in Neoplatonic and Patristic Texts." *StPat* 11 (1972): 278-81.

———. "The God of the Greeks and the Nature of Religious Language." In *Early Christian Literature and the Classical Intellectual Tradition*, edited by William R. Schoedel and Robert L. Wilken, 48-53. Paris: Beauchesne, 1979.

———. *The Use of Sacrificial Ideas in Greek Christian Writers from the New Testament to John Chrysostom.* Cambridge, Mass.: Philadelphia Patristic Foundation, 1979.

Zahavy, Tzvee. "Three Stages in the Development of Early Rabbinic Prayer." In *From Ancient Israel to Modern Judaism: Essays in Honor of Marvin Fox*, vol. 1, edited by Jacob Neusner, Ernest Frerichs, and Nahum Sarna, 233-65. Atlanta: Scholars, 1989.

Zeller, Dieter. "God as Father in the Proclamation and in the Prayers of Jesus." In *Standing before God: Studies on Prayer in Scriptures and in Tradition with Essays*, edited by Asher Finkel and Lawrence Frizzell, 117-30. New York: Ktav, 1981.

INDEX OF SUBJECTS

baptism, 163, 216-17, 230-34
berakah, 23, 85

communication model, 9-10, 147-65, 178, 183, 233, 237

divine predicates
  aloneness, 136, 138
  eternal, 132-33
  imperishable, 128-29, 136
  inaccessible, 136
  ineffable, 129
  invisible, 129
  unseen, 137
doxology, 85-90, 127-37
  1 Tim 1:17 as, 127-33
  1 Tim 6:15-16 as, 133-37
  form of, 86-87, 127
  types of, 85-86

Eucharist, 163, 218-19, 235-36
eucharisteō, 23-26, 218-19, 228

foot washing, 112-13

glory, 131-32, 141-42,
God
  attributes of, 138-39
  blessed, 133
  eternal, 132-33
  as Father, 64, 68-70, 75-76
  hallowed/holy, 71-72
  honor of, 20-21, 90
  honorable qualities of, 88-89
  names of, 41, 46, 64, 70-71, 83, 88, 92, 134
  as King, 70, 128
  as King of Kings, Lord of Lords, 72, 134-35
  as *paterfamilias,* 69
  and *patria potestas,* 69-70
  as Patron, 52-56, 76-77
  power of, 66, 77, 89, 92-93, 138-39
  sovereign, 81-84, 134. *See also* divine predicates
group-oriented person, 61-62

high-context society, 89
holy and wholeness, 71-72, 215
Holy Spirit, 181, 187-90
honor
  definition of, 37-38
  displayed, 69-74, 88
  names for, 70-71, 81, 83, 88
  synonyms for, 38, 42-43, 132
honor, achieved
  benefaction, 38, 40-41
  challenge/riposte, 41-43

virtue, 39, 88-90
honor, ascribed, 38

Isis, 120

Jesus
    as broker and mediator, 94-95, 102-9,
        148-49, 200-203, 246
    farewell prayer of, 94-110
    as prophet, 179-86
    as secret keeper, 180-82, 186
justice, 39, 209-14

Kerygma tou Petrou, 143

Magnificat, 90-94
meals, 235-37
media of exchange, 43-46, 53-56, 84, 92-
    93, 105-9, 136, 219
Moses, as broker, 102-3

negative theology, 121-22, 128-31, 139-40,
    142-43

Our Father, 63-80, 217-18
    John 17 as Our Father, 95-97

patron-broker-client, 52-56, 75-79, 84,
    89-90, 91-93, 101, 104-5
patronage/benefaction, 219-20
prayer
    definition of, 8-9
    types of, 10, 14-28
        acknowledgment, 21-22, 81-82, 87,
            90-91, 143, 177-78, 228
        appreciation, 23, 164, 219-20, 228,
            235, 241
        heuristic, 19-20
        imaginative, 20
        interactional, 16
        petitionary, 12-13, 45, 66, 81-82, 172-
            76, 185, 219-21, 227, 233, 238
        praise, 12-13, 97-98
        regulatory, 15

    self-focused, 16-19, 99, 172-76
    thanksgiving, 12-13, 25-26
purity, 61, 215

reciprocity, 46-52
rhetoric, deliberative, 155, 183-85, 209-15
rituals and ceremonies, 56-60, 68, 81, 87,
    110-11, 159-64, 216-19, 224-26, 229-30,
    233-35, 238-40, 241-43

social science models, 1-4, 7, 29-30, 245-
    50
space
    being in/dwelling in, 196-97
    fixed v. fluid, 190-93
    model of territoriality, 191-93
    as relationships, 193-97
    rooms in my Father's house, 169, 193-
        96

table fellowship, 236-37
Tanchuma, 191
time, 34-35, 57-59
    forthcoming, 109, 179
    future, 73-74
    of God: eternity, 90, 109, 128-29, 132-
        33, 136,
    past, 84, 94, 109
    present, 73-74, 80, 84, 94, 109-10

uniqueness, 112-33
    as first, 115-16, 117, 120, 121
    incomparableness, 122-23
    as most, 120
    as no one else, 126-27
    as only/alone, 115-16, 117, 120-21, 125,
        127, 130-31, 136, 138
    as one of a few, 115-16
    as one who most, 115-16. *See also*
        negative theology

value system, 31-37, 80, 84-85, 90, 93-94,
    109-10

worship
definition of, 144, 147-48
descriptions of, 145-47
elements of, 170-71
almsgiving, 213-14, 217, 237-39, 243
calendar, 217, 224-25, 238, 239, 243
as confessing God, 149-50
doxologies, 208, 219
exhortations, 156-58, 208-16, 226-27
fasting as, 217, 225, 227, 238, 240
food blessing, 218-19
hearing the story of Jesus, 151-52,
185-86, 228-29

homily, 152-56, 182-85
honoring Jesus, 152-54
kiss, 234, 242
oracles, 159, 186-90, 225-26
personnel, 213-14, 221-25, 229, 235
prayers, 148-50, 171-78, 217-18, 219-
20, 234-35, 240-41
prophecy, 158-59, 178, 221-24
rituals, 159-65, 216-17, 224-25, 229-
30, 231-34, 239, 241-44
Scripture reading, 150-51, 239

INDEX OF SCRIPTURE AND OTHER ANCIENT TEXTS

OLD TESTAMENT

Genesis
4:26	8
6:8	51
12:1-3	55
15:13-16	55
18:22-23	102

Exodus
12	58
3:20	21
8:10	122
9:14	124
15:9	21
15:11	123
15:12	21
15:16	21
20:7	70
20:13-17	229
20:18-20	102
20:19	102
32:11	8, 13
32:11-14	102
33:20	129

Leviticus
11:44-45	71
14	161

22:32	70

Deuteronomy
3:24	124
4:2	229
4:34	21
4:35	124, 131
5:15	21
6:4	131, 177
6:4-5	126
6:13	125
7:6-7	55
10:17	135
12:32	229
21:18-21	69
33:26	122

Joshua
10:12	13

Judges
16:30	14

1 Samuel
2:2	122
4:4	72

2 Samuel
7:8-16	55

7:16	55

1 Kings
3:12	123
3:13	123
3:16-28	88
4:22-28	88
10:23	123
28:6	8

2 Kings
17:36	21
18:5	123
23:25	123

1 Chronicles
16:36	235
29:10-11	85
29:11	141

2 Chronicles
20:6	122

Nehemiah
5:13	235
13:26	123

Job
1:8	123

2:3	123	89:10	21
3:11-15	19	89:13	21
6:8-13	19	95:7-11	37
9:1-10	19	96:2-3	22
12:2-25	19	100:3	21
42:1-6	20	103:1	22
		104:27	78
Psalms		105:1	23
38	58	108:1	17
51	45, 58	116:12	50
56	58	118:15-16	21
59	58	131:1-2	99
113–116	60	131:1-3	17
2:7	80	135:1	71
8:1	22	136:1-2	24
9:1	23	136:2-3	135
9:7	72	139:1	45
10:16	72	145:1	91
13:1	16	145:13	39
18:49	22	148:1	22
19:1	22	148:5	71
20:1	71		
22:1	42	**Proverbs**	
29:2	70	1:8	69
29:10	72	4:1	69
30:1	91		
33:8	22	**Isaiah**	
35:10	123, 124	1:18	232
40:10-11	17	6:3	71
43:4	17	29:33	64
44:24	16	33:22	71
47:1	22	44–45	131
48:1	22	53:10	8
54:1	70		
59:16-17	21	**Ezekiel**	
62:1-2	17	20:33	64
62:1-7	99	26:7	72
62:5-6	17		
66:2	70	**Daniel**	
66:10	66	2:37	72
69:30	91		
74:1	16	**Habakkuk**	
86:8	122	1:5	155
89:8	123		

Malachi	
1:11	229
1:14	229
NEW TESTAMENT	
Matthew	
5	210
24	229
3:7-10	159
4:10	125
5:16	74
5:23	229
5:23-24	225
5:26	229
5:33	229
5:38-39	228
5:39	151
5:40-41	228
5:42	229
5:44	151
5:48	228
6:1-16	229
6:1-18	217, 238
6:9-13	63, 67-80
6:11	36
6:11-13	28
6:33	74
7:6	229
7:7	15
7:11	47
7:12	228
7:21	65
10:10	47, 229
11:25	13
11:25-26	28
11:27	126
12:13-17	151
12:28-34	151
12:31	229
15:19	229
18:5-17	163
18:12-15	225

18:14	65	1:49	91	3:2	105, 108
18:15-17	159, 188	1:64	12	3:3	96, 232
18:23-34	65, 79	1:68	85	3:5	96
18:34	79	1:68-79	28	3:13	126
21:9	229	2:13	12	3:22-26	205
21:28-31	69	2:29	37	3:32	107
22:37-39	228	2:29-32	28	3:34	107
23:9	69	4:8	125	3:35	104
24:4	229	4:18	163	4:6	103
24:31	229	4:21	37, 80	4:7	103
24:36	125	5:21	125	4:8	103
24:36-44	226	10:7	47	4:14	107
26:30	12	10:22	126	4:19	179
26:39	218	10:30	47	4:20	168, 190
26:42	218	10:33-35	47	4:21	168
26:44	218	11:3	36	4:23	168
28:18	75	11:11-13	47	4:31	108
28:19	229	12:58	79	4:31-34	103
		13:13	24	4:34	96, 104, 106
Mark		18:11-12	28, 99	5:3-5	188
1:5	13	18:13	28	5:19-20	106
1:15	65	18:13-14	161	5:21	106
1:44	161	18:43	12	5:21-29	106
2:7	125	19:5	80	5:22	106
3:35	74	19:22	47	5:25	106
6:21	58	22:14-34	58	5:26	106
7:15	151	23:43	80	5:27	106
10:18	126	24:27	151	5:28-29	106
11:23	151			5:30	103, 106
12:29	177	**John**		5:44	125
12:29-30	126	1:1-2	107	6:1-13	107
12:32	126, 177	1:1-3	106	6:14	179
13:32	73	1:1-18	103	6:25	108
14:26	60	1:12	106	6:29	96
14:36	74, 98	1:14	103	6:32-56	205
14:38	28	1:18	108, 126, 196	6:33-51	168
		1:38	108	6:38	103, 106
Luke		1:49	108	6:39	106
1:13	13, 15	1:50-51	196	6:39-40	107
1:28	91	2:7-10	107	6:44	106
1:30	92	2:19	167	6:46	108
1:46	28	2:19-22	190	6:54	106
1:46-55	63	2:21	168	6:59	108
1:48-49	28	2:22	186	7:14	108

7:16-17	108
7:28	108
7:37-38	107, 169
7:40	179
7:52	179
8:12	107, 169
8:18	107
8:20	108
8:28	108
9:2	108
9:17	179
9:22	188, 191
9:32-33	105
9:34	188
10:17-18	106
10:18	107, 127
10:22	58
10:28-29	106
11:8	108
11:28	108
11:41	95
11:43	106
12:27-28	95
12:42	188
12:42-43	191
12:49	108
13:1	104
13:1-3	103
13:3	105
13:12-17	205
13:13	108
13:16	180
13:31	110
13:34	104
14–17	165, 167-205, 207
14–16	186
14–15	196-97
14:1-4	181
14:2	96, 168, 169, 191, 193-96
14:2-3	103, 106
14:3	179
14:4	180
14:5	180, 181

14:6	127, 180, 181, 194, 203
14:7	181
14:8	181
14:9	181
14:9-11	181
14:10	197
14:10-11	103, 181
14:11	197
14:13	203
14:13-14	172
14:14	107, 203
14:15-16	172
14:17	189, 197
14:18-19	179
14:18-21	181
14:19	189
14:20	103, 197
14:21	105, 107, 196
14:21-24	191-93
14:22	181, 189
14:23	103, 105, 106, 110, 195, 196
14:23-24	181
14:24	108
14:26	108, 187
14:27	189
14:28	103
14:28-29	179
14:30	179
15–16	183
15:1-2	106, 183
15:1-8	183, 184, 185
15:1-17	185
15:2	183, 184
15:3-8	110
15:4	183, 184, 197
15:5	183, 184, 197
15:6	183, 184
15:7	110, 172, 183, 197
15:8	183
15:9	184, 185
15:9-10	107, 184
15:9-17	103, 183, 184

15:10	185
15:12-13	107
15:15	106
15:16	172, 184, 185, 203
15:17	184
15:18	189
15:18-25	180, 197
15:19	189
15:20	180
15:26	108, 187
16:1-2	179, 188, 191, 197
16:4	179
16:5	103, 181
16:7-10	187
16:7-11	188, 189
16:8	189
16:12	187
16:15	105
16:16	179, 181
16:17	103
16:17-18	181
16:19-24	181
16:20	189
16:20-24	181
16:23-24	172
16:24	203
16:25	181
16:25-27	181
16:26	15, 172, 203
16:28	189
16:29-30	181
16:31-33	181
16:33	189
17	17, 63, 94-110
17:1	95, 98, 101, 173
17:2	106, 109, 175, 196
17:3	103, 108, 109, 125, 169, 173, 177, 201
17:4	17, 96, 100, 104, 108, 109, 176, 202
17:5	98, 101, 103, 109, 173, 175, 196, 201
17:6	17, 95, 100, 104,

	107, 109, 173, 176,		175, 195, 196, 201,	27:23-24	159
	202		202	27:29	15
17:6-8	174, 175	17:24-25	101		
17:6-9	109	17:25	95, 100, 103, 176	**Romans**	
17:7	196	17:25-26	175	1:1	157
17:8	17, 100, 103, 104,	17:26	17, 95, 100, 104,	1:20	129
	108, 109, 176, 196,		107, 109, 176	3:23	37
	202	18:15-17	188	4:17	139
17:9	15, 97, 98, 174,	18:20	108	7:25	149
	175	18:36	96	8:26-27	13
17:10	175	19:23-24	95	10:9	150
17:11	95, 97, 98, 101,	19:26-27	106	11:25-26	158
	110, 174, 175, 195,	19:33-34	169	11:36	12, 86, 132
	219	20:1	169	12:1	156
17:11-12	107, 196	20:16	108	12:12-13	156
17:12	18, 95, 97, 100,	20:23	205	12:14	151
	104, 109, 174, 175,	20:26	169	12:17	151
	176, 202			13:7	151
17:13	202	**Acts**		13:8-9	151
17:13-14	174, 175	1:6-7	73	13:8-10	156
17:14	17, 100, 104, 108,	2:38-39	155	14:14	151
	109, 176, 195, 196	2:42	145, 170, 182	15:9	12, 13, 22
17:14-16	97	4:24-30	33, 63, 81-83	15:30	13
17:15	97, 98, 104, 174,	4:29	15	16:25	86, 89
	195, 202	4:34-35	239	16:25-26	125
17:15-16	175	8:30-38	151	16:25-27	12, 63, 87
17:16	174, 175	11:28	158	16:27	125, 132, 149
17:17	98, 101, 174, 175	13:2	159		
17:18	18, 100, 103, 108,	13:9-11	159	**1 Corinthians**	
	176	13:14-41	154, 155	1:1	157
17:18-19	174, 175	13:16-26	155	1:17	157
17:19	18, 100, 104, 176,	13:16-33	155	4:1	157
	202	13:26	155	5	163, 188
17:20	175	13:27-37	155	5:3-5	159
17:20-21	98, 109, 175	13:33	80	7:10	151
17:21	95, 101, 103, 104,	13:33-37	155	8:6	150
	110, 201	13:38-39	155, 156	9—10	156
17:22	18, 100, 104, 109,	13:38-41	156	9:3-12	47, 224
	176, 196	13:40-41	155, 156	9:14	151
17:22-23	175	17:24	75	11:2	157
17:23	103, 104, 105, 109,	18:9	159	11:2-16	158
	110	21:4	159	11:17	157
17:24	95, 98, 101, 109,	23:11	159	11:20ff.	145, 170
		26:29	15	11:23	151, 237

12:3	150, 159	6:18	13	**2 Timothy**	
13	156			1:5	157
13:2	151	**Philippians**		1:6	157
14	158	1:11	85	4:18	132
14:1-36	145, 170	2:11	13		
14:6-26	20, 28	4:6	13	**Titus**	
14:37-38	159	4:20	12, 86, 132	2:1	158
15:3-7	237			2:15	158
15:51-52	158	**Colossians**			
15:53-54	37	1:15	129	**Hebrews**	
15:57	149	3:16	12	3:1–4:13	185
16:22	159	3:18–4:1	156	3:7–4:13	37
		3:20	74	5:6	200
2 Corinthians				6:1-12	185
1:3	86	**1 Thessalonians**		6:20	200
5:16	151	1:9	150	7:7	42
12:1-3	20	2:10	71	7:17	200
12:9	159	2:12	74, 156	7:25	200
13:7	15	4:1	156	7:26	149
13:9	15	4:2-6	159	8:3	149
		4:3	74	8:6	200
Galatians		4:3-11	156	9:15	200
1:1	157	4:15-17	158	11:27	129
1:5	86, 132	5:1-9	156	12:24	200
1:8-9	159	5:19-20	158	13:15	12
4:6-7	164			13:21	132
5:16-25	156	**1 Timothy**			
5:19-21	156	1:1	157	**James**	
5:21	159	1:17	63, 85, 87, 88,	1:5	15
5:22-24	156		127-32, 136, 137,	1:13	66
			141	3:9	12
Ephesians		1:18	157	4:3	15
1:3-10	86	2:1	13, 14, 156	5:14-16	163
1:6	12	2:5	149, 200	5:15	13
3:20	89	2:5-6	150	5:16	13, 15
3:20-21	12, 63, 87	3:4	69		
3:21	132	4:6	157	**1 Peter**	
4:1	156	4:11	157	1:3	86
4:2-3	156	4:13	151, 157	1:7	85
5:3-6	156	4:14	157	1:15-16	71
5:19	12	6:2	157	4:11	86, 132
5:21–6:9	156	6:15	72, 141		
6:1	74	6:15-16	133-37, 141	**2 Peter**	
6:13-17	156	6:16	132, 141, 142	3:18	86

1 John

2:1   149

Jude

24   89
24-25   12, 63, 87
25   3, 90, 132, 142, 149

Revelation

1:6   133
1:8   159
1:17-20   159
3:10   65
4:8   71
4:9   13
4:11   80, 132
5:9   12
5:12-13   12
5:13   132
7:12   13
14:13   159
19:9   159
22:7   159

APOCRYPHA

1 Maccabees

4:30   85
10:29-30   79

2 Maccabees

1:24-25   138-39
10:7-8   58

3 Maccabees

2:3   139
5:35   135

Sirach

51:12   24

Tobit

8:15-17   85
12:6   24

PSEUDEPIGRAPHA

Joseph and Aseneth   247-48

Testament of Asher   215

RABBINIC LITERATURE

Exodus Rabbah   138

Talmud
b. Berakoth   18, 65, 66, 75

OTHER EARLY LITERATURE

Aelius Theon
Progymnasmata   115-16

Apostolic Constitutions   131, 140

Aristotle
Rhetoric   114, 176-77, 209

Cicero
De inventione rhetorica   39, 116

Nature of the Gods   76, 132, 134

De oratore   114, 116

Cleanthes
"Hymn to Zeus"   119-20

Clementine Homilies   236

Cyprian
On the Lord's Prayer   69-70

Demosthenes
Funeral Oration   118-19

Dio Cassius
Roman History   135

Dio Chrysostom
Orations   76, 120, 135

Diodor of Sicily
Historical Library   128, 134, 135

Diogenes Laertius
Lives of the Philosophers   142

Diognetus   129

Iamblichus
Life of Pythagoras   76

Ignatius
To the Magnesians   129

Irenaeus
Against Heresies   143

Isaeus
On the Estate of Dicaeogenes   40

Isocrates
Evagoras   119, 136-37

On the Team of Horses   113

Josephus
Against Apion 62

Jewish Antiquities 40-41, 50, 75, 78, 83, 95, 129

Jewish War 79

Lucretius
Nature of Things 134

Lysias
Funeral Oration 117-18

Origen
On Prayer 13, 149

Orphic Hymns 121-22, 130-31, 132, 133, 142

Pausanias
Descriptions of Greece 191

Philo
Against Flaccus 83

On Agriculture 11

On the Cherubim 135-36

On the Creation of the World 129

On Dreams 102, 134, 136

On Flight and Finding 95, 136

On the Life of Abraham 134

On the Life of Moses 83, 102, 139

On Planting 10-11

On the Posterity of Cain 102

On the Sacrifices of Cain and Abel 134

On the Special Laws 129

Unchangeableness of God 51, 134

Who Is the Heir? 83

Plato
Euthyphro 11

Menexenus 118

Politics 11

Republic 191

Pliny
Letter to Trajan 145, 170

Plutarch
Common Conceptions 134

Dinner of the Seven Wise Men 34, 143

E Delphi 129

Letter to Apollonius 34

Old Men in Public affairs 119

Oracles at Delphi 20

Stoic Self-Contradictions 134

Talkativeness 34

Pseudo-Aristotle
Virtues and Vice 39, 210

Quintilian
Institutio oratoria 76, 115, 116, 209

Rhetoric to Herennius 39, 116, 177

Seneca
Benefits 22

Sextus Empiricus
Against the Physicians 128

Strabo
Geography 119

Tacitus
Annals 79

Tertullian
Against Marcion 133

On Prayer 69-70

Thucydides
History 118